Hicken, Mandy.

Now read on.

DATE			

NOW READ ON

Now read on

A guide to contemporary popular fiction

Second edition

Mandy Hicken
Ray Prytherch

Published by
SCOLAR PRESS
Gower House
Croft Road
Aldershot
Hants GU11 3HR
England

Ashgate Publishing Company
Old Post Road
Brookfield
Vermont 05036
USA

British Library Cataloguing in Publication Data

Now read on: a guide to Contemporary Popular Fiction. – 2Rev. ed
I. Hicken, Marilyn E. II. Prytherch, R. J.
016.823009

ISBN 1–85928–008–0

Typeset by P Stubley, Sheffield
Printed in Great Britain by Hartnolls, Bodmin, Cornwall

CONTENTS

INTRODUCTION

In the four years since the first edition of *Now read on* was compiled, there has been a steady expansion in the numbers of new fiction titles published. In this second edition there are many new authors, and new works by authors who were represented before. Reviews and critical comments on the earlier edition were generally favourable, and the book has sold well; remarks by reviewers have been noted in preparing the new edition.

This book is not, nor is it intended to be, an exhaustive guide to fiction. It is, rather, a guide to the work of popular contemporary authors, who write in a specific genre. Many of the novelists who have been chosen are very well-known, and in their case the book will serve as a reminder of published titles; others are less well-established, and the relevant entries will provide new sources of reading material for devotees of a particular genre. All the authors write in the English language, and are, for the most part, British, though American, Australian and African novelists also appear. With very few exceptions, the authors mentioned are still writing regularly; those who are not have died within the last few years.

The purpose of the book is to answer the question so often put to staff in public libraries and bookshops: 'I've read all Catherine Cookson's or Wilbur Smith's books. Does anyone else write like them?' The information given has been tested on a sample of public library users, and should prove to be a valuable tool for libraries, in answering readers' enquiries, and in training library staff in fiction selection. It will also, it is hoped, have a place in the bookshop, and may well attract the attention of those members of the public who wish to widen their reading of contemporary fiction. The details of each author's publications are up to date to the middle of 1993, and it is intended to produce regular revisions of the book as new titles and new authors emerge.

The book contains information about twenty different genres in fiction. Some, like Detective stories and Police work, and Fantasies and Science fiction, overlap to a great extent, but have their own individual characteristics and exponents. Some authors write in more than one genre, and frequent cross-references have been made in this case. Some major exponents of a genre, for instance Agatha Christie and Dorothy L. Sayers in Detective stories, have been mentioned as a comparison, but have no entry of their own, simply because they are so well-known as to need no further discussion, and because they are no longer writing.

There are significant omissions from the book. No mention has been made of writers of Westerns, or light romantic novels. The 'literary' novel has also been excluded, since it is always reviewed in the media, and is, in any case, rather outside the scope of this particular book. In listing Science fiction, a genre which has been exhaustively surveyed, attention has been focused on comparative newcomers to this field, with a mention of the seminal figures.

The choice of authors is essentially a personal one, but based on a survey of popular material read by public library users. Readers of this guide may well have other choices, and comments, critical or otherwise, on the contents would be gratefully received. Nearly sixty new authors have been listed in this second edition, and new titles by the authors listed in the previous edition have been added.

The book is arranged alphabetically by genre, then alphabetically by author within each genre. Each author's entry contains biographical details, comments about the content, style and quality of the novels, and a complete list of publications, with bibliographical details. It then lists the names of other authors who write in a similar style.

There are two indexes. The first lists every author mentioned in the text, and includes pseudonyms where they have been used; bold page numbers signify main entries. The second lists series and recurring characters in an author's work. An appendix lists the winners of prizes awarded for specific genres.

The opportunity has been taken in this second edition to improve a number of features in the layout, and the modified format should assist the location of information and overall legibility. The compilers would like to express their appreciation to Peter Stubley for his advice and assistance in the production of the final camera-ready copy.

ADVENTURE STORIES

These are identified with fast-moving plots, exotic settings, and larger-than-life main characters. Their authors are mainly concerned with holding the reader's interest by involving their hero (for there are few women as main characters in this type of novel) in hair-raising adventures which demand tough action, escapes and chases, and ingenious solutions to seemingly insurmountable problems. The tradition was established by writers like Rider Haggard, John Buchan and Dornford Yates, and is continued by a number of extremely popular, best-selling authors such as Hammond Innes and Alistair MacLean, who have dominated the scene for many years. Recently, a new generation has emerged, whose plots are equally fast-moving, but whose characterisation and analysis of situations have much greater depth.

This is essentially a type of fiction for picking up at airports and station bookstalls, and is an integral part of the stock of standard fiction in public libraries. Collins have always been a leading publisher of this genre.

Bagley, Desmond

Born in England in 1923, he worked in the British Aircraft Industry during 1940–6. He then travelled overland to Africa, where he worked in Uganda, Kenya and Rhodesia, before going to South Africa in 1950. He became a freelance journalist in 1956, and a professional novelist in 1962. His major hobby was travel, and his books are almost invariably set in foreign locations, ranging from the jungles of South America to the interior of Iceland. He lived latterly in Guernsey, and died in 1983. His last two books were not of the same standard as the earlier ones, but were still enjoyable and enthusiastically received by his readers.

All his books were published by Collins, and most are still available in a standard edition.

Publications

The golden keel   1963
High citadel   1965
Wyatt's hurricane   1966
Landslide   1967
The Vivero letter   1968
The spoilers   1969
Running blind   1970
The freedom trap   1971
The tightrope men   1973
The snow tiger   1975
The enemy   1977
Flyaway   1978
Bahama crisis   1980
Windfall   1982
The plutonium factor   1982
Juggernaut   1985 (published posthumously)

Now read
Hammond Innes, Geoffrey Jenkins, Alistair MacLean, Duncan Kyle, Ken Follett, Wilbur Smith, Clive Cussler, Bob Langley.

Driscoll, Peter

British, born in London in 1942. His parents moved to South Africa when he was a child, and he was educated there. He took a degree at the University of the Witwatersrand in Johannesburg in 1967, and became a journalist in Johannesburg after serving in the South African army. He moved to London to work as a script-writer and sub-editor on Independent Television News from 1969 to 1973, then decided to devote all his time to writing. He now lives in Ireland.

Peter Driscoll has been compared to John Buchan and Eric Ambler in his choice of plot and setting. He believes that a good thriller should have the depth and insight of a 'straight' novel, within the limitations of the genre, and says that he 'tries his hardest to communicate authenticity, atmosphere, and – an elusive but essential ingredient – the quality of fear'.

His plots are set in countries which are undergoing socio-political problems, in which his heroes become inadvertently involved. The books are researched in depth, giving real authenticity, and the atmosphere of tension is carefully built up. Driscoll does not gloss over the brutalities of the regimes in the countries in which he places his books. Whether writing about South Africa, in *The Wilby conspiracy*, or Northern Ireland in *In connection with Kilshaw*, he brings realism to the plot.

Publications

The white lie assignment　Macdonald　1971
The Wilby conspiracy　Macdonald　1973
In connection with Kilshaw　Macdonald　1974
The Barboza credentials　Macdonald　1976
Pangolin　Macdonald　1979
Heritage　Granada　1983
Spearhead　Bantam　1988
Secrets of state　Bantam　1991

Now read
Ken Follett, Colin Forbes, Jack Higgins, Bob Langley, Ken Royce, Wilbur Smith, Craig Thomas.

Follett, James

British. He was trained as a marine engineer, and worked as a technical writer for the Ministry of Defence. He also spent some time searching for underwater treasure, filming sharks and designing powerboats before becoming a full-time writer. He now lives in a small village in Surrey with his family and a collection of back numbers of New Scientist.

He is the author of a number of radio and television plays, as well as producing novels at regular intervals. His books are full of excitement and action, and he draws on his engineering and scientific background to add realism to the plots. Many of his books are about weaponry and modern methods of warfare, and feature sophisticated aircraft and boats. His plots are ingenious and inventive, with mounting tension and a convincing climax. In some cases characterisaion is secondary to technology, but his dialogue is crisp, and the life of the modern soldier is described in authentic detail.

Publications

> *The doomsday ultimatum* Weidenfeld 1977/
>   Mandarin 1991
> *Ice* Weidenfeld 1978/Mandarin 1989
> *U-700* Weidenfeld 1979/Severn House 1991
> *Churchill's gold* Weidenfeld 1980
> *The tip-toe boys* (*Who dares wins*) Corgi 1982/
>   Severn House 1992
> *Earthsearch* BBC 1981
> *Deathship* BBC 1982/Severn House 1990
> *Dominator* Methuen 1984
> *Swift* Methuen 1986
> *Mirage* Methuen 1988
> *A cage of eagles* Severn House 1990
> *Torus* Methuen 1990
> *Trojan* Lime Tree 1991
> *Savant* Heinemann 1993

Now read
Clive Cussler, Colin Forbes, Geoffrey Jenkins, Craig Thomas.

Follett, Ken

British, born in Cardiff in 1949. Took a degree in philosophy at University College, London, and made journalism his career. He wrote his first novel to pay a car repair bill, and sold it as a serial to the *London Evening News*, for whom he was working. He achieved real success with his tenth novel, *Storm Island*, and has written best-sellers ever since. He specialises in the sort of fast-moving action stories popularised by Alistair MacLean. Some of his books could also be categorised as spy stories, since many of them have a political background, or war stories, since the action takes place in a Second World War setting. The backgrounds are well-researched, and the characters have depth. *Pillars of the earth* is an historical saga.

Publications

> *The bear raid*   Harwood, Smart   1976
> *Shakeout*   Harwood, Smart   1977
> *Storm Island*   H. Hamilton   1978   (later retitled
>   and filmed as *The eye of the needle*)
> *Triple*   H. Hamilton   1979
> *The key to Rebecca*   H. Hamilton   1981
> *The man from St Petersburg*   H. Hamilton   1982
> *On wings of eagles*   Collins   1983
> *Lie down with lions*   Collins   1985
> *Pillars of the earth*   Macmillan   1989
> *Night over water*   Macmillan   1991
> *A dangerous fortune*   Macmillan   1993

Now read
Colin Forbes, Jack Higgins, Alistair MacLean, Craig Thomas.

Forbes, Colin

British. He served in the Mediterranean during the Second World War, and then went into business, where he had various occupations before deciding to become a writer. He is one of the authors who add authenticity and depth of character to an exciting plot. His books are stories of high adventure, sometimes in a wartime setting, or in espionage. He started writing in the late 1960s, and achieved his first success in 1969 with *Tramp in armour*.

Publications

>*Tramp in armour*   1969
>*The heights of Zervos*   1970
>*Palermo ambush*   1972
>*Target five*   1973
>*The stone leopard*   1975
>*Avalanche express*   1977
>*The Stockholm syndicate*   1981
>*Double jeopardy*   1982
>*The leader and the damned*   1983
>*The year of the golden ape*   1983
>*Terminal*   1984
>*Cover story*   1985
>*The Janus man*   1986
>*Deadlock*   1987
>*The Greek key*   1988
>(All published by Collins.)
>*Shockwave*   Pan   1989
>*Whirlpool*   Pan   1990
>*Cross of fire*   Pan   1991
>*By stealth*   Pan   1992

Now read
Peter Driscoll, Alistair MacLean, Jack Higgins, Wilbur Smith, Craig Thomas.

Francis, Dick

Born in Pembrokeshire in 1920, and became a Flying Officer in the RAF in the Second World War. He then became an amateur National Hunt jockey, and turned professional in 1948. On retiring from competitive racing he became racing correspondent for the *Sunday Express* from 1957 to 1973. After writing his autobiography in 1957,

7

he decided to try his hand at thrillers, and the first was published in 1962. He has produced one a year since then. All his books are set in the world of horse racing, and are adventure stories in the truest sense, with fast-moving plots, chases, and heroes who succeed in spite of overwhelming odds. His knowledge of flying helps in the authenticity of detail. His success has encouraged other sportsmen to write similar material.

Publications

Dead cert 1962
Nerve 1964
For kicks 1965
Odds against 1965
Flying finish 1966
Blood sport 1967
Forfeit 1968
Enquiry 1969
Rat race 1970
Bonecrack 1971
Smokescreen 1972
Slay-ride 1973
Knock-down 1974
High stakes 1975
In the frame 1976
Risk 1977
Trial run 1978
Whip hand 1979
Reflex 1980
Twice shy 1981
Banker 1982
Danger 1983
Proof 1984
Break in 1985
Bolt 1986
Hot money 1987
The edge 1988
Straight 1989
Longshot 1990

Comeback 1991
Driving force 1992
Decider 1993
(All published by Michael Joseph in England and
Harper in the USA.)

Now read
Jon Breen, John Francome, Michael Maguire (horse racing); Ille
Nastase (tennis); Keith Miles (golf); Gerald Hammond (shooting);
Douglas Rutherford (motor racing); Alan Synge, Michael Marquesee
(cricket).

Higgins, Jack (Harry Patterson)

British. Born in 1929 in Newcastle-upon-Tyne, but he was educated
at Roundhay School and Beckett Park Teachers' Training College,
Leeds, followed by a sociology degree at LSE. He tried various jobs
in the education and clerical professions, mainly in Leeds and other
areas in Yorkshire, after army service, and became a full-time writer
at the age of 41. He has dual British/Irish citizenship, and now lives
in Ireland. He has written under a variety of pseudonyms: Martin
Fallon, James Graham, Hugh Marlowe, Harry Patterson, but most
titles have been reprinted under the name of Jack Higgins.
   Jack Higgins writes many different types of thriller, from the pure
adventure story, like *The eagle has landed*, to the private detective
novel, as Hugh Marlowe, and the spy story, as Martin Fallon. He is
currently writing political thrillers, set in Northern Ireland, which
feature Liam Devlin in conflict with the IRA. His novels are listed
under the heading of adventure stories because many of them come
into that category. Several of his books have become successful films.

Publications

as Jack Higgins
East of desolation Hodder 1968
In the hour before midnight Hodder 1969
Night judgment at Sinos Hodder 1970
The last place God made Collins 1971

9

The savage day   Collins   1972
A prayer for the dying   Collins   1973
The eagle has landed   Collins   1975
Storm warning   Collins   1976
Day of judgement   Collins   1978
Solo (*The Cretan lover* in US)   Collins   1980
Luciano's luck   Collins   1981
Touch the devil   Collins   1982
Exocet   Collins   1983
Confessional   Collins   1985
Night of the fox   Collins   1986
A season in hell   Collins   1989
Memoirs of a dance hall Romeo   Collins   1989
Cold harbour   Heinemann   1990
The eagle has flown   Chapmans   1991
Eye of the storm   Chapmans   1992
Thunder point   M. Joseph   1993

as Harry Patterson
Sad wind from the sea   1959
Cry of the hunter   1960
The thousand faces of night   1961
Comes the dark stranger   1962
Hell is too crowded   1962
The dark side of the island   1963
(All published by John Long.)
Pay the devil   Barrie & Rockcliff   1963
A phoenix in the blood   Barrie & Rockcliff   1964
Thunder at noon   1964
Wrath of the lion   1964
The graveyard shift   1965
The iron tiger   1966
Brought in dead   1967
Hell is always today   1968
Toll for the brave   1971
(All published by John Long.)
The Valhalla exchange   Hutchinson   1976
To catch a king   Hutchinson   1979
Dillinger   Hutchinson   1983

as Martin Fallon
The testament of Caspar Schultz   1962
Year of the tiger   1963
The keys of hell   1965
(All published by Abelard Schuman.)
Midnight never comes   1966
Dark side of the street   1967
A fine night for dying   1969
(All published by John Long.)

as James Graham
A game for heroes   1970
The wrath of God   1971
The Khufra run   1972
Bloody passage   1974
(All published by Macmillan.)

as Hugh Marlowe
Seven pillars to hell   1963
Passage by night   1964
A candle for the dead   1966
(All published by Abelard Schuman, though the last
was reissued by Hodder in 1969 as *The violent
enemy*.)

Now read
Ken Follett, Colin Forbes, Geoffrey Jenkins, Alistair MacLean,
Craig Thomas.

Innes, Hammond

British. Born in Sussex in 1913. He was educated in Kent, and
joined the staff of the *Financial News* in 1934. He served in the
Royal Artillery in the Second World War, where he continued to
write, and became a full-time author after the war. His hobbies are
travel and ocean racing, and these are reflected in his plots. He was
awarded a CBE in 1978.

Hammond Innes writes in the tradition of Buchan and Haggard.

His plots, though well-researched and detailed, are full of cliff-hanging situations and daring escapades. His knowledge of the sea and of life in other countries is self-evident in the locations of his novels. The books have remained consistently popular, and Collins have reprinted most of them in a standard edition. Several have been filmed.

He has also written children's books as Ralph Hammond, and travel books. Two of his later novels, *The big footprints*, about the elephant poachers in Africa, and *The last voyage: Captain Cook's lost diary*, were not really thrillers.

Publications

Wreckers must breathe 1940
The Trojan horse 1940
Attack alarm 1941
Dead and alive 1946
Killer mine 1947
The lonely skier 1947
Maddon's Rock 1948
The blue ice 1948
The white south 1948
The angry mountain 1950
Air bridge 1951
Campbell's kingdom 1952
The strange land 1954
The Mary Deare 1956
The land God gave to Cain 1958
The doomed oasis 1960
Atlantic fury 1962
The Stode Venturer 1965
Levkas man 1971
Golden soak 1973
North star 1975
The big footprints 1977
The last voyage 1978
Solomon's seal 1980
The black tide 1982
High stand 1985

Medusa   1988
(All published by Collins.)
Isvik   Chapmans   1991

Now read
Desmond Bagley, Clive Cussler, James Follett, Geoffrey Jenkins,
Duncan Kyle, Alistair MacLean.

Jenkins, Geoffrey

British. He is one of the generation of writers of high adventure who
emerged in the 1960s, writing to a formula, with fast-moving plots
and lots of action. Many of Geoffrey Jenkins' books have a naval
setting. He also writes naval historical novels under the name of
Patrick O'Brian, and these novels are listed under Sea stories.

Publications

The river of diamonds   1964
A twist of sand   1966
The watering place of good peace   1969
Scend of the sea   1971
A grue of ice   1973
A cleft of stars   1973
A bridge of magpies   1974
Southtrap   1979
A ravel of waters   1981
The unripe gold   1983
Fireprint   1984
In harm's way   1986
Hold down a shadow   1988
A hive of dead men   1991
(All published by Collins.)

Now read
Desmond Bagley, Ken Follett, Hammond Innes, Duncan Kyle,
Alistair MacLean.

Kyle, Duncan

British. Born in Bradford. He worked as a journalist until 1970, when his first novel was accepted, and has been a full-time writer ever since. He now lives in deepest Suffolk. Kyle is another writer in the tradition of Buchan and his successors, with action-filled plots and dashing heroes.

Publications

> *A cage of ice* 1970
> *Flight into fear* 1971
> *A raft of swords* 1973
> *Terror's cradle* 1974
> *In deep* 1976
> *Whiteout* 1977
> *Black Camelot* 1978
> *Green River high* 1979
> *Stalking point* 1981
> *The King's commissar* 1983
> *The dancing men* 1985
> *Exit* 1993
> (All published by Collins.)

Now read
Desmond Bagley, Ken Follett, Hammond Innes, Geoffrey Jenkins, Alistair MacLean.

Langley, Bob

British. Born in Newcastle-upon-Tyne. He joined the BBC as a news presenter in 1969, working on both regional and national programmes. He presented 'Pebble Mill at One' and 'Saturday Night at the Mill' before leaving to become a freelance presenter and author. He lives in the Lake District, where his great hobby is fell-walking.

Bob Langley writes taut, fast-moving thrillers, with foreign settings, which always involve manhunts and often mountain climbing. Some are spy stories, but of the adventure type rather than the Intelligence Service procedural type. He draws on his own experiences in the news-reporting field to add authenticity.

Publications

> *Death stalk*   1977
> *War of the running fox*   1978
> *Hour of the gaucho*   1979
> *Traverse of the gods*   1980
> *Autumn tiger*   1981
> *Warlord*   1983
> *East of Everest*   1984
> *Conquistadores*   1985
> *The Churchill diamonds*   1986
> *Avenge the Belgrano*   1988
> *Blood River*   1989
> (All published by Michael Joseph.)

Now read
Jack Higgins, Colin Forbes, Craig Thomas.

MacLean, Alistair

Born in Glasgow in 1922. He served in the Royal Navy in the Second World War, and then became a history teacher. He began writing short stories, and moved on to novels with great success. He is by far the best known of the thriller writers who emerged in the 1950s and 1960s, and set the pattern for many of his successors. His plots are simply laid out, with cliff-hanging suspense in every chapter, and plenty of action to occupy the hero until the last page. The settings for the stories are varied; some are war stories, like *The guns of Navarone*, others are sea stories, like *HMS Ulysses*, and some, like *Caravan to Vaccares* and *Puppet on a chain* are set in post-war Europe. Many of the books have been filmed, and lend themselves eminently well to screen adaptations.

Alistair MacLean retired as a tax exile to Switzerland, where he died in 1987. However, he left a number of story outlines,

commissioned by an American film company, to be written by other
authors. It must be said that his last books were not as well received
as the earlier ones, and appeared stale. Nevertheless, Collins
continue to keep all his books in print. He also wrote as Ian Stuart.

Several novels, based on his outlines, have appeared since his death.

Publications

> *HMS Ulysses*   1955
> *The guns of Navarone*   1957
> *South by Java Head*   1957
> *The last frontier*   1959
> *Night without end*   1960
> *Fear is the key*   1961 (as Ian Stuart)
> *The golden rendezvous*   1962
> *Ice station Zebra*   1963
> *When eight bells toll*   1966
> *Where eagles dare*   1967
> *Force 10 from Navarone*   1968
> *Puppet on a chain*   1969
> *Caravan to Vaccares*   1970
> *Bear Island*   1971
> *The way to dusty death*   1973
> *Breakheart Pass*   1974
> *Circus*   1975
> *The golden gate*   1976
> *Seawitch*   1977
> *Goodbye California*   1978
> *Athabasca*   1980
> *River of death*   1981
> *Partisans*   1982
> *Floodgate*   1983
> *San Andreas*   1984
> *Santorini*   1986
> By John Denis: *Hostage tower*   1985
> *Air Force One is down*   1987
> By Alistair MacNeill: *Death train*   1988
> *The Rembrandt affair*   1989
> *Night watch*   1989

Red alert   1990
Time of the assassins   1992
Dead halt   1992
(All published by Collins.)
By Simon Gandolfi: *Golden girl*   Chapmans   1992

Now read
Desmond Bagley, Clive Cussler, Ken Follett, Hammond Innes, Geoffrey Jenkins, Duncan Kyle.

Peters, Elizabeth

American. Real name Barbara Mertz. She was born in Illinois in 1927, and read Archaeology at the University of Chicago. She has written several works about Egyptology under her own name, and her archaeological and museum training is reflected in her novels. She is one of the few women who write this type of material, and her books are not only full of action and suspense, but contain a good deal of humour. She writes about two heroines; Vicky Bliss, who is an American working in a German museum, and Amelia Peabody, a nineteenth-century archaeologist who works in Egypt. The Peabody books, as well as being adventure stories, are splendid parodies of the Victorian confession novel.

Elizabeth Peters also writes as Barbara Michaels, and another entry will be found in the section on Gothic romances.

Publications

The Jackal's head   Jenkins   1969 (reissued by
  Souvenir Press 1982)
The Dead Sea cipher   Cassell   1975
Shadows in the moonlight   Hodder   1975 (reissued
  by Severn House 1986)
The seventh sinner   Hodder   1975 (reissued by
  Severn House 1984)
The Camelot caper   Cassell   1976
Ghost in green velvet   Cassell   1977
Summer of the dragon   Souvenir Press   1980

The love talker   Souvenir Press   1981
The murders of Richard III   Piatkus   1989
Naked once more   Piatkus   1990

VICKY BLISS

The Copenhagen connection   Souvenir Press   1983
Silhouette in scarlet   Souvenir Press   1984
Die for love   Souvenir Press   1985
Trojan gold   Piatkus   1987
Street of the Five Moons   Piatkus   1988

AMELIA PEABODY

Crocodile on the sandbank   Souvenir Press   1976
Curse of the Pharaohs   Souvenir Press   1982
The mummy case   Souvenir Press   1986
Lion in the valley   Piatkus   1987
The deeds of the disturber   Piatkus   1989
The last camel died at noon   Piatkus   1991
The snake, the crocodile and the dog   Piatkus   1993

For similar authors see Gothic romances.

Savarin, Julian

Born in Dominica, of African, Mayan and French ancestry. At the age of 12, he moved to Britain, where he finished his education. He served for a period in the RAF, and then devoted his time to music and writing.

His first books were science fiction, then he turned to writing thrillers. His plots are set in exotic locations, and have an atmosphere of tension. His latest books feature Gordon Gallagher, an adventurer, who becomes embroiled in political situations in unfriendly countries. The stories are tough and fast-moving.

Publications

GORDON GALLAGHER SERIES

Waterhole   1982

Wolfrun   1984
Windshear   1985
Naja   1986
Hammerhead   1987
The Quiraing list   1988
(All published by Allison & Busby.)

OTHERS

Lynx   1984
Gunship   1985
(Both published by Secker & Warburg.)
Trophy   Century   1989

Now read
Clive Cussler, Colin Forbes, Jack Higgins, Wilbur Smith.

Smith, Wilbur

Born in 1933. He is a British subject, but was brought up and educated in Rhodesia, where he took a degree in economics, and worked for the Inland Revenue. He wrote his first novel in 1963 at the age of 30, and achieved immediate success with it, though it was banned in South Africa. After writing two more successful novels, he decided to become a full-time writer, and moved to South Africa. He has written a book almost every year since then.

Wilbur Smith writes about the Africa which he knows so well. His novels are meticulously researched, and have great depth of character. The plots are exciting and fast-moving, but tell the reader a great deal about wildlife in Africa, and social conditions. The books are set in the jungle, or in the gold mines, and some deal with the Boer War and the 1914–18 war in Africa, but all have a courageous and heroic central character. They are long – often 180,000 words – and complex at times, but are eagerly awaited, and translate well to the screen.

Publications

When the lion feeds   1964

The dark of the sun   1965
The sound of thunder   1966
Shout at the devil   1968
Gold mine   1970
The diamond hunters   1971
The sunbird   1972
Eagle in the sky   1974
The eye of the tiger   1975
Cry wolf   1976
A sparrow falls   1977
Hungry as the sea   1978
Wild justice   1979
A falcon flies   1980
Men of men   1981
The angels weep   1982
The leopard hunts in darkness   1984
The burning shore   1985
Power of the sword   1986
Rage   1987
A time to die   1989
(All publications by Heinemann.)
Golden fox   Macmillan   1990
Elephant song   Macmillan   1991
River God (an historical novel, set in ancient Egypt)
   Macmillan   1993

Now read
Frederick Forsyth, Peter Driscoll, Julian Savarin.

Thomas, Craig

Born in Cardiff in 1942. He obtained an MA at University College, Cardiff in 1967 and became a teacher. His first two books were published while he was still a schoolmaster, and the success of the second, *Firefox*, enabled him to become a professional novelist. He lives in Lichfield, and lists his hobbies as gardening, watching cricket and listening to music.

His books are deeply researched and carefully plotted, with good characterisation and convincing locations. They deal with political situations and world crises, with a build-up of tension as the plot unfolds.

Publications

Rat trap   1976
Firefox   1977
Wolfsbane   1978
Snow falcon   1979
Jade tiger   1981
Sea leopard   1982
Firefox down   1983
The bear's tears   1985
Winter hawk   1987
All the grey cats   1988
Last raven   1990
A hooded crow   1992
(All published by Collins.)
Playing with cobras   HarperCollins   1993

Now read
Ken Follett, Colin Forbes, Jack Higgins, Peter Driscoll.

COUNTRY LIFE

This is a genre which has always been extremely popular with readers, and which reached its heyday in the 1930s and 1940s, when authors of the calibre of H. E. Bates, Adrian Bell and Henry Williamson were writing regularly about the countryside. There has been a decline in this sort of writing and, though many of the sagas and family stories convey the atmosphere of rural life, there are few traditional country and animal stories published now.

The authors selected for this section write in a variety of styles, some of which overlap with other genres. For example, Frank Parrish writes thrillers, and L. G. J. Layberry has written a long family saga. They have been chosen for this section, however, because a feeling for the countryside and a knowledge of its ways are paramount in their work.

Adams, Richard

British. He was born in 1920. He was awarded an MA in Modern History at Oxford, and entered the Civil Service in 1948. He retired in 1974 as Assistant Secretary at the Department of the Environment. He has been an active campaigner for animal rights for many years, and was President of the RSPCA during 1980–82. His concern for animals and for the conservation of their environment is reflected in his novels, many of which feature animals as their main characters.

He had an extraordinary success with his first novel, *Watership Down*, which, though ostensibly written for children, and awarded the Carnegie Medal in 1972, became a cult novel among adults, and was filmed as a full-length cartoon. His animal characters are drawn with real feeling, and have distinct personalities. He writes about the harshness and brutality of the countryside, as well as its beauty, and his books have a moral theme about man's lack of feeling for his fellow creatures. The books are long and detailed, with many threads to their plot, and, though not an easy read, sustain the reader's interest to the end. His books are now concerned with natural history, or are stories for children.

Publications

> *Watership Down*   Allen Lane   1972
> *Shardik*   Viking/Lane   1974
> *The plague dogs*   Viking   1977
> *The girl in a swing*   Viking   1980
> *Traveller*   Hutchinson   1989

Now read
Jack London, Henry Williamson.

Fitzroy, Rosamond

British. She lives in the West Country in an old house with a large garden, which, with looking after her dogs, takes up much of her time. She lists her other interests as bridge, patience, crossword puzzles and antiques.

She writes very much in the style of Angela Thirkell, and her settings are also similar. Her novels are set in the fictional county of Mallamshire, and revolve around the lives of the aristocracy and squirearchy, and their influence on the lives of the rural inhabitants. Everyday village life is shrewdly observed, with its feuds and families realistically portrayed. The books are light-hearted and easy to read, with credible characterisation and considerable wit. They form a series, but stand up equally well as individual novels.

Publications

THE MALLAMSHIRE SERIES

The manor of Braye   1979
The widow's might   1980
The American Duchess   1980
(All published by Arlington Press.)
Ill fares the land   1987
Barnaby's charity   1988
The Rockport rubies   1989
(All published by Hale.)

Now read
Miss Read, Angela Thirkell.

Horwood, William

British. He was born in Oxford in 1944, and read Geography at the University of Bristol. He was a journalist for ten years, and was latterly Features Editor of the *Daily Mail*. His first novel became a bestseller, and he decided to become a full-time writer. He lives on the Kent coast.

His novels are long sagas, intricately plotted and beautifully described. Each of his animals has a character of its own, and the events in their lives are totally credible. His major novels form a trilogy about a colony of moles living in Duncton Wood, but he has written others about birds and other creatures.

Publications

> DUNCTON CHRONICLES
>
> *Duncton Wood*   Century Hutchinson   1980
> *Duncton quest*   Century Hutchinson   1988
> *Duncton found*   Century Hutchinson   1989
> *Duncton tales*   HarperCollins   1991
> *Duncton rising*   HarperCollins   1992
> *Duncton stone*   HarperCollins   1993
>
> *The Stonor eagles*   1982
> *Callanish*   1984
> *Skallagrigg*   1986
> (All published by Century Hutchinson.)

Now read
Richard Adams.

Layberry, L. G. J. (Joe)

British. He was born near Burton on Trent, and educated at the village school at Rolleston. He learned about farming in the rural area of South Derbyshire, and in 1934 moved to Kent, where he studied agriculture at the Farm Institute. He spent many years in farm management, but ill-health in his fifties put a stop to his physical activities, and he joined the Civil Service. He is now retired, and lives near Folkestone, with a view of the arable fields of the chalk hills, and retains an interest in farming, as well as writing about it.

His novels are set in South Derbyshire and follow the lives and fortunes of the inhabitants of Oakleigh Farm from just before the First World War to the 1950s. He writes well and authentically about farm life and techniques in a peaceful and fertile area. His descriptions of village life and customs early in this century are excellent. His plots are slight, being mainly a chronicle of everyday life, but the action is well-sustained, and the style, though a little stilted, is good enough to retain the reader's interest. His characterisation is perceptive, and the main characters are built up and acquire depth as the series progresses.

Publications

OAKLEIGH FARM

Hayseed 1980
Gleanings 1981
To be a farmer's girl 1982
A pocket full of rye 1984
Tangled harvest 1984
(All published by Midas.)
The last mophrey 1987
As long as the fields are green 1987
A new earth 1988
(Published by Spellmount Press.)

Now read
Adrian Bell.

Lloyd, A. R.

British. He was born in 1927, and lives on a farm in Kent. He has always lived in the country, and avoided school as far as possible when he was a child, preferring to work on one of the local farms. He served in the army, in a unit which still used horses, and then became a journalist before turning to writing history and biography. He began to write novels about country life and animals in 1984.

His novels evoke the spirit of the countryside. Most are about animals, which he understands well, and to which he gives individual characters. His descriptions of the countryside are graphic and perceptive, and the plots are full of interest. *The farm dog* is a moving study of a working dog's relationship with his master.

Publications

The last otter 1984
The farm dog 1986

KINE SAGA

Marshworld (*Kine*) 1988
Witchwood 1989
Dragonpond 1990
(All published by Muller.)

Now read
Richard Adams, Brian Carter, Brian Parvin.

Miss Read

British. The pen name of Dora Jane Saint. She is the wife of a retired schoolteacher, and was a teacher herself for many years, in schools in small rural communities. She began to write after the Second World War, mainly light pieces about country matters for a variety of magazines. Her first novel, *Village school*, was published in 1955, and she has written another almost every year since then. She lives with her family in a Berkshire village.

Her books are evocative and nostalgic, conveying the peaceful atmosphere of a small enclosed rural community, seen through the eyes of the village headteacher. Her descriptions of the changing seasons and the wildlife of the countryside are excellently done, as are her perceptive portrayals of the local characters who make up the population of the village. The books epitomise country life, with its small dramas, gossip and humour.

Publications

FAIRACRE

Village school 1955
Village diary 1956
Storm in the village 1960
Miss Clare remembers 1962
Over the gate 1964
Village Christmas 1966
Fairacre festival 1969
Tyler's Row 1972

29

Further afield   1974
No holly for Miss Quinn   1976
Village affairs   1977
The white robin   1979
Village centenary   1980
Summer at Fairacre   1984
Mrs. Pringle   1989
Changes at Fairacre   1991

THRUSH GREEN

Thrush Green   1960
Winter in Thrush Green   1961
News from Thrush Green   1970
Battles at Thrush Green   1975
Return to Thrush Green   1978
Gossip from Thrush Green   1981
Affairs at Thrush Green   1983
At home in Thrush Green   1985
The school at Thrush Green   1987
Friends at Thrush Green   1990
Celebrations at Thrush Green   1992

CAXLEY SERIES

The market square   1966
The Howards of Caxley   1967
Emily Davis   1971
(All published by Michael Joseph.)

Now read
Rosamond Fitzroy.

Parrish, Frank

British. He lives deep in the Dorset countryside, but is otherwise
reticent about personal details. He writes thrillers set in Dorset,
about a central character called Dan Mallett, a bank clerk turned
poacher and amateur detective. The books are full of action and

humour, with a satisfying dénouement as Dan evades the law once again, while bringing the criminal to justice. The main feature of the novels is the author's remarkable sense of the atmosphere of the countryside and knowledge of country lore. The descriptions are so vivid that the reader can almost hear and smell the fields and hedgerows, as Dan moves quietly through them.

Publications

> *Fire in the barley*   1977
> *Sting of the honeybee*   1978
> *Snare in the dark*   1982
> *Bait on the hook*   1983
> *Face at the window*   1984
> *Fly in the cobweb*   1986
> *Caught in the birdlime*   1987
> (All published by Constable.)

Now read
A. R. Lloyd, Brian Parvin.

Parvin, Brian

British. He was born in Nottinghamshire. He started his career as a journalist in Nottingham, working later in London. His job involved travelling widely, but he has now returned to the English countryside which he loves. He is deeply concerned with the issues involved in the preservation of wild life, a concern which is mirrored in his books.

He began by writing thrillers, but has now turned his attention to animal stories, mainly about the small mammals of the countryside – hedgehogs, badgers and rabbits. He imbues his animals with individual characters, and describes their environment and habits with accuracy and feeling. His books are short and easy to read, and provide a useful contribution to the literature of the genre.

Publications

> *The singing tree*   1987

Now read on

> *The golden garden*   1987
> *The moonkeepers*   1988
> *The dawn boys*   1989
> (Published by Hale.)

Now read
William Horwood, A. R. Lloyd.

DETECTIVE STORIES

The detective story achieved popular acclaim in the 1930s, when authors like Dorothy L. Sayers, C. B. Kitchin, G. D. H. Cole and Margery Allingham lifted the books from their blood and thunder, pulp fiction image, and turned them into an art form, with credible characterisation, well-constructed plots and a good literary style. They are very much the province of women authors, with Agatha Christie, Ngaio Marsh, Gladys Mitchell and Mignon G. Eberhart writing from the 1930s to the 1960s, and the literary tradition is kept alive by writers such as P. D. James and Ruth Rendell.

Detective stories fall into two distinct groups; those which have a background of police procedures, in which the detectives are members of the CID, and those in which the detective is an amateur with an interest in criminology allied to his or her own career. Their authors often have a working background or special interest in the subject about which they write.

The hallmark of the good detective story is a clever plot, which offers clues as the story unfolds, thus enabling the reader to apply logic and powers of observation to solve the problem and unmask the murderer at the same time as the detective. Police work overlaps to a large extent, but merits its own section because of the differences in presentation, and its emphasis on police work across the board. As in other genres, some authors write both types of novel.

Aird, Catherine

British. Her real name is Kinn Hamilton Mackintosh and she was born in Huddersfield, Yorkshire in 1930. She works for the Girl Guide Association as Chair of the Finance Committee, and now lives in Canterbury. She was Chair of the Crime Writers' Association in 1990/91. In October 1992 she was the first recipient of the Crime Writers' Association/Hertfordshire Libraries Golden Handcuffs Award for her outstanding contribution to detective fiction.

Her style is that of the domestic murder, set usually in a village or small town in the fictional county of Calleshire, and her detective, Inspector C. D. Sloan, is a straightforward policeman with no psychological hang-ups.

Publications

INSPECTOR SLOAN SERIES

The religious body   Macdonald   1966
A most contagious game   Macdonald   1967
Henrietta who?   Macdonald   1968
The complete steel   Macdonald   1969
A late phoenix   Collins   1971
His burial too   Collins   1973
Slight mourning   Collins   1975
Parting breath   Collins   1977
Some die eloquent   Collins   1979
Passing strange   Collins   1980
Last respects   Collins   1982
Harm's way   Collins   1984
Dead liberty   Collins   1986
The body politic   Macmillan   1990
A going concern   Macmillan   1993

Now read
Agatha Christie, Elizabeth Lemarchand, Patricia Moyes, Emma Page.

Braun, Lilian Jackson

American. She has written since the age of two, and began to write her series of mysteries when one of her own Siamese cats fell to its death from her apartment block. She now divides her time between her two homes, one in North Carolina, and the other a remote island retreat.

The novels feature Jim Qwilleran, an ex-reporter who inherited a large estate in Moose County, and his two Siamese cats, Koko and Yum-Yum, who have an amazing talent for solving mysteries. The same characters recur in each book, and are a fine collection of eccentrics. The plots are ingenious and diverse, with plenty of action. There is a great deal of information about the habits of Siamese cats, and also about life in what amounts to an enclosed community. Jim Qwilleran is an endearing character, gentle yet shrewd, who brings his journalists' eye to gathering information about crime. The books are funny and light-hearted, with crisp dialogue, and clever characterisation.

Publications

The cat who could read backwards   Constable 1966
The cat who ate Danish modern   Constable   1967
The cat who turned on and off   Constable   1968
The cat who played Brahms   Collins   1969
The cat who played Post Office   Collins   1987
The cat who knew Shakespeare   Headline   1987
The cat who saw red   Headline   1990
The cat who sniffed glue   Headline   1991
The cat who went underground   Headline   1991
The cat who talked to ghosts   Headline   1992
The cat who lived high   Headline   1992
The cat who knew a cardinal   Headline   1992
The cat who moved a mountain   Headline   1992
The cat who wasn't there   Headline   1993

Now read
Gerald Hammond, Neville Steed

Brett, Simon

British. Born in Surrey in 1945, and awarded an Honours Degree in English at Oxford in 1967. He was President of the Oxford University Dramatic Society, and the theatre is still his hobby. He joined the BBC as a Radio Producer in 1967, and moved to London Weekend Television as a Producer in 1977. He writes scripts for TV and radio as well as his detective stories, including those for the comedy series 'After Henry'. His detective is an actor, Charles Paris, and his plots reflect his knowledge of the theatre and television. Characterisation is good, with the minor and major characters equally well-rounded. He has recently introduced a new series featuring Mrs. Pargeter, the widow of an astute but rather shady businessman.

Publications

CHARLES PARIS SERIES

Cast, in order of disappearance   1975
So much blood   1976
Star trap   1977
An amateur corpse   1978
A comedian dies   1979
Dead side of the mike   1980
Situation tragedy   1981
Murder unprompted   1982
Murder in the title   1983
Not dead, only resting   1984
Dead giveaway   1985
A shock to the system   1986
What bloody man is that?   1987
A series of murders   1989
Corporate bodies   1991
(All published by Gollancz.)

MRS PARGETER SERIES

A nice class of corpse   1986
Mrs., presumed dead   1988
Mrs. Pargeter's package   1990

Mrs. Pargeter's pound of flesh   1992
(All published by Macmillan.)

Dead romantic   Macmillan   1986

Now read
Antonia Fraser, Ngaio Marsh, Anne Morice, John Sherwood.

Burley, W. J.

British. Born in Cornwall in 1914, and trained originally as a gas engineer. He worked for the South Western Gas and Water Board during 1936–50 and then went to Balliol College, Oxford, where he gained an MA. He then became a teacher of biology, and retired to become a full-time writer in 1974.

He says that his work is very much influenced by Georges Simenon and his detective, Detective Superintendent Charles Wycliffe, uses methods based on Gestalt psychology. All his books are set in Cornwall and reflect his love of and knowledge about his home county. He has tried to inject both humour and originality into his main character, and one of his strengths is in his portrayal of the characters involved in Wycliffe's cases, and the psychological effects on them. He wrote two books about a character called Henry Pym, before dropping him for Wycliffe, and has also written some psychological thrillers, which, he says, have more of himself in them.

Publications

DR. HENRY PYM NOVELS

A taste of power   1966
Death in willow pattern   1969

DET. SUPERINTENDENT WYCLIFFE SERIES

Three-toed pussy   1969
To kill a cat   1970
Guilt edged   1971
Death in a salubrious place   1972
Death in Stanley Street   1973

Wycliffe and the pea green boat 1975
Wycliffe and the schoolgirls 1976
Wycliffe and the scapegoat 1978
Wycliffe in Paul's Court 1980
Wycliffe's wild goose chase 1982
Wycliffe and the Beales 1983
Wycliffe and the four Jacks 1985
Wycliffe and the quiet virgin 1986
Wycliffe and the Winsor blue 1987
Wycliffe and the tangled web 1988
Wycliffe and the cycle of death 1990
Wycliffe and the dead flautist 1991
Wycliffe and the last rites 1992
Wycliffe and the dunes mystery 1993

OTHERS

The sixth day 1968
The schoolmaster 1977
Charles and Elizabeth 1979
(All published by Gollancz.)

Now read
Douglas Clark, Martha Grimes, S. T. Haymon, Sheila Radley, Jonathan Ross, June Thomson.

Clark, Douglas

British. Born in the 1920s. After serving in the army, he made his career in the pharmaceutical industry, working for well-known drug manufacturers. This experience is reflected in his books, which all feature Detective Chief Superintendent George Masters, and his team, based at Scotland Yard. Masters is attached to the Murder Squad, and specialises in cases of death by poisoning. The settings of the books are provincial towns all over the country, and the locations are carefully researched, as are the many different and sometimes obscure poisons used as a method of murder. Characterisation is one of Douglas Clark's strengths. As the series progresses he builds a very real and convincing picture of Masters, his assistant, Bill Green, and their families, and the interaction between the police and the people whom they encounter in their cases. Police methods are also authentically described, in some detail.

Publications

DETECTIVE CHIEF SUPT. MASTERS SERIES

Nobody's perfect   1969
Death after evensong   1969
Deadly pattern   1970
Sweet poison   1970
Sick to death   1971
The miracle makers   1971
Premedicated murder   1975
Dread and water   1976
Table d' hôte   1977
The Gimmel flask   1977
The libertines   1978
Heberden's seat   1979
Poacher's bag   1979
Golden rain   1980
Roast eggs   1981
The longest pleasure   1981
Shelf life   1981
Doone Walk   1982
Vicious circle   1983
The Monday theory   1983
Bouquet garni   1984
Dead letter   1984
Performance   1985
The jewelled eye   1985
The big grouse   1986
Storm centre   1986
Plain sailing   1987
(All published by Gollancz.)

Now read
W. J. Burley, Martha Grimes, Sheila Radley, Jonathan Ross, June Thomson.

George, Elizabeth

American. She lives in New Jersey.

She is another American author who, like Martha Grimes, has captured the essence of the English detective story. The books have four main protagonists: Detective Chief Inspector Thomas Lynley, a member of the English aristocracy who prefers not to use his title (a device borrowed from Ngaio Marsh); his close friend Simon St. James, a forensic scientist; Deborah, Simon's wife, who is a talented photographer; and Lady Helen Clyde, whom Lynley would very much like to marry. In complete contrast is Barbara Havers, Lynley's Detective Sergeant, who comes from a very poor background, and who despises Lynley's affluent life-style, and family background.

The books are long, and very detailed, and are obviously carefully researched in this country. The plots are often sombre, with psychological undertones, and concern the vicissitudes of family life. Murder is always involved, usually with a devious motive, and often with an unexpected ending. Lynley is a complex character, guilt-ridden and full of self-doubt. The style is literary, full of classical allusions, but the diversity of the plot, and the depth of the characterisation hold the reader's interest throughout the book.

Publications

>*A great deliverance*   Bantam   1989
>*Payment in blood*   Bantam   1989
>*Well-schooled in murder*   Bantam   1990
>*A suitable vengeance*   Bantam   1991
>*For the sake of Elena*   Bantam   1992
>*Missing Joseph*   Bantam   1993

Now read
P. D. James, S.T. Haymon, Ruth Rendell, Peter Robinson.

Grant-Adamson, Lesley

British. A comparative newcomer to the field of crime writers. Her stories are well-constructed and written in a taut style, with a careful build-up of suspense. Her detective is the chief reporter for a gossip column, Rain Morgan, and the settings are those of the contemporary business world. There is a good deal of psychological insight in her characterisation, and her plots are intelligent and skilful, with an underlying sense of evil.

Publications

RAIN MORGAN SERIES

Patterns in the dust   1984
The face of death   1985
Guilty knowledge   1987
Wild justice   1987
Curse the darkness   1990

OTHERS

Threatening eye   1988
Flynn   1991
A life of adventure   1992
The dangerous edge   1993
(All published by Faber.)

Now read
Amanda Cross, Antonia Fraser, P. D. James, Ruth Rendell.

Grimes, Martha

American. Lives in Washington, DC. Martha Grimes does the research for all her books in the English countryside, which she loves. All her novels are set in England, usually in Yorkshire or the Cotswolds, and their titles are derived from English pub names. She writes in the style of Agatha Christie and the other exponents of the country house detective story, and employs the device of having two detectives, a policeman, Det. Chief Inspector Richard Jury, and an amateur, in her case the dilettante poet and ex-peer, Melrose Plant. Her plots are intricate, with several interwoven threads, and her characters, many of whom recur in each book, are credible, with memorable quirks of personality and eccentricities. The police procedures are carefully researched, but there is also insight into the character and domestic life of Jury.

Publications

CHIEF INSPECTOR JURY SERIES

The man with a load of mischief   Brown, Little
   1981
The old fox deceiv'd   Brown, Little   1982
The anodyne necklace   Brown, Little   1984
   Reprinted by Michael O'Mara   1989
The dirty duck   Michael O'Mara   1986
I am the only running footman   Michael O'Mara
   1987
Jerusalem Inn   Michael O'Mara   1987
The Five Bells and Bladebone   Michael O'Mara
   1988
The deer leap   Michael O'Mara   1988
Help the poor struggler   Michael O'Mara   1989
The old silent   Headline   1990
The old contemptibles   Headline   1991
The horse you came in on   Headline   1993

Now read
W. J. Burley, Roy Lewis, Emma Page, Sheila Radley, June Thomson.

Haymon, S. T.

British. Born in Norwich in the 1920s. She writes with great local knowledge, and most of her books are set in the Norwich area. Her detective, Chief Inspector Ben Jurnet, is an introspective character, much given to self-doubt, and troubled by questions of religion. Some of the books have a religious flavour, and involve the building and staff of Norwich Cathedral. Her plots are well-constructed, meticulously worked out and full of detail. She applies psychological insight to her characters, who have depth and credibility. Her output has been small, a reflection of the care and craft which goes into her writing.

Publications

CHIEF INSPECTOR JURNET SERIES

Death of a pregnant virgin 1980
Ritual murder 1982
Stately homicide 1985
Death of a god 1987
A very particular murder 1989
Death of a warrior queen 1991
(All published by Constable.)

Now read
P. D James, Ruth Rendell, Sheila Radley, June Thomson.

Hilton, John Buxton

British. Born in Buxton, Derbyshire in 1921, and educated there and at Pembroke College, Cambridge, where he took a degree in languages. He became, in turn, teacher, headmaster (at Chorley Grammar School, Lancashire), Inspector of Schools, 1964–70, and Tutor-Counsellor for the Open University, 1971–78. He died in 1987.

He applied his knowledge of and interest in history to his books, and many of their plots are built around local customs and legends. There is very little violence in the books, though most of them concern murder. He says, 'I believe that the distinction between suspense fiction and the "literary novel" is an unreal one, and my effort is to bridge the gap. Consequently, I believe that my books should appeal to readers of some literary sensitivity who do not normally read thrillers.'

He wrote three series of books, with different and distinctive characters. His mainstream contemporary detective stories were about Superintendent Simon Kenworthy, attached to Scotland Yard, and apparently careless in his methods, some of which were unorthodox. The character of Kenworthy was carefully built up until the reader began to understand his motivation and beliefs. The second series concerned Sergeant Thomas Brunt, and were set in the High Peak of Derbyshire in the late nineteenth and early twentieth century. There is a great deal of local knowledge, both of terrain and of the character of the Derbyshire people in this series, and some of them are rather more psychological thrillers than straightforward detective stories. The brooding atmosphere of the Derbyshire hills and the quality of life of the inhabitants of isolated communities are described with great authenticity. The third series was written under the name of John Greenwood and features a splendidly idiosyncratic detective, Inspector Mosley, whose particular territory was the wild border country between Lancashire and Yorkshire. Again, the life of the people in remote villages is graphically described, and the characters have colour and a great deal of humour.

Publications

SUPERINTENDENT KENWORTHY SERIES

Death of an alderman   1968
Death in midwinter   1969
Hangman's tide   1972
No birds sang   1975
Some run crooked   1977
The anathema stone   1979
Playground of death   1980
Surrender value   1981
The green frontier   1982
The sunset law   1982
The asking price   1983
Corridors of guilt   1984
The Hobbema prospect   1984
Passion in the peak   1985
The innocents at home   1986
Moondrop to murder   1986
Displaced person   1987

SERGEANT BRUNT SERIES

The quiet stranger   1985 (chronologically first)
Gamekeeper's gallows   1973
Rescue from the rose   1975
Dead nettle   1977

Mr. Fred   1983
Slickensides   1987
(All the above published by Collins Crime Club.)

INSPECTOR MOSLEY SERIES

Murder Mr. Mosley   1983
Mosley by moonlight   1984
Mosley went to mow   1985
Mists over Mosley   1986
The mind of Mr. Mosley   1987
What me? Mr. Mosley   1987
(All published by Quartet Books.)

Now read
W. J. Burley, H. R. F. Keating, Roy Lewis, Jonathan Ross.

James, P. D.

Phyllis Dorothy James was born in 1920, and has a background of work in the Civil Service. She is the widow of a doctor. She was an administrator in the National Health Service from 1949 to 1968, when she joined the Home Office as a Principal, working with the Police Department and later the Criminal Department. Her novels are academic and well-constructed, and her situations are based on her own sound knowledge of police procedures. The characters in her books are rounded and fully developed. Most of the books concern Adam Dalgleish, a Detective Superintendent in the Metropolitan Police, and a published poet. Dalgleish's character has matured with each book, and the reader becomes aware of the acute psychological pressures involved in police work as the series continues. Her writing is of a high literary standard and compares favourably with many contemporary 'serious' novelists.

Publications

ADAM DALGLEISH SERIES

Cover her face   1962

A mind to murder 1963
Unnatural causes 1967
Shroud for a nightingale 1971
The black tower 1975
Death of an expert witness 1977
A taste for death 1985
Devices and desires 1989

CORDELIA GRAY SERIES

An unsuitable job for a woman 1972
The skull beneath the skin 1982
(All published by Faber.)

Now read
Amanda Cross, W. J. Burley, Martha Grimes, S. T. Haymon, Ruth
Rendell, D. L. Sayers, Dorothy Simpson, June Thomson.

Lemarchand, Elizabeth

British. Born in Barnstaple, Devon in 1906. Took a degree at London
University in 1927 and became a teacher. She ended her career as
Headmistress at Lowther College in Abergele, Wales. She started
writing detective stories in 1967, after her retirement, and is still
producing them at regular intervals. Her style is that of the cosy
village murder, with little violence, very reminiscent of those written
by Agatha Christie, Ngaio Marsh, Patricia Wentworth and the other
writers of that generation, to which, of course, she belongs. The books
are pleasant and uncomplicated, with traditional settings, usually in
Devon, and the crimes are solved by Inspector Pollard. The
characterisation is good, and the plots reflect the time-honoured device
of giving clues to the reader, but there is often a twist to the ending.

Publications

INSPECTOR POLLARD SERIES

Death of an old girl 1967
The Affacombe affair 1968

Alibi for a corpse 1969
Death on doomsday 1970
Cyanide with compliments 1972
Let or hindrance 1973
Buried in the past 1974
A step in the dark 1976
Unhappy returns 1977
Suddenly while gardening 1978
Change for the worse 1980
Nothing to do with the case 1981
(All published by Hart-Davis.)
Troubled waters 1982
The wheel turns 1983
Light through glass 1984
Who goes home? 1986
The Glade Manor murder 1988
(All published by Piatkus.)

Now read
Catherine Aird, Agatha Christie, Anne Morice, Emma Page.

Lewis, Roy

British. Born in Glamorgan in 1933. Gained an LL.B at Bristol University in 1954, followed by a Dip. Ed. at Exeter in 1957. He became a teacher and college lecturer, though he was called to the Bar in 1965. He moved to Northumberland in 1967, where he became an Inspector of Schools, then deputy Principal of New College, Durham. Since 1974, he has been Managing Director of Felton Press in Newcastle.

He began writing detective stories in 1969, as a change from the many legal textbooks he had published. He wrote several perceptive stories with great attention to character and location, but also began to write the traditional type of police procedural story, with Inspector John Crow as the detective. In recent years he has introduced two more main characters, both amateur detectives; Eric Ward, who is a solicitor, and Arnold Landon, who is a surveyor with a local Planning Department. These novels are all set in and around Newcastle. His knowledge of the law and the world of business is used to provide convincing plots and description, and his love of the Northumberland countryside is obvious. Perhaps his greatest strength lies in his characterisation, which is carefully observed, and developed in depth.

Publications

INSPECTOR CROW SERIES

A lover too many   1967
Wolf by the ears   1970
Error of judgement   1971
A secret singing   1972
Blood money   1973
A part of virtue   1976
A question of degree   1976
Nothing but foxes   1977
A relative distance   1981

ERIC WARD SERIES

A certain blindness   1980
Dwell in danger   1982
A limited vision   1983
Once dying, twice dead   1984
A blurred reality   1985
Premium on death   1986
The salamander chill   1988
A necessary dealing   1989
A kind of transaction   1991

ARNOLD LANDON SERIES

A gathering of ghosts   1983
Most cunning workmen   1984
A trout in the milk   1986
Men of subtle craft   1987
The devil is dead   1989
A wisp of smoke   1991
A secret dying   1992
Bloodaxe   1993

OTHERS

The Fenokee project   1971
A fool for a client   1972
Of singular purpose   1973
Double take   1975
Witness my death   1976
A distant banner   1976
An uncertain sound   1978
An inevitable fatality   1978
(All published by Collins.)

Now read
J. B. Hilton, Reginald Hill, June Thomson.

Livingston, Nancy

British. She was born in Stockton-on-Tees, and has worked as a cook, an air hostess, a musician, an actor, and as a production assistant in television. She started her writing career with plays for radio. She now lives with her husband in an old house in Nottinghamshire. Her detective stories have an unusual investigator in the shape of a retired tax inspector, Mr. Pringle, aided by his flamboyant mistress, Mavis Bignell, who works as a barmaid. Pringle has a keen eye for wrong-doing, and a strong sense of justice. Mavis has sound common-sense, and a certain intuitive flair for detection. The novels are set in England and, latterly, in Australia and the Western states of America. The plots are imaginative, with great attention to detail, and a sense of humour.

Nancy Livingston also writes family sagas, and another entry may be found in the chapter devoted to the saga.

Publications

The trouble at Aquitaine   1985
Fatality at Bath and Wells   1986
Incident at Parga   1987
Death in a distant land   1988
Death in close-up   1989

Mayhem in Parva   1990
Unwillingly to Vegas   1991
A quiet murder   1992
(All published by Gollancz.)

Now read
Simon Brett, Roy Lewis, Gwen Moffat, John Sherwood.

Moyes, Patricia

Irish. Born in Bray, Co. Wicklow in 1923. She was a Flight Officer in the WAAF during the Second World War, then became secretary to Peter Ustinov, until 1953, when she joined *Vogue* as an Assistant Editor. She has lived abroad since 1958, successively in Switzerland, Holland, Washington DC and the Virgin Islands.

She writes well-plotted, ingenious and amusing stories, often set in the countries in which she has lived. Her detective is Chief Superintendent Henry Tibbett, of Scotland Yard, an ordinary and unassuming man, who solves his cases without ostentation, ably assisted by his wife Emmy. The Tibbett's domestic life is emphasised, and the reader builds up a detailed picture of their characters, and those of their friends, as the series progresses.

Publications

DET. CHIEF SUPERINTENDENT TIBBETT SERIES

The sunken sailor   1961
Death on the agenda   1962
Murder à la mode   1963
Falling star   1964
Johnny underground   1965
Murder fantastical   1967
Death and the Dutch uncle   1968
Who saw him die?   1970
Season of snows and sins   1971
The black widower   1975

To kill a coconut   1976
Who is Simon Warwick?   1978
Dead men don't ski   1979
Angel death   1980
A six-letter word for death   1983
Night ferry to death   1985
Black girl, white girl   1990
(All published by Collins.)

Now read
Agatha Christie, Elizabeth Lemarchand, Anne Morice, Emma Page.

Page, Emma

British. Real name, Honoria Tirbutt. Born in West Hartlepool, Durham. She gained a degree at Oxford, and writes radio plays under her own name. She lives in Worcestershire, an area which is the setting for most of her books. She is another exponent of the domestic murder story, set in small towns. Her plots are carefully worked out, and her characters have both charm and credibility. She started writing detective stories in 1970, and introduced her character, Chief Inspector Kelsey, in 1981.

Publications

INSPECTOR KELSEY SERIES

Every second Thursday   1981
Last walk home   1982
Cold light of day   1983
Scent of death   1985
Final moments   1986
Deadlock   1991
Mortal remains   1992

OTHERS

In loving memory   1970
Family and friends   1972
A fortnight by the sea   1973

Element of chance 1975
(All published by Collins.)

Now read
Catherine Aird, Elizabeth Lemarchand, Ngaio Marsh, Patricia
Moyes, Anne Morice.

Radley, Sheila

British. Lives in Norfolk. She had a variety of jobs in the Civil
Service, adult education and advertising before deciding to move to
the country in the 1960s, to run a village store and Post Office. She
wrote three romantic suspense novels as Hester Rowan: *Overture in
Venice* (1976), *The linden tree* (1977) and *Snowfall* (1978), before
turning to the classic detective story. Her chief character is Det.
Superintendent Douglas Quantrill, a conscientious and overworked
detective, who sees his marriage and family life disintegrating as
duty takes up more of his time. The tension is enhanced by conflict
with his ambitious son-in-law, who is rapidly outstripping him in the
race for promotion. The novels are all set in East Anglia, with
intricate plots and good characterisation.

Publications

DET. SUPTERINTENDENT QUANTRILL SERIES

Death and the maiden 1980
The Chief Inspector's daughter 1981
A talent for destruction 1982
Blood on the happy highway 1984
Fate worse than death 1985
Who saw him die? 1987
This way out 1989
Cross my heart and hope to die 1991
(All published by Constable.)

Now read
W. J. Burley, S. T. Haymon, P. D. James, Ruth Rendell, Jonathan
Ross, June Thomson.

Rendell, Ruth

British. Born in London in 1930. She worked as a journalist in Essex before her children were born. She has now remarried and lives in Suffolk. Ruth Rendell's work is of an extremely high quality, and she shares with P. D. James the respect of the literary critics. She says that her chief interest as a writer is in the creation of character, a fact that is apparent in all her books. Her chief characters are Chief Inspector Reg Wexford, his family and his colleagues, in particular Inspector Mike Burden. Wexford is tolerant, shrewd and outgoing, with a strong sense of moral values, and an appreciation of literature. Burden, on the other hand, is cold and unyielding, intolerant of weakness, and the contrast between the two is an integral part of the series. The people involved in Wexford's cases are seen through his eyes, and judged according to his values. The plots of the novels are intricate, with many sub-plots and psychological twists. They are far removed from the cosy country house murder stories which form a large percentage of the genre, and appeal to the reader who does not habitually read detective stories. Many of the Wexford novels have been adapted for television, starring George Baker as Wexford.

Ruth Rendell has also written a number of psychological thrillers which do not feature Wexford. They are often chilling stories about social misfits or introverted families. She has recently started to write under the name of Barbara Vine, in a slightly more Gothic style, but with the same literary standard.

Publications

INSPECTOR WEXFORD SERIES

From Doon with death   1965
A new lease of death   1967
Wolf to the slaughter   1968
The best man to die   1969
A guilty thing surprised   1970
No more dying then   1971
Murder being once done   1972
Some lie and some die   1973
Shake hands forever   1975
A sleeping life   1978

Make death love me   1979
Put on by cunning   1981
The speaker of mandarin   1983
An unkindness of ravens   1985
The veiled one   1988
Kissing the gunner's daughter   1992

OTHERS

To fear a painted devil   1965
Vanity dies hard   1965
The secret house of death   1968
One across, two down   1971
The face of trespass   1974
A demon in my view   1976
A judgement in stone   1977
Means of evil (short stories)   1979
Master of the moor   1982
The killing doll   1984
Lake of darkness   1984
The new girl friend (short stories)   1985
Live flesh   1986
Talking to strange men   1987
Heartstones: a novella   1987
The bridesmaid   1989
Going wrong   1990
The crocodile bird   1993
(All published by the Hutchinson Group.)

as Barbara Vine
A dark adapted eye   1986
Fatal inversion   1987
The house of stairs   1988
Gallowglass   1990
King Solomon's carpet   1991
Asta's book   1993
(Published by Viking Press.)

Now read
S. T. Haymon, P. D. James, Dorothy Simpson, June Thomson.

Richardson, Robert

British. He was born in 1940, is a journalist, and lives in Old Hatfield, Hertfordshire. His first book won the John Creasey Memorial Award given by the Crime Writers' Association for the best first crime novel in Britain in 1985. He is Chairman of The Crime Writers' Association for 1993–94. He writes very much in the style of Dorothy L. Sayers. His detective, Augustus Maltravers, is witty, erudite and perceptive. The plots are intricate and ingenious, and have an atmosphere of evil, in which the tension is sustained until the denouement, which is often unexpected. Characterisation is good, with Maltravers and his fiancee, Tess, developed in some depth. Locations are interesting; a cathedral, a community of artists in Cornwall, a remote Yorkshire village, and all concern the cause and effect of murder on an enclosed community.

Publications

> *The Latimer Mercy*   1985
> *Bellringer Street*   1988
> *The book of the dead*   1989
> *The dying of the light*   1990
> *Sleeping in the blood*   1991
> *The Lazarus tree*   1992
> *The hand of strange children*   1993 (not Maltravers)
> (All published by Gollancz.)

Now read
Martha Grimes, S. T. Haymon, P. D. James.

Ross, Jonathan

British. Real name, John Rossiter. Born in Devon in 1916. Served in the police force, except for wartime service in the RAF, reaching the rank of Detective Chief Superintendent in the Wiltshire Constabulary. He retired to Spain, but returned to live in Salisbury in 1976. He writes police procedural novels about Det. Superintendent George Rogers, a complex man who regrets his failed marriage but knows himself well enough to realise that much of the fault lay with him and his job. The police detail is, as one would expect, totally authentic, but the novels are more than an account of police investigations because of the depth of characterisation and atmospheric settings. He also writes adventure thrillers under his own name, about an agent called Roger Tallis.

Publications

DET. SUPERINTENDENT ROGERS SERIES

The blood running cold　1968
Diminished by death　1968
Dead at first hand　1969
The deadest thing you ever saw　1969
Here lies Nancy Frail　1970
The burning of Billy Topper　1974
I know what it's like to die　1976
A rattling of old bones　1978
Dark blue and dangerous　1981
Death's head　1982
Dead eye　1983
Dropped dead　1984
Burial deferred　1985
Fate accomplished　1987
Sudden departures　1988
A time for dying　1989
Daphne dead and done for　1990
Murder be hanged　1992

ROGER TALLIS SERIES (as John Rossiter)

The murder makers　1969
The deadly green　1970
A rope for General Dietz　1970
The golden virgin　1975
(All published by Constable.)

Now read
W. J. Burley, Douglas Clark, J. B. Hilton, Sheila Radley, Dorothy Simpson, June Thomson.

Shepherd, Stella

British. She was born in 1953, in Oldham, Lancashire. She studied medicine at the University of Nottingham, and has worked in hospitals, mainly concentrating on radiotherapy. She is now married to a pharmacist, John Martin, and lives near Colchester.

Her novels are all set in and around hospitals, and have the authenticity of detail which one might expect from a practising doctor. They are all concerned with murder, usually by some devious method, not easily detected by those outside the medical fraternity. The plots are ingenious and fast-moving, and the medical procedures, though faithfully described, are easily followed by the reader. She does not have a recurring character in her novels, though they do follow a pattern in that the police are assisted by one of the doctors.

Publications

> *Black justice* 1988
> *Murderous remedy* 1989
> *Thinner than blood* 1991
> *A lethal fixation* 1993
> (All published by Constable.)

Now read
Roy Lewis, John Sherwood.

Simpson, Dorothy

British. She lives near Maidstone, Kent. She began her career as a teacher of French, then married and had three children. Her first detective story was published in 1980, and she won the Crime Writers' Association Silver Dagger Award in 1985, with *Last seen alive*.

Her plots are concerned as much with the effects of murder on a closely-knit group of people, as with the solution of the crime, and show deep insight into human relationships, as well as great ingenuity. The character of her detective, Inspector Luke Thanet, is explored in some detail, on a professional and personal level. His wife, who works in the Probation Service, is often brought in as a sounding board for his philosophy, adding extra realism to the story.

Publications

INSPECTOR LUKE THANET SERIES

The night she died   1980
Six feet under   1982
Puppet for a corpse   1983
Close her eyes   1984
Last seen alive   1985
Dead on arrival   1986
Element of doubt   1987
Suspicious death   1988
Dead by morning   1989
Doomed to die   1991
Wake the dead   1992
No laughing matter   1993
(Published by Michael Joseph.)

Now read
S. T. Haymon, P. D. James, Sheila Radley, Ruth Rendell, June Thomson.

Staynes and Storey

British. Jill Staynes and Margaret Storey first met at St. Paul's Girls' School in London, where they collaborated on bizarre serial stories. Jill went to Oxford, then into advertising, while Margaret went to Cambridge, and worked in publicity. They remained friends, and later, both became teachers. They now devote all their time to writing.

The novels have good, intricate plots, with a logical outcome. Superintendent Robert Bone is a caring man, as concerned about the less pleasant aspects of his job as he is for the welfare of his disabled daughter, Charlotte. He is a widower, and the books explore the dilemma of a single parent, who has a demanding job to do. Family and school life, and police work are neatly interwoven.

Publications

SUPERINTENDENT ROBERT BONE SERIES

Goodbye, Nanny Gray   Barrie and Jenkins   1987
A knife at the opera   Bodley Head   1988
Body of opinion   Bodley Head   1988
Grave responsibility   Barrie   1990
The late lady   Century   1992
Bone idle   Century   1993

Now read
W. J. Burley, Sheila Radley, Dorothy Simpson.

Thomson, June

British. Born in Kent in 1930. Gained a BA in English at London University in 1952, and taught, both full- and part-time for some years. All her novels are set in rural Essex, a mysterious and enclosed part of the country, and usually concern an individual who is at odds with society, and is therefore an outsider. She describes the life of a small community with great insight, and her characters are carefully developed. The policeman in the books is Inspector Finch, a self-sufficient man who lives with his sister, and has few friends outside his work. Because of this, he can readily understand the psychological make-up of the people he has to deal with in his cases.

Publications

INSPECTOR FINCH SERIES

Not one of us   1972
Death cap   1973
The long revenge   1974
Case closed   1977

A question of identity   1978
Deadly relations   1979
Alibi in time   1980
Shadow of a doubt   1981
To make a killing   1982
Sound evidence   1984
A dying fall   1985
Dark stream   1986
No flowers, by request   1987
Rosemary for remembrance   1988
The spoils of time   1989
Past reckoning   1990
Foul play   1991

OTHERS

Secret files of Sherlock Holmes   1990
The secret chronicles of Sherlock Holmes   1992
Flowers for the dead, and other stories   1992
(All published by Constable.)

Now read
S. T. Haymon, J. B. Hilton, P. D. James, Sheila Radley, Ruth
Rendell, Jonathan Ross, Dorothy Simpson.

FAMILY STORIES

A genre which is very closely allied to the saga. The authors of this type of novel write about the everyday life of the family, and the impact on it of outside events. The books are usually long, with credible plots and characters, and written in a style which is absorbing and satisfying, without demanding too much in the way of concentration from the reader. The novels of Catherine Cookson are the foremost examples of the genre, and are certainly the most popular with women readers. However there are now a number of female novelists writing in this style, for it is very much the province of women writers, to great effect. They may not be great literature, but they are the mainstay of public library stocks, and give enormous pleasure to their many readers.

See also The Saga and 'Perceptive' women's novels.

Allen, Charlotte Vale

She was born in Toronto, where she still has close friends and family. After a brief spell in England, she emigrated to the United States in 1966. She worked in a variety of jobs, but became a nightclub/cabaret performer, working in clubs throughout the Midwest before settling in New York. She began to write during her pregnancy in 1971, and published her first novel in 1976. Since then she has been a full-time writer. She now lives in Connecticut.

She has a good narrative style, with well-crafted plots, dealing with modern issues. The books are easy to read, and very popular with women of all ages.

Publications

Promises   Hutchinson   1980
Gifts of love   Magnum   1980
Meet me in time   NEL   1980
Times of triumph   NEL   1980
Perfect fools   NEL   1980
Love life   NEL   1981
The marmalade man (later retitled *Destinies*)
   Hutchinson   1981
Moments of meaning   NEL   1983
Dream train   Arrow   1982
Daddy's girl   NEL   1983
Believing in giants   NEL   1983
Acts of kindness   NEL   1983
Intimate friends   Hutchinson   1983
Pieces of dreams   Hutchinson   1984
Hidden meanings   Severn House   1984
Matters of the heart   Hutchinson   1985
Julia's sister   Severn House   1985
Time/Steps   Weidenfeld   1988
Illusions   Weidenfeld   1988
Night magic   Weidenfeld   1988
Gentle stranger   Severn House   1990
Mixed emotions   Severn House   1991
Running away   Severn House   1991

Leftover dreams Severn House 1992
Painted lives Chivers 1992
Chasing rainbows Severn House 1993

Now read
Janet Dailey, LaVyrle Spencer, Danielle Steel.

Binchy, Maeve

Irish. Born in Dublin, where she worked as a journalist for many years, before becoming Fleet Street columnist for the *Irish Times*. She spends part of the year in London, and the rest in Ireland, where she and her husband, Gordon Snell, have a house. She says that when she is writing a novel, she starts at 5.30 am, to get three hours' work done before leaving for Fleet Street at 8.30 am.

Maeve Binchy's novels are long, carefully plotted, and with depth of characterisation. They are usually set in Ireland, from the 1940s onward, and concern a large and closely-knit family. Their problems are explored with sympathy and concern, and the situations in which they find themselves are within the experience of their reader.

Publications

Light a penny candle 1984
Echoes 1985
Firefly summer 1987
Silver wedding 1988
Circle of friends 1990
The copper beech Orion 1992

SHORT STORIES

Dublin 4 1983
London Transport 1983
The lilac bus 1986
(All published by Century except where stated.)

Now read
Catherine Cookson, Audrey Howard, Shelagh Kelly, Beryl Kingston, Belva Plain.

Blair, Emma

British. Born in Glasgow, but now lives in Devon. Emma Blair is actually a pseudonym used by a male author, who is married with two children, which, presumably, gives him his insight into family life. The novels are long family sagas, set mainly in Scotland, some at the turn of the century, and others in the present. They are extremely popular, and easy to read. There are good descriptions of family life and conflicts, set in credible surroundings, and with rounded characters and lively dialogue.

Publications

Nellie Wildchild   Severn House   1984
Hester Dark   Severn House   1984
This side of heaven   Severn House   1985
Jessie Gray   Severn House   1985
The Princess of Poor Street   Joseph   1986
Street song   Joseph   1987
When dreams come true   Joseph   1987
A most determined women   Joseph   1988
The blackbird's tale   Joseph   1989
Maggie Jordan   Bantam   1990
Scarlet ribbons   Bantam   1991
The water meadows   Bantam   1992
The sweetest thing   Bantam   1993

Now read
Catherine Cookson, Iris Gower, Nancy Livingston, Jessica Stirling.

Bowling, Harry

British. He was born in Bermonsey, London, in the 1930s. He left school at the age of 14 to help support his family and then did National Service in the 1950s. He has had a variety of jobs – lorry driver, milkman, carpenter, decorator and butcher – all of which enriched his experience of community life, and he is now a community worker. He lives with his wife and three children in

Deptford. The novels are full of gritty realism, set in the poverty and deprivation of the East End of London in the 1920s and 30s. Well-crafted plots, good characterisation and a natural flair for storytelling have made his books instant best-sellers.

Publications

> *Connor Street's war*　Headline　1987
> *Tuppence to Tooley Street*　Headline　1988
> *Ironmonger's daughter*　Headline　1989
> *Paragon Place*　Headline　1990
> *Gaslight in Page Street*　Headline　1991
> *The girl in Cotton Lane*　Headline　1992
> *Backstreet child*　Headline　1993

Now read
Josephine Cox, Marie Joseph, Lena Kennedy, Mary Jane Staples.

Clarke, Brenda

British. Born in Bristol, and still lives in Somerset. She writes fairly light family stories, with attention to detail in both plot and characters, and a good literary style, but her books are not as long as many of those in the genre. Some are historical, but with the emphasis on the family rather than historical events. She also writes light historical novels under the name of Brenda Honeyman.

Publications

> *The glass island*　Collins　1978
> *The lofty banners*　Hamlyn　1980
> *The far morning*　Hamlyn　1982
> *All through the day*　Hamlyn　1983
> *A rose in May*　Hutchinson　1984
> *Three women*　Hutchinson　1985
> *Winter landscape*　Century　1986
> *Under heaven*　Bantam　1987
> *An equal chance*　Bantam　1988

Sisters and lovers   Bantam   1989
Beyond the world   Bantam   1992
A durable fire   Bantam   1993

Now read
Lena Kennedy, Mary Minton, Sarah Shears.

Cookson, Catherine

British. Born in Tyne Dock, Co. Durham in 1906. She has been a prolific author since 1950, producing at least one book a year. Her books are set in various periods from the nineteenth century onwards, but they are all based in Tyneside. Because she knows the area so well, her locations are totally authentic, and she researches the historical background thoroughly. Many of her novels concern the poverty and deprivation in the North East, and are culled from her own experiences as a child, and from the reminiscences of her family and friends.

Her style is simplistic, but the plots, albeit predictable, are engrossing, and her characters, particularly those of women, are shrewdly observed. The idea of a matriarchal society with a strong woman holding the family together is obvious in many of her books. She has written several series about the same characters, but is included here, rather than in the section on The Saga, because so many of her books are about one individual family.

Although she is now in her 80s, and confined to bed for much of the time, she continues to write as vigorously as ever, and is, without doubt, the most requested author in libraries and bookshops.

She also writes as Catherine Marchant, in a lighter style, and not always about the North East.

Publications

MARY ANN SHAUGHNESSY SERIES

A grand man   1954
The Lord and Mary Ann   1956
The devil and Mary Ann   1958
Love and Mary Ann   1961

Life and Mary Ann   1962
Marriage and Mary Ann   1964
Mary Ann's angels   1965
Mary Ann and Bill   1967
(All published by Macdonald.)

THE MALLEN FAMILY

The Mallen streak   1973
The Mallen girl   1973
The Mallen litter   1974
(Published by Heinemann.)

TILLY TROTTER

Tilly Trotter   1980
Tilly Trotter wed   1981
Tilly Trotter widowed   1982
(Published by Heinemann.)

HAMILTON

Hamilton   1983
Goodbye Hamilton   1984
Harold   1985
(Published by Heinemann.)

BILL BAILEY

Bill Bailey   1986
Bill Bailey's lot   1987
Bill Bailey's daughter   1988
(Published by Bantam.)

OTHERS

Kate Hannigan   1950
The fifteen streets   1952
Colour blind   1953
Maggie Rowan   1954
Rooney   1957
The menagerie   1958

Fanny McBride 1959
Fenwick Houses 1960
The garment 1962
The blind miller 1963
Hannah Massey 1964
The long corridor 1965
The unbaited trap 1966
Katie Mulholland 1967
The round tower 1968
The glass virgin 1969
The nice bloke 1969
The invitation 1970
The dwelling place 1971
Feathers in the fire 1971
Pure as the lily 1972
(All published by Macdonald.)
The invisible cord 1975
The gambling man 1975
The tide of life 1976
The girl 1977
The cinder path 1978
The man who cried 1979
The whip 1982
The black velvet gown 1984
A dinner of herbs 1985
The moth 1986
(All published by Heinemann.)
The parson's daughter 1987
The cultured handmaiden 1988
The Harrogate secret 1989
The black candle 1989
Gillyvors 1990
My beloved son 1991
The rag nymph 1992
The house of women 1992
The Maltese angel 1992
The year of the virgins 1993
The golden straw 1993
(Published by Bantam.)

as Catherine Marchant
Heritage of folly 1962
The fen tiger 1963
House of men 1963
(Published by Macdonald.)
Miss Martha Mary Crawford 1975
The iron façade 1976
The slow awakening 1976
(Published by Heinemann.)

Now read
Valerie Georgeson, Marie Joseph, Lena Kennedy, Beryl Kingston,
Sarah Shears.

Crane, Teresa

British. She was born in Essex, where she still lives with her family.
She began to write in 1977, and her first novel was published in
1980. She writes long stories, full of incident and interest, with well-
sustained plots and considerable depth of characterisation. She pays
great attention to detail in the background and location of her books,
and tackles issues like poverty and deprivation and the role of
women in the family with skill and perception.

Publications

Spider's web 1980
Molly 1982
A fragile peace 1984
The rose stone 1986
Sweet songbird 1987
The Hawthorne heritage 1988
Tomorrow, Jerusalem 1989
Green and pleasant land 1991
Strange are the ways 1993
(All published by Collins.)

Now read
Audrey Howard, Lena Kennedy, Beryl Kingston, Mary Minton.

Freeman, Cynthia

American. Born in New York, and educated at the University of Berkeley, California. She worked as an interior designer before becoming a novelist. Her novels very often have backgrounds of displacement, particularly of Jews, and of the struggles of immigrant families to retain roots in a new society. Some of the books are almost sagas in their breadth of plot and scope of characters. She is an expert at building her characters, whom she explores in real depth.

Publications

> *A world full of strangers*   1976; hardback Piatkus 1983
> *Fairytales*   1978; hardback Piatkus   1980
> *The days of winter*   Piatkus   1979
> *Portraits*   Piatkus   1980
> *Come pour the wine*   Piatkus   1981
> *No time for tears*   Collins   1982
> *Illusions of love*   Collins   1984
> *Seasons of the heart*   Collins   1986
> *The last princess*   Collins   1988

Now read
Audrey Howard, Margaret Pemberton, Belva Plain, Katherine Yorke.

Haines, Pamela

British. Born in Harrogate, Yorkshire in 1926. Gained an MA in English from Cambridge in 1952. She married in 1955, and had five children before she became a writer. She received the *Spectator* New Writing Prize in 1971.

Pamela Haines' books are about the underlying conflicts in family life, and are seen through the eyes of a young girl coming to terms with womanhood. There is an element of tragedy and suffering running through each book. The conventional happy ending is not for her; she prefers to pursue each situation to its logical and inevitable conclusion. She explores the psychological makeup of her characters in considerable depth, and there is a great deal of interaction between members of families. The books are not always an easy read, and are by no means escapist reading, but are so well written, with such compelling characterisation, that they will be remembered and reread.

Publications

> *Tea at Gunter's* Heinemann 1974
> *A kind of war* Heinemann 1976
> *Men on white horses* Collins 1978
> *The kissing gate* Collins 1981
> *The diamond waterfall* Collins 1984
> *The golden lion* Collins 1986
> *Daughters of the Northern fields* Collins 1988

Now read
Maeve Binchy, Belva Plain, Erin Pizzey.

Howard, Audrey

British. Born in Liverpool, but has lived in St Anne's on Sea for most of her life. She worked in the Civil Service for many years, writing as a hobby, but did not consider herself a real author until she entered a literary competition which resulted in the publication of her first novel, *The skylark's song*. She writes long novels, with detailed plots and a wealth of characters, set in Liverpool with locations that she knows from first-hand experience, though *The juniper bush*, with which she won the 1988 Boots Romantic Novel of the Year Award, is set in nineteenth-century Cumbria.

Publications

> *The skylark's song* 1984
> *Morning tide* 1985
> *Ambitions* 1986
> *The juniper bush* 1987
> *Between friends* 1988
> (Published by Century Hutchinson.)

The mallow years Hodder 1990
A day will come Hodder 1992
All the dear faces Hodder 1992

Now read
Maeve Binchy, Brenda Clarke, Marie Joseph, Shelagh Kelly, Beryl Kingston, Margaret Pemberton, Katherine Yorke.

Joseph, Marie

British. Born in Lancashire, and educated at Blackburn High School for Girls. She worked in the Civil Service before her marriage. She now lives in Middlesex with her husband, who is a retired chartered engineer, and enjoys the company of her eight grandchildren. Although she suffers from rheumatoid arthritis, she writes steadily, and produces a novel a year. She began writing short stories for women's magazines, then moved on to full-length novels. They are set in the mill towns of Lancashire, where poverty and hardship were the norm in the 1930s, and depict the struggle to improve the quality of life in an environment of unemployment and deprivation. In spite of the settings, there is humour and courage in the stories, and the characters are drawn with affection and perception. Her female characters are particularly strong, and hold the narrative together. She won the Romantic Novelists' Association Award in 1987, with *A better world than this*.

Publications

Guilty party Macdonald 1975
Footsteps in the park Macdonald 1979
Ring a-roses Hurst & Blackett 1979
Maggie Craig 1980
A leaf in the wind 1980
Emma Sparrow 1981
Gemini girls 1982
The listening silence 1982
Lisa Logan 1984
The clogger's child 1985

Polly Pilgrim   1985
A better world than this   1987
A world apart   1988
The travelling man   1989
When love was like that, and other stories   1991
Since he went away   1992
(All published by Century Hutchinson.)

Now read
Catherine Cookson, Audrey Howard, Lena Kennedy, Beryl Kingston, Pamela Oldfield.

Kelly, Shelagh

British. Born in Yorkshire, and still lives in York. She is another example of authors who write about their own regional environment, in her case, West Yorkshire. She says, 'The love of writing stories has been with me since I was very small, a debt owed to my parents who enhanced my infant years with a character called Tiny Tot. Tot lived in Clifford's Tower, an ancient monument in York, and I am sure that was responsible for my interest in the city's history. It was this combined love of make-believe and history which led to my success as a novelist. I took up genealogy as a hobby, and, knowing only that my ancestors were Irish immigrants in the 1840s, I was appalled to discover the prejudice and poverty that they had to face in the slums of Walmgate. Thus, at last, I was provided with the inspiration for my first novel.' Her books are long, detailed family stories, and could equally well be classed as sagas. They concern large families, struggling against poverty and adversity, and reflect the social conditions of the period in which they are set. Her plots are well-constructed and her characterisation is deep and very typical of their Yorkshire background.

Publications

THE FEENEY FAMILY

A long way from heaven   1985
For my brother's sins   1986

Erin's child   1987
Dickie   1989

My father, my son   1988
Jorvik   1992
(All published by Century.)

Now read
Audrey Howard, Beryl Kingston, Genevieve Lyons, Mary Minton, Belva Plain.

Kennedy, Lena

British. Born in London in 1912, she was 67 when her first book, *Maggie*, was published, and wrote at least one book a year until her death in 1986. She lived in the East End of London, and wrote with great authenticity about family life in the area. Like Catherine Cookson and Marie Joseph, her strongest characters are indomitable women, prepared to fight against the odds for a better way of life. She said of her writing, 'I never take anything straight from life, but there are bits of me in all my books. Writing a novel is like knitting a great big knobbly jumper with lots of different patterns that come together to make one big pattern.' *Lady Penelope* and *The dandelion seed* are historical novels, set in the sixteenth and seventeenth centuries. She left a number of manuscripts, which have been published since her death.

Publications

Maggie   1979
Autumn Alley   1980
Nelly Kelly   1981
Lizzie   1982
Lady Penelope   1983
Lily, my lovely   1985
Down our street   1986
The dandelion seed   1987
The Inn on the marsh   1988

>*Eve's apples*   1989
>*Owen Oliver*   1990
>(All published by Macdonald.)
>*Ivy of the Angel*   Little, Brown   1993

Now read
Catherine Cookson, Audrey Howard, Marie Joseph, Beryl Kingston, Pamela Oldfield.

Kingston, Beryl

British. She was born and brought up in Tooting, London, and after taking a degree at London University taught English and Drama at a number of London schools. She now lives in Sussex.

She writes long, detailed novels about London in the early years of the century. The plots concern the everyday life of ordinary families, and the characters are lively, likeable and true to life.

Publications

>*Hearts and farthings*   1985
>*Kisses and ha' pennies*   1986
>*A time to love*   1987

>THE EASTER FAMILY

>*Tuppenny times*   1988
>*The fourpenny flyer*   1989
>*Sixpenny stalls*   1990

>*London pride*   1990
>*War baby*   1991
>(All published by Macdonald.)
>*Two silver crosses*   Century   1993

Now read
Catherine Cookson, Marie Joseph, Lena Kennedy, Mary Minton, Sarah Shears.

Lyons, Genevieve

Irish. Born and educated in Dublin, where she became a successful actress, and one of the founders of the Dublin Globe Theatre. She gave up her acting career to bring up her daughters, and began to write plays. This led on to novels. She now lives in London, but spends much of the year travelling abroad. She writes about Ireland in the early years of this century, and involves the families about whom she writes in the historical events of the time. Her novels are carefully researched to provide authentic historical detail, and the plots involve many strands. Her characterisation is good, and the effect of outside events on the structure of family life is well portrayed.

Publications

> *Slievelea*   1986
> *The green years*   1987
> *Dark Rosaleen*   1988
> *A house divided*   1989
> *Zara*   1990
> *The Palucci vendetta*   1991
> (All published by Macdonald.)
> *Summer in Dranmore*   Little, Brown   1992

Now read
Maeve Binchy, Shelagh Kelly, Mary Minton, Belva Plain.

Minton, Mary

British. A teacher of Creative Writing at Leicester Education Centre. Her stories are set in the period before and during the Second World War, and are about family life in times of crisis. They have well-constructed plots, strong characterisation, and good interaction between the characters.

Publications

> *Beggars would ride*   1985
> *Yesterday's road*   1986

The marriage bowl   1987
The weeping doves   1987
Don't laugh at fools   1988
Spinner's end   1989
Every street   1990
Paradise corner   1992
The house of destiny   1993
(All published by Century.)

Now read
Maeve Binchy, Brenda Clarke, Genevieve Lyons, Belva Plain, Sarah Shears, Elizabeth Walker.

Monk, Connie

British. She is one of a family of musicians, is married, and lives in Devon. She writes family stories, in which the central character is a woman. They are often set in the nineteenth century, and contain accurate historical detail, with flowing plots. *Jessica* was shortlisted for the Romantic Novelists' Association Award in 1987.

Publications

Season of change   Piatkus   1984
Fortune's daughter   Piatkus   1985
Jessica   Piatkus   1986
Hannah's Wharf   Piatkus   1987
Rachel's way   Piatkus   1989
Reach for the dream   Piatkus   1990
Tomorrow's memories   Piatkus   1991
Flame of courage   Piatkus   1992

Now read
Teresa Crane, Marie Joseph, Anne Melville, Mary Minton.

Pemberton, Margaret

British. She has written in different styles for various publishers, but is now established as the author of romantic family stories. There is little sex in her novels, and by no means as much of the deprivation and suffering as is found in the books of many of the writers in the genre. Her books are a 'good read', enjoyed by readers who are looking for escapism.

Publications

Tapestry of fear   1979
Vengeance in the sun   1979
The guilty secret   1981
(Published by Hale.)
Rendezvous with danger   1978
The mystery of Saligo Bay   1979
The flower garden   1982
Silver shadows, golden dreams   1985
Never leave me   1986
A multitude of sins   1988
(Published by Macdonald.)
White Christmas in Saigon   Bantam   1990
An embarrassment of riches   Bantam   1992
Moonflower madness   Severn House   1993

Now read
Cynthia Freeman, Danielle Steel.

Pizzey, Erin

British. Born in 1939, and educated in Dorset. She has devoted her career to campaigning and fund-raising for Women's Aid, which has led to many clashes with the law. She founded the first Shelter for Battered Wives in 1971, and now acts as a counsellor for abused women and their children.

She became well-known after the publication of her first book, *Scream quietly or the neighbours will hear*, an exposé of violence to women, and went on to write autobiography and novels. She writes from a feminist viewpoint, though not aggressively so, with real insight into women's emotions, and with a strong story-line.

Publications

> *The watershed*   H. Hamilton   1983
> *In the shadow of the castle*   H. Hamilton   1984
> *The pleasure palace*   H. Hamilton   1986
> *The first lady*   Collins   1987
> *The consul-general's daughter*   Collins   1988
> *The snow-leopard of Shanghai*   Collins   1989
> *Other lovers*   Collins   1991
> *Morningstar*   HarperCollins   1992
> *Swimming with dolphins*   HarperCollins   1993

Now read
Maeve Binchy, Cynthia Freeman, Pamela Haines, Belva Plain.

Plain, Belva

American. She lives in New Jersey. She wrote stories for major magazines for many years before her first novel, *Evergreen*, was published in 1978, and became an immediate bestseller. She writes the family novel on the grand scale, with intricate plot and subplot, and an extended family setting, seen in relation to the events of twentieth century America. Her characters are deep and rounded, and her style literary, while easy to read.

Publications

> *Evergreen*   1978
> *Random winds*   1980
> *Eden burning*   1982
> *Crescent City*   1988
> *The golden cup*   1986
> *Tapestry*   1988
> (All published by Collins.)

Blessings New English Library 1990
Harvest New English Library 1990
Treasures New English Library 1992
Whispers New English Library 1993

Now read
Maeve Binchy, Cynthia Freeman, Pamela Haines, Margaret Pemberton.

Rhodes, Elvi

British. She was born and educated in Bradford, the eldest of five children. She left school at sixteen and became the main financial supporter of her family. She now lives in Rottingdean, Sussex.

Her novels are all set in Yorkshire in the early part of the century, and reflect her own background. She writes about women who struggle against poverty and deprivation to make a better life for themselves. The settings are authentic, and the plots are absorbing and well-constructed. The main characters are credible and explored in some depth, but the books are easy to read and very popular.

Publications

Opal Century 1984
Doctor Rose Century 1984
Ruth Appleby Bantam 1988
The golden girls Corgi 1988
Madeleine Bantam 1989
The House of Bonneau (sequel) Bantam 1990
Summer promise and other stories Bantam 1990
Cara's land Bantam 1991
The rainbow through the rain Bantam 1993

Now read
Catherine Cookson, Marie Joseph, Shelagh Kelly, Lena Kennedy, Sarah Shears.

Robertson, Denise

British. She was born in, and writes about, North East England. She lives near Sunderland with her family and an assortment of dogs. She has worked extensively in television, both as writer and presenter, and is well known for her agony aunt slot in Granada TV's morning programme. She also writes a column in national newspapers. Her books are set among the mining communities in the North East, and confront issues like the miners' strike, and the hardships which it caused to families. Her characters are strong and uncompromising, and her insight into the problems of family life is deep and perceptive. Her first novel *The land of lost content*, won the Constable Trophy for fiction in 1984.

Publications

> *The land of lost content*   1985
> *A year of winter*   1986
> *Blue remembered hills*   1987
> (These form the Belgate trilogy.)
>
> *The second wife*   1988
> *None to make you cry*   1989
> *Remember the moment*   1990
> *The stars burn on*   1991
> *The anxious heart*   1992
> *Strength for the morning*   1993
> (All published by Constable.)

Now read
Catherine Cookson, Iris Gower, Audrey Howard, Beryl Kingston, Nancy Livingston.

Shears, Sarah

British. Born in Kent, before the First World War. She left school at 14 and was apprenticed as a Post Office clerk. She then had numerous occupations – nanny, gardener, housekeeper, and assistant matron – until the Second World War, when she worked as a housemaid in a factory hostel, writing all the time. She spent seven years as a writer of children's books and magazine stories, but then moved to London, to take up a new career in selling, and finally as warden in an old people's home. After her retirement, she began to write successful novels, and now has over twenty titles to her credit.

Her novels are about country people, and are simple in style, but with a good, flowing narrative, characters who engage the sympathy of the reader, and a practical approach to everyday family life, drawn from her own wealth of experience. She is popular among older women readers, who find the gentleness in her books a refreshing change from the sex and violence so often found in modern novels.

Publications

COURAGE SERIES

Child of gentle courage 1973
Courage in darkness 1974
Courage to serve 1974
Courage in war 1976
Courage in parting 1977
(Published by Elek and reprinted by Chivers.)

LOUISE

Louise 1975
Louise's daughters 1976
Louise's inheritance 1977
(Published by Elek and reprinted by Piatkus.)

ANNIE PARSONS

Annie Parsons Elek 1978; reprinted Piatkus
Annie's boys Elek 1979; reprinted Piatkus
Annie's kingdom Piatkus 1980

THE NEIGHBOURS

The neighbours 1982
The neighbours' children 1983

THE VILLAGE

The village   1984
Family fortunes   1985
The young generation   1986
Return to Russets   1990

OTHERS

The landlady   1980
Deborah Hammond   1981
The apprentice   1981
Martha Craddock   1982
The old woman   1987
The sisters   1988
Thomas (sequel)   1989
Son of Thomas   1991
(All published by Piatkus since 1980.)

Now read
Brenda Clarke, Marie Joseph, Margaret Pemberton.

Spencer, LaVyrle

American. She lives in Stillwater, Minnesota, with her husband.

She is a prolific writer, and is considered to be one of America's most successful exponents of romantic fiction. Her books are fairly lightweight family stories, some of which are historical, bordering on Gothic romance. Others have contemporary settings, always with a woman as the central character.

The books are extremely popular, especially among younger readers, and can be classed as easy-to-read, escapist fiction.

Publications

A heart speaks   Futura   1987
The gamble   Futura   1988
Years   Worldwide   1989
Vows   Worldwide   1989

Separate beds   Piatkus   1990
Twice loved   Piatkus   1990
Morning glory   Grafton   1990
The endearment   Severn House   1991
Bitter sweet   Grafton   1991
Spring fancy   Worldwide   1992
The fulfilment   Grafton   1992
Forgiving   Collins   1992
Bygones   Collins   1992
November of the heart   HarperCollins   1993

Now read
Charlotte Vale Allen, Janet Dailey, Danielle Steel.

Staples, Mary Jane

British, born in Walworth, London. Her stories are all set in London, among the poverty and hardship of the working class, but in spite of deprivation, there is a note of cheerful optimism. Her portrayals of London life are excellently drawn, and her characters are warm, colourful Cockneys. She, too, produces instant best-sellers.

Publications

Down Lambeth way   1988
Our Emily   1989
King of Camberwell   1990
Two for three farthings   1990
The lodger   1991
Rising summer   1991
Pearly Queen   1992
Sergeant Joe   1992
On Mother Brown's doorstep   1993
(All published by Bantam.)

Now read
Harry Bowling, Josephine Cox, Lena Kennedy, Beryl Kingston, Marie Joseph.

Walker, Elizabeth

British. Born in 1949, she lives in West Yorkshire where her husband is a banker. Her novels are long and detailed, and she spends a long time on research to ensure authenticity. The plots are full of incident and the settings are convincing, particularly those based in Yorkshire.

Publications

> *Voyage*   Piatkus   1987
> *Rowan's Mill*   Piatkus   1988
> *The court*   Piatkus   1989
> *Conquest*   Piatkus   1990
> *Dark sunrise*   Headline   1990
> *Wild honey*   Headline   1990
> *Summer frost*   Headline   1991
> *Hallmark*   Headline   1992
> *Day dream*   Headline   1992

Now read
Barbara Taylor Bradford, Judith Glover, Mary Minton.

Yorke, Katherine (Nicola Thorne)

British. She was born in Cape Town, South Africa, of an English father and a New Zealand mother, but was brought up and educated in England. She took a degree in sociology and, after several different types of job, became a writer.

She writes pleasant, romantic family stories, often about the conflicts of marriage and career, but with happy endings. She uses fast-paced plots, and contemporary settings. She also writes in a different style as Nicola Thorne, where her settings are wider-ranging, and her characters more fully developed.

Publications

> as Katherine Yorke
> *A woman's place*   Macdonald   1983

The pair-bond   Macdonald   1984
Swift flows the river   Macdonald   1988

as Nicola Thorne
Bridie climbing   Milton House   1975
The girls   Mayflower   1978
A woman like us   Heinemann   1979
A perfect wife and mother   Heinemann   1980
The daughters of the house   Granada   1981
Where the rivers meet   Granada   1982
Affairs of love   Granada   1983
Enchantress saga   Piatkus   1986
Champagne   Grafton   1989
Champagne gold (sequel)   Grafton   1992
Pride of place   Grafton   1989

THE ASKHAM CHRONICLES

Never such innocence   Granada   1985
Yesterday's promises   Grafton   1986
Bright morning   Grafton   1986
A place in the sun   Grafton 1987

Bird of passage   Grafton   1990
A wind in summer   HarperCollins   1993

as Rosemary Ellerbeck (her real name)
The people of this parish   Heinemann   1991

Now read
Cynthia Freeman, Audrey Howard, Margaret Pemberton.

FANTASIES

A genre which is becoming increasingly popular, and in which the number of titles increases rapidly, as their readership grows. Some are no more than paperback pulp fiction; others have real literary merit.

Fantasy has its roots in the sagas and eddas, the folk and fairy tales, the 'gothick' stories of the eighteenth and nineteenth centuries, and has close links with both science fiction and the horror story. It differs from science fiction in that it does not rely on technology or science as integral parts of its plots, but instead conjures up an imaginary world of 'sword and sorcery', a term used by Fritz Leiber to describe the type of novel concerned with an heroic figure fighting evil, equipped only with a magic sword.

It has been difficult to select a handful of authors from the many people who write fantasies, but we have consulted several avid readers of the genre, and have tried to list novels which have some depth of characterisation, and a skilful plot. J. R. R. Tolkien has to be taken as the yardstick against which other writers are measured, and we have chosen authors who write with a similar theme, but without being quite as scholarly.

Anthony, Piers

Born in England in 1934, but moved with his family to Spain and then to the United States in 1940. He became an American citizen in 1958. Before becoming a full-time writer, he worked for a communications company, and also taught English. He started writing short stories for science fiction magazines in 1963, and published in this medium for the next ten years. He has turned increasingly to full-length novels, and has maintained a high output, both in volume and quality. His style is original and inventive, with mind-twisting plots, full of imagery and cosmic fantasy. The books are set on far-distant, imaginary planets, but have considerable depth of characterisation, and are spiced with humour.

Publications

Chthon   Macdonald   1967
Phthor   Macdonald   1970
Steppe   Millington   1980
Anthonology   Grafton   1986

BATTLE CIRCLE

Sos the rope   Faber   1968
Var the stick   Faber   1971
Neq the sword   Faber   1971
(One-volume edition   Corgi   1984)

CLUSTER

Vicinity   1979
Chaining the lady   1979
Kirlian quest   1979
Thousandstar   1980
Viscous circle   1981
(Published by Millington in hardback; Panther in
   paperback.)

APPRENTICE ADEPT

Split infinity   1981

Blue adept   1981
Juxtaposition   1983
Out of phaze   1988
The robot adept   1989
Phaze doubt   1991
(Published by NEL in hardback and Granada in
  paperback.)

TAROT TRILOGY

God of Tarot
Vision of Tarot
Faith of Tarot
(All published in paperback by Panther in 1982.)

XANTH

A spell for Chameleon   1977
A source of magic   1979
Castle Roogna   1979
Centaur Isle   1982
Ogre, ogre   1982
Night mare   1983
Dragon on a pedestal   1985
Crewel Lye   1987
Golem in the gears   1988
Vale of the vole   1988
Heaven cent   1989
The man from Mundania   1990
Unicorn point   1990
Isle of view   1991
Question quest   1992
The colour of her panties   1992
Demons don't dream   1993
(Published by Futura/Macdonald and NEL.)

INCARNATIONS OF IMMORTALITY

On a pale horse   1986
Bearing an hour glass   1986

With a tangled skein   1987
Wielding a red sword   1987
Being a green mother   1988
For love of evil   1990
And eternity   1990
(Published by Grafton in paperback and Severn
   House in hardback.)

BIO OF A SPACE TYRANT

Refugee   1985
Mercenary   1985
Politician   1986
Executive   1986
Statesman   1987
(Published by Grafton in paperback.)

OF MAN AND MANTA

Omnivore   Faber   1969
Orn   Corgi   1987
Ox   Corgi   1987

OTHERS

Prostho plus   Gollancz   1971
Race against time   Sidgwick & Jackson   1974
Rings of ice   Millington   1975
Triple detente   Sphere   1975
Hasan   Tor Books (US)   1986
The Ring (with Robert Margroff) Tor Books   1986
The ESP worm (with Robert Margroff) Tor Books
   1986
Macroscope   Grafton   1985
Shade of the tree   Grafton   1987
Ghost   Grafton   1988
Total recall   Legend   1990
Mute   Severn House   1991
Virtual mode   HarperCollins   1991
Fractal mode   HarperCollins   1992

Mercycle   Grafton   1993
(with Robert E. Margroff)
Dragon's gold   Severn House   1992
Serpent's silver   Severn House   1992
Chimaera's copper   Severn House   1993

Now read
Marion Zimmer Bradley, Harry Harrison, Michael Moorcock, Peter Morwood.

Brooks, Terry

American. Born in Illinois in 1944. He has been a practising attorney since 1969, but has written ever since he was at school. His first novel was published in 1977 and became an immediate best seller. He writes long sagas about mythical kingdoms, with quests and dragons and elves. The plots are detailed and imaginative, and there is a good deal of humour, especially when the hero makes mistakes.

Publications

SHANNARA SERIES

The sword of Shannara   1977 (UK 1981)
The elfstones of Shannara   1982
The wishsong of Shannara   1984
The scions of Shannara   1990
The Druid of Shannara   1991
The elf-queen of Shannara   1993

THE MAGIC KINGDOM

Magic kingdom for sale/sold   1986
The black unicorn   1987
Wizard at large   1988
(All published by Macdonald/Futura.)

Now read
David Eddings, Harry Harrison, Katherine Kurtz, Michael Moorcock, Tolkien.

Cook, Hugh

Born in New Zealand in 1956. He wrote two single fantasies, before turning to the 'sword and sorcery' style of writing. He writes with emotional impact, with detailed characterisation, and a lot of interaction between the characters. The books are well-written, in a literary style, but with wit, and an element of horror.

Publications

Plague summer   1980
The shift   1985

CHRONICLES OF AN AGE OF DARKNESS

The wizards and the warriors   1986
The wordsmiths and the warguild   1987
The women and the warlords   1987
The walrus and the warwolf   1988
The wicked and the witless   1989
The wishstone and the wonderworkers   1990
The Wazir and the witch   1990
The werewolf and the wormlord   1991
The worshippers and the way   1992
(All published by Colin Smythe in hardback and by
   Corgi in paperback.)

Now read
David Eddings, David Gemmell, G. G. Kay, Peter Morwood, Gene Wolfe, Tolkien.

Cooper, Louise

British. A comparatively new writer, published only in paperback. She writes in the 'sword and sorcery' style; well-constructed novels with good characterisation, intricate and exciting plots and vivid descriptions. Her books are usually part of multi-volume works, though they can be read singly.

Publications

TIME MASTER TRILOGY

The initiate   1985
The outcast   1985
The master   1986

INDIGO

Mirage   1987
Nemesis   1988
Inferno   1988
Infante   1989
Nocturne   1990
Troika   1991
Avatar   1991
Revenant   1992
(All published by Unwin paperbacks.)

Now read
Hugh Cook, David Eddings, Raymond Feist, Roberta MacAvoy, Jack Vance.

Donaldson, Stephen R.

American. Born in 1947 in Cleveland, Ohio. He lived in India during his childhood, where his father was a surgeon working in a leper colony. He graduated in 1968, and spent two years doing hospital work in the Third World, as a conscientious objector, before reading for an MA in English at Kent State University.

He writes in the tradition of epic fantasy. His main character, Thomas Covenant, is a leper, conceived from hearing one of his father's lectures about leprosy, and drawn from recollections of his own childhood experiences. His descriptions of suffering and alienation are very convincing, and his style is almost allegorical.

The books are very derivative of Tolkien, and are extremely popular, though by no means an easy or comfortable read.

Publications

CHRONICLES OF THOMAS COVENANT, THE UNBELIEVER

Lord Foulsbane   1980
The Illearth war   1980
The power that preserves   1980
(Published originally in paperback by Fontana 1977/8.)

THE SECOND CHRONICLES

The wounded land   1980
The one tree   1982
White gold wielder   1983
Gildenfire   1983 (links the two series)
Regal's daughter   1984

MORDAUNT'S NEED

The mirror of her dreams   1986
A man rides through   1987
(All published by Collins.)

GAP INTO POWER

Gap into conflict: the real story   HarperCollins   1990
The gap into vision: forbidden knowledge
   HarperCollins   1991
A dark and hungry god arises   HarperCollins   1992

Now read
David Eddings, David Gemmell, Peter Morwood, Julian May, Gene Wolfe, Tolkien.

Eddings, David

American. Born in Washington in 1931, and grew up near Seattle. He took a BA in English at Washington University and joined the US army, before becoming a buyer for the Boeing Corporation. He later taught English at college level. His first novel was a straightforward adventure story, but he quickly turned to fantasy, with immediate success. Perhaps more than any other writer, he has assumed the mantle of Tolkien. He writes long, detailed sagas, in the tradition of heroic adventure and sword and sorcery, and his books are extremely popular. His descriptions are graphic and imaginative, and his characters are developed in depth throughout the books. His mythical lands are vividly portrayed, with historical and geographical detail, and the struggle of good against the power of evil is sustained throughout the books.

Publications

THE BELGARIAD

The pawn of prophecy   1982
Queen of sorcery   1982
Magician's gambit   1983
Castle of wizardry   1984
Enchanter's endgame   1985
(All published by Century in hardback.)

THE MALLOREON

Guardians of the west   1987
King of the Murgos   1988
Demon Lord of Karanda   1988
Sorceress of Darshiva   1989
Seeress of Kell   1991
(All published by Bantam in hardback.)

THE ELENIUM

The diamond throne   Grafton   1989
The ruby knight   Grafton   1990
The sapphire rose   HarperCollins   1991

TAMULI

Domes of fire   HarperCollins   1992

The losers   HarperCollins   1993 (not a fantasy, but about Good v. Evil)

Now read
Hugh Cook, Stephen Donaldson, David Gemmell, Katherine Kurtz, Julian May.

Feist, Raymond E.

American. He was born in Southern California, and now lives in San Diego. He has had a varied career, working in the film industry, for a community health service, and as an assistant dean at a California college. He has also sold cars, built swimming pools, and designed games. He, too, writes in the sword and sorcery style. His books are detailed and well-plotted, with exciting situations and good description. The characters are rounded, with marked contrast between good and evil.

Publications

THE RIFTWAR SAGA

Magician   1983
Silverthorn   1985
A darkness at Sethanon   1986
Prince of the blood 1989

OTHERS

Daughter of the Empire (with Janny Wurts)   1987
Servant of the Empire (with Janny Wurts)   1990
Faerie tale   1988
(All published by Grafton.)
The King's buccaneer   HarperCollins   1992

Now read
Hugh Cook, David Eddings, David Gemmell, Peter Morwood, Jack Vance, Gene Wolfe.

Gemmell, David

British. He lives in Hastings, and is a full-time writer. He is a comparative newcomer to the field of fantasy, but has achieved success and acclaim. He writes about the heroic quest, and his books are full of magic and Celtic imagery. Some are based around the Arthurian legends; others are derivative of the Norse sagas. They are imaginative and well-constructed, with a build-up of suspense as the hero fights the powers of darkness.

Publications

THE DRENAI SAGA

Waylander   1986
Legend   1984
The king beyond the gate   1985
Quest for lost heroes   1990
Waylander II: in the realm of the wolf   1992

SIPSTRASSI TALES

Wolf in shadow   1987
Ghost king   1988
Last sword of power   1988
The last guardian   1989
Knights of dark renown   1990
Dark prince   1991
Lion of Macedon   1991
Morningstar   1992
(All published by Century Hutchinson.)

Now read
Hugh Cook, Louise Cooper, David Eddings, Robert Holdstock, Patricia A. McKillip.

Harrison, Harry

American. Born in Stamford, Connecticut, but grew up in New York City. He was drafted into the US army on his eighteenth birthday, and did not return to civilian life for some years. He became an artist, art director and editor, before becoming a full-time writer. He has lived with his family in twenty-seven countries around the world, but has now settled in Ireland.

He writes both fantasy and science fiction, and sometimes a mixture of the two. The books have humour as well as excitement and are easy to read. Many were originally published in paperback format, but the later ones are in hardback.

Publications

THE STAINLESS STEEL RAT SERIES

The Stainless Steel Rat   1961
The Stainless Steel Rat's revenge   1971
The Stainless Steel Rat saves the world   1973
The Stainless Steel Rat wants you   1975
The Stainless Steel Rat for President   1983
The Stainless Steel Rat is born   1985
The Stainless Steel Rat gets drafted   1987
(Published by Faber in hardback and Sphere in
   paperback.)
Stainless Steel visions   Legend   1993

TO THE STARS

Starworld   Panther   1981
Homeworld   Severn House   1986
Wheelworld   Severn House   1988
Deathworld (3 volumes)   Sphere   1985
The technicolour time machine   Futura   1976
Planet of the damned   Futura   1976
Queen Victoria's revenge   Severn House   1977
Make room! Make room!   Ace Books (US)   1984
Rebel in time   Granada   1984
The California iceberg   Grafton   1987
Montezuma's revenge   Tor Books (US)   1987
The QE2 is missing   Severn House   1987
A Transatlantic tunnel, hurrah!   Tor Books   1988
The Turing option   Viking   1992

BILL THE GALACTIC HERO

Bill the galactic hero   Avon (US)   1979

Bill the galactic hero on the planet of robot slaves
  Gollancz   1989
Bill the galactic hero on the planet of bottled brains
  Gollancz   1990
*Bill the galactic hero on the planet of tasteless
  pleasure*   Gollancz   1991
*Bill the galactic hero on the planet of zombie
  vampires*   Gollancz   1992
*Bill the galactic hero on the planet of the hippies
  from hell*   Gollancz   1992

West of Eden   Granada   1984
Winter in Eden   Grafton   1986

Now read
Marion Zimmer Bradley, Michael Moorcock, Jack Vance, Gene
Wolfe.

Holdstock, Robert

British. Born in 1948. He lives in rural Herefordshire, which is the
setting for his books. He started writing intelligent science fiction,
but moved to fantasy in 1984. The books are set in Ryehope Wood,
Herefordshire, an ancient area of forest uninhabited for centuries,
and full of mysterious forces dating from the Stone Age, known as
mythagos. These beings are capable of drawing images from the
human mind, and taking on fleshly form. When humans enter the
forest, they assume the role of hero. This device serves to lead the
plot into different directions, and brings in elements of the Arthurian
and Robin Hood legends, and others from the Roman period and the
Iron Age. *Mythago Wood* won the World Fantasy Award in 1985,
well-deserved because of its imagery and construction.

Publications

Eye among the blind   Faber   1976
Where time winds blow   Faber   1982

Mythago Wood   Gollancz   1984
Lavandyss (sequel)   Gollancz   1988
The bone forest   Grafton   1991
The fetch   Orbit   1991

Now read
David Eddings, David Gemmell, G. G. Kay, Katherine Kurtz, Peter Morwood.

Kay, Guy Gavriel

Canadian. Born in Toronto in 1954. He has the reputation of being a Tolkien scholar, and helped Christopher Tolkien to edit his father's posthumous book, *The Silmarillion*. Predictably, his books are very much influenced by Tolkien, but instead of using the inhabitants of his imaginary world as heroes, he uses the device of transporting people from the real world (in this case, five students from Toronto University) to the fantasy one, to fight evil forces, and save their own world. This creates the opportunity to explore the modern characters in depth, as well as creating a complete contrast in the exotic inhabitants of Fionavar, the fantasy kingdom. The books are full of mythological elements, in particular the Arthurian legend, which is played out against the background of Fionavar.

Publications

THE FIONAVAR TAPESTRY

The summer tree   1985
The wandering fire   1986
The darkest road   1987
(Published by Allen & Unwin.)
Tigana   Viking   1990
A song for Arbonne   HarperCollins   1992

Now read
David Eddings, David Gemmell, Robert Holdstock, Katherine Kurtz, Tolkien.

Kurtz, Katherine

American. She writes long, intricate sagas, full of Celtic imagery and historical fantasy, but spiced with humour and with lively, interesting characters. There are elements of sword and sorcery but they are not as strong as in the works of other fantasy writers. The books are mainly published in paperback format, with one or two hardbacks, and are linked sagas.

Publications

DERYNI SERIES

Deryni rising   1985
Deryni checkmate   1985
High Deryni   1986
The Deryni archives   1988

THE HISTORIES OF KING KELSON

The bishop's heir   1986
The king's justice   1986
The quest for Saint Camber   1987

LEGENDS OF CAMBER OF CULDI

Camber of Culdi   1986
Saint Camber   1986
Camber the heretic   1987
The harrowing of Gwynnedd   1989
(Published by Century.)

(with Deborah Harris)
The adept   Severn House   1992
The lodge of the lynx   Severn House   1993

Now read
Terry Brooks, David Gemmell, Harry Harrison, Roberta MacAvoy, Michael Moorcock, Nancy Springer.

MacAvoy, Roberta A.

American. She writes books which are part fantasy, part thriller, with characters who are helped by supernatural powers. Some of her books have an historical setting; for example, the Damian Trilogy, which is set in Renaissance Italy. Others are set in ancient Ireland. The books have fast-moving plots, and lively characters. They are essentially light reading, and are published in paperback form.

Publications

THE DAMIAN TRILOGY

Damiano 1985
Damiano's lute 1985
Raphael 1985
The Book of Kells 1985
Tea with the Black Dragon 1987
Twisting the rope 1987
The grey horse 1988
(All published by Bantam.)
Lens of the world Headline 1992
King of the dead (sequel) Headline 1992

Now read
Piers Anthony, Harry Harrison, Michael Moorcock.

McKillip, Patricia A.

American. She writes romantic fantasy, very much slanted towards women, with female main characters. This is somewhat unusual in fantasy, but she was influenced by Andre Norton and Anne McCaffrey, who had written similar material. Her work has a dream-like, gentle, fairy-tale quality, with poetical imagery.

Publications

CHRONICLES OF MORGAN, PRINCE OF HED

Riddlemaster of Hed 1976

Heir of sea and fire   1977
Harpist in the wind   1979
(All published in paperback by Futura in 1979.)
Forgotten beasts of Eld   1974 (Futura 1987)
(Published originally in paperback by Collins and
    later in hardback.)
The sorceress and the cygnet   Pan   1991

Now read
Anne McCaffrey, Nancy Springer, Jack Vance.

May, Julian

American. Lives in Mercer Island, Washington. Her first novel,
Dune Roller, published in 1951, has become a minor classic. She is
another contender for the mantle of Tolkien. Her books are long,
detailed sagas, full of imagery, and set in a country which is
graphically and meticulously described. Her characters are portrayed
in depth, and her style is literary and polished.

Publications

THE EXILES

The many coloured land
The golden torc
The non-born King
The adversary
(Published in hardback in 1985.)
Intervention   1987
(All published by Collins.)
Jack the bodiless   HarperCollins   1992

Now read
Hugh Cook, Stephen Donaldson, David Eddings, G. G. Kay, Gene
Wolfe, Tolkien.

Moorcock, Michael

British. Born in 1939. He was one of the first British writers of fantasy, and has been a major influence on younger authors. He is a prolific writer, and has written series about a number of different heroes, mainly of the sword and sorcery type. He also writes the Jerry Cornelius series, with an anarchical anti-hero, and has recently written straight historical novels, albeit with an unusual angle.

Publications

THE CORNELIUS CHRONICLES

The final programme   1969
A cure for cancer   1970
The English assassin   1972
The lives and times of Jerry Cornelius   1975
The condition of Muzak   1976
The entropy tango   1981
*The adventures of Una Persson and Catherine
    Cornelius in the 20th century*   1984
(Published by New English Library.)

THE DANCERS AT THE END OF TIME

An alien heat   1974
The hollow lands   1975
The end of all songs   1976
Legends from the end of time   1976
The transformation of Miss Mavis Ming   1977
(Published by W. H. Allen; collected volume
    Granada 1983.)

HAWKMOON: THE HISTORY OF THE
    RUNESTAFF

The jewel in the skull   1973
The mad god's amulet   1973
The sword of dawn   1973
The runestaff   1974

HAWKMOON: THE CHRONICLES OF CASTLE
  BRASS

Count Brass
The champion of Garathorm
The quest for Tanelorn
(Published by Grafton in one volume 1986.)

EREKOSE

The eternal champion   Mayflower   1970
Phoenix in Obsidian   Mayflower   1970
The dragon in the sword   Grafton   1987

ELRIC

Stormbringer   Mayflower   1968
Elric of Melnibone   Hutchinson   1972
Sailor on the seas of fate   Mayflower   1981
The vanishing tower   Granada   1983
The weird of the white wolf   Granada   1984
The bane of the Black Sword   Granada   1984
Elric at the end of time   Granada   1985
The fortress of the pearl   Gollancz   1989
The revenge of the rose   Grafton   1991

THE BOOKS OF CORUM

The Knight of the Swords   1971
The Queen of the Swords   1971
The King of the Swords   1972
The bull and the spear   1979
The oak and the ram   1981
The sword and the Stallion   1981
(Published by Mayflower.)

MICHAEL KANE

The city of the beast
The lord of the spiders
Masters of the pit
(Reprinted in one volume as *Warriors of Mars*   NEL.)

THE NOMAD OF TIME

The war lord of the air   Grafton   1973
The land leviathan   Grafton   1974
The steel tsar   Grafton   1981

OTHERS

The time dweller   Mayflower   1971
The distant suns   Unicorn   1975
The winds of Limbo   Penguin   1993
The ice schooner   Granada   1985
The rituals of infinity   NEL   1986
The shores of death
Gloriana   Allison & Busby   1978
The war hound and the world's pain   NEL   1982
The city in the autumn stars   Grafton   1986

Now read
Piers Anthony, David Gemmell, Katherine Kurtz, Roberta MacAvoy,
Jack Vance.

Morwood, Peter

British. He writes historical fantasy, full of quests and sorcerors,
about a mythical kingdom, the Drusalan Empire. The books have
well-constructed plots, and rounded characters, and are much
influenced by the novels of Tolkien.

Publications

ALDRIC TALVARIN

The horse lord   Century Hutchinson   1986
The demon lord   Century Hutchinson   1987
The dragon lord   Century Hutchinson   1988
The warlord's domain   Century Hutchinson   1989

Prince Ivan   Legend   1990

Now read
David Eddings, Raymond Feist, David Gemmell, Julian May.

Springer, Nancy

British. She writes mythological fantasy, set in the imaginary land of Catena. The books have depth and subtlety, with vivid description, but with a gentle quality. They are reminiscent of the medieval legends of chivalry.

Publications

THE BOOK OF ISLE

The white hart   1984
The silver sun   1984
The sable moon   1985
The black beast   1985
(Published by Richard Drew in hardback and Corgi in paperback.)
Wings of flame   Arrow   1986
Chains of gold   Macdonald   1987
Madbond   Arrow   1990
Mindbond   Arrow   1991

Now read
Katherine Kurtz, Roberta MacAvoy, Patricia McKillip, Jack Vance.

Vance, Jack

American. Born in 1920. He is a prolific writer of science fiction as well as fantasy. After producing work for such magazines as *Amazing*, and writing a number of science fiction novels, he turned to fantasy. He writes lyrical and colourful stories, set in the far future, in worlds peopled with monsters and magic. His plots are ingenious and entertaining, with humour as well as imagery.

Publications

The dying earth   1950 (Granada 1972 UK)
The eyes of the Overworld   1966 (Granada 1972 UK)

Fantasms and magic 1978
Trullion: Alastor Mayflower 1979
The blue world 1980
The dragon masters 1981
Cugels saga 1983
Rhialto the Marvellous 1984
To live forever 1987
(Published by Grafton.)

PLANET OF ADVENTURE

City of the Chasch 1974
Servant of the Wankh 1974
The Dirdir 1975
The Pnume 1975
(Published in hardback by Dobson.)

LYONESSE

Suldrum's garden 1983
The green pearl 1985
Madouc 1990
(All published in paperback by Grafton.)

CADWAL CHRONICLES

Araminta station New English Lib. 1989
Ecce and old earth New English Lib. 1992

Now read
Piers Anthony, Michael Moorcock, Patricia McKillip, Nancy
Springer.

Warrington, Freda

British. She was born in Leicestershire and grew up in the
Charnwood Forest area, which she says inspired a feeling for nature,
colour and atmosphere. She trained at Loughborough College of Art
and Design, and worked in graphic design and illustration, writing in
her spare time. She now lives in south Derbyshire.

Her books are in the tradition of sword and sorcery, but have a lyrical quality, and are influenced by classical mythology. The plots are detailed and intricate, with many strands. She uses imaginary worlds as her setting, described in graphic detail, and peopled with extraordinary beings. The heroic quest is a feature of many of the books, though *A taste of blood wine* is the first of a sequence of vampire fantasies.

Publications

THE BLACKBIRD QUARTET

A blackbird in silver   1986
A blackbird in darkness   1986
A blackbird in amber   1988
A blackbird in twilight   1988
(All published by NEL.)

The rainbow gate   NEL   1989
Darker than the storm   NEL   1992
A taste of blood wine   Pan   1992
Sorrow's light   Pan   1993

Now read
David Gemmell, Guy G. Kay, Patricia McKillip, Peter Morwood.

Wolfe, Gene

American. Born in 1931. His first book was published in the United States in 1975, and was, in effect, a Book of the Dead. It has become a classic, though it is, perhaps, his least-known novel. He later turned to fantasy of the more traditional type, with sword and sorcery and imaginary worlds. The books are long and detailed, with intricate plots, and characterisation in depth.

Publications

Peace   1975 (Chatto 1984 in UK)

THE BOOK OF THE NEW SUN

Shadow of the torturer   1980
The claw of the conciliator   1981
The sword of the Lictor   1982
The citadel of the Autarch   1983
The Urth of the new Sun   1987
The free live free   1984
Soldier of the mist   1986
There are doors   1989
(Published by Gollancz.)
Castleview   New English Lib.   1991

Now read
Stephen Donaldson, David Eddings, Julian May, Peter Morwood,
Michael Moorcock, Jack Vance.

FOREIGN LOCATIONS

The authors selected for this section, are, as in the section devoted to Country life, exponents of different genres. They have been included here because they give a detailed and accurate picture of life in other countries, based on first-hand knowledge. Many of them are natives of other countries, or have lived abroad for many years. They give an unbiased account of social life and politics, and the conditions under which the inhabitants of their chosen country live. Most are very well known, and attract much critical attention.

There are a number of authors listed elsewhere who give a vivid and accurate picture of foreign countries. See the entries for Julian Savarin and Wilbur Smith for books about Africa; Bob Langley for the Middle East; Elizabeth Peters for Egypt and Germany; Patricia Moyes for the West Indies; Mary Wells for Hong Kong and the Philippines; Jan van de Wetering for the Netherlands; Christopher Nicole for the Far East and the West Indies; and many of the authors of spy stories for accounts of life behind the Iron Curtain.

Barber, Noel

British. He was for many years the chief foreign correspondent of the *Daily Mail*, and led an adventurous life in pursuit of his stories. He was the first Briton to reach the South Pole since Scott, was injured in the Moroccan wars, and in the Hungarian uprising, and walked the Himalayas to report the Dalai Lama's escape to India. He wrote several volumes of non-fiction before publishing his first novel.

The novels are very long, totally authentic, based on his own experiences in the countries in which they are set, and graphically descriptive. The plots have many facets, neatly dove-tailed, and the characters are explored in some depth. They appear to have equal appeal to both male and female readers.

Publications

> *Tanamera*   1981
> *Farewell to France*   1983
> *A woman of Cairo*   1984
> *The other side of Paradise*   1986
> *The weeping and the laughter*   1988
> *Daughers of the Prince*   1989
> (All published by Hodder.)

Now read
James Clavell, T. N. Murari.

Chand, Meira

She was born and educated in London, though her mother is Swiss and her father Indian. She is married to an Indian businessman and, except for a brief period in India, they have lived in Japan since 1962.

Her novels explore domestic life in Japan, and in particular the condition of women. They are acutely observed, and characterised in depth. Their great strength lies in their perception of the impassive and aesthetic way of life of the Japanese, which masks turbulent and sometimes violent emotions. Her style is powerful and her prose elegant.

Publications

> *The gossamer fly*   1979
> *Last quadrant*   1981
> *The bonsai tree*   1983
> *The painted cage*   1986
> (All published by Murray.)
> *House in the sun*   Hutchinson   1989

Now read
Anita Desai, Ruth Prawer Jhabvala.

Clavell, James

Australian American. He was born in Sydney in 1924, but has lived in the United States for most of his life. He served in the artillery as a young officer in World War II, and was captured by the Japanese in Java. He was imprisoned in the infamous Changi jail, where he first became interested in the Japanese culture. He returned from service to become a screen producer and director, involved with *The Fly* and *The Great Escape*, among others.

He began to write what he calls his Asian Saga in 1962, when *King Rat* was published. It was mainly auto-biographical, and helped heal the wounds inflicted by his wartime experiences, by re-telling the story of a group of prisoners in a Japanese camp. His later books have shown a depth of feeling for, and admiration of the Japanese culture. The books are very long, extremely detailed, and scholarly in their approach to their subject, in the sense of meticulous research and authentic settings. They are stories of high adventure, and panoramic breadth, following the fortunes of a high-bred Japanese dynasty from the beginning of the 17th century to the end of the 19th century. They offer a remarkable insight into the relationship between Japanese honour and Western imperialism, through the eyes of the people of Japan. The characters are developed in depth, with the Oriental way of life acutely observed.

120

Publications

> *King Rat* Hodder 1962
> *Taipan* Hodder 1966
> *Shogun* Hodder 1975
> *Noble House* Grafton 1981
> *Gai-Jin* Hodder 1993

Now read
James Melville, T. N. Murari.

Desai, Anita

Indian. She was born in 1937, of a Bengali father and a German mother. She was educated in Delhi, and is a member of the Advisory Board for English at the National Academy of Letters. She is also a Fellow of the Royal Society of Literature in London. She is married with four children and lives in India.

She began to write in the 1970s, and her work includes novels, short stories and children's books. Two of her novels, *Clear light of day* and *In custody*, were shortlisted for the Booker Prize, and *The village by the sea* won the Guardian Award for Children's Fiction in 1982. Her books are concerned with family life in India, with its strict rules and taboos. Her characters are portrayed in depth, and the women are depicted as strong and resourceful, but restricted by the customs of the country. The descriptions of Indian locations and social conditions are vivid and graphic.

Publications

> *Where shall we go this summer?* PNK 1975
> *The peacock garden* Heinemann 1979
> *Clear light of day* Heinemann 1980
> *Fire on the mountain* Penguin 1981
> *Games at twilight* Penguin 1982
> *Voices in the city* Orient, Delhi 1982
> *Cry, the peacock* Orient, Delhi 1983

In custody   Heinemann   1984
Baumgarten's Bombay   Heinemann   1988

Now read
Meira Chand, Buchi Emecheta, Ruth Prawer Jhabvala.

Emecheta, Buchi

Nigerian. She came to England in 1962, and lives in London with her five children. She graduated in sociology at London University, and writes for learned journals, and for radio and television, as well as writing novels for adults and children. She was appointed Senior Research Fellow in the Department of English and Literary Studies at the University of Calabar, Nigeria, in 1980, and also serves on the Advisory Council to the Home Secretary on Race and Equality, and on the Arts Council, in Britain.

Her novels are mainly set in Nigeria, and depict the struggle against corruption and poverty encountered in the daily life of the ordinary people. She, again, is particularly concerned with the condition of women, and their fight for recognition. Some of the books concern the plight of Nigerians in Britain, and their subjection to racial prejudice. The atmosphere of African countries is vividly conveyed, and the characters are memorably drawn.

Publications

Second class citizen   1977
The bride price   1978
In the ditch   1979
The slave girl   1979
The joys of motherhood   1979
Destination Biafra   1982
(Published by Fontana.)
Naira power   Macmillan   1982
Double yoke   Fontana   1984
Gwendolen   Collins   1989

Now read
Anita Desai, Meira Chand.

Jhabvala, Ruth Prawer

She was born in Poland in 1927, and came to England at the age of 12. She was educated here, and took her degree at London University. She is married to an Indian architect, and lived in Delhi from 1951 to 1975. Since then, they have divided their time between Delhi, London and New York.

She is a prolific writer of novels and short stories, and has also produced a number of film scripts, including her own *Heat and Dust* and E. M. Forster's *Room with a View*. Her novels conjure up the essence of India, with its colour and contrasts, and its richness of character. They are also penetrating studies of human relationships, with sharp dialogue and a deep understanding of character. She has been widely praised by the critics, and has received the Booker Prize for *Heat and Dust* in 1975, the Neil Gunn International Fellowship in 1979, and the MacArthur Foundation Award in 1986.

Publications

To whom she will   Allen & Unwin   1955
The nature of passion   Allen & Unwin   1956
Esmond in India   Allen & Unwin   1958
The householder   Murray   1960
Get ready for battle   Murray   1962
A backward place   Murray   1965
A new dominion   Murray   1973
Heat and dust   Murray   1975
In search of love and beauty   Murray   1983
Three continents   Murray   1987
Poet and dancer   Murray   1993

SHORT STORIES

Like birds, like fishes   Murray   1963
A stronger climate   Murray   1968
An experience of India   Murray   1971
How I became a Holy Mother   Murray   1976
Out of India (selected stories)   Murray   1987

Now read
Anita Desai, Shiva Naipaul.

Jolley, Elizabeth

She was born in England, but moved to Western Australia with her husband and three children in 1959. She runs a small goose farm and orchard, and conducts writing workshops in community centres and prisons.

She writes novels and collections of short stories which capture the atmosphere of life in the less populated areas of Australia, where, in some cases, there is still a battle for survival. Her stories are ironic, with overtones of fantasy, and are powerful studies of individuals and eccentrics, against a minutely observed background.

Publications

Palomino   Melbourne House   1980
Woman in a lampshade (stories)   Melbourne House   1982
Miss Peabody's inheritance   Viking   1984
Mr. Scobie's riddle   Penguin   1984
Foxybaby   Viking   1986
The well   Viking   1986
Milk and honey   Viking   1987
The newspaper of Claremont Street   Viking   1987
Five Acre virgin (stories)   Viking   1988
The travelling entertainer (stories)   Viking   1988
The sugar mother   Viking   1989
My father's moon   Viking   1989
Cabin fever   Sinclair Stevenson   1991

Now read
Shiva Naipaul.

Keating, H. R. F.

British. He was born in St Leonard's-on-Sea, Sussex in 1926. He was educated at Merchant Taylor's School, London, then served in the British Army, 1945–48. He attended Trinity College, Dublin, and was awarded a BA in 1952. He became a journalist and was sub-editor of the *Wiltshire Herald*, the *Daily Telegraph* and *The Times*, successively, from 1953 to 1967. Although he has been a full-time writer for many years, he still acts as Crime Books Reviewer for *The Times*. He is married, with four children, and lives in London.

His first novels were detective stories with considerable humour, well-received by the critics. He went on to write a series set in Bombay, about Inspector Ganesh Ghote of the Bombay Crime Branch. The first of these won him the Crime Writers Association Golden Dagger in 1964, and the Mystery Writers of America Edgar Allan Poe Award in 1965.

Keating has a wide-ranging interest in Indian life and culture, and a sharp ear for the cadences of Indian speech and the native use of Indian English. He says: 'While the books provide a reasonably accurate picture of today's India – a picture conditioned, I admit, by the fact that for the first ten years I wrote about Ghote I had not actually visited his country – I like to think that they put a recognizable human being into broad general situations which could happen to any of us.' The picture, in fact, is a remarkably accurate one of India, Indians and foreigners in India. The descriptions are vivid, and locations diverse – the Indian railways, the film industry, and life among India's high caste. Ghote himself is typically Indian; shrewd yet self-effacing, charming and humane.

Publications

> *Death and the visiting firemen*   1959
> *Zen there was murder*   1960
> *A rush on the ultimate*   1961
> *The dog it was that died*   1962
> (Published by Gollancz.)
> *Death of a fat god*   Collins   1963
> *Is skin deep, is fatal*   Collins   1965

> INSPECTOR GHOTE

> *The perfect murder*   1964
> *Inspector Ghote's good crusade*   1966
> *Inspector Ghote caught in meshes*   1967
> *Inspector Ghote hunts the peacock*   1968

Inspector Ghote plays a joker   1969
Inspector Ghote breaks an egg   1970
Inspector Ghote goes by train   1971
Inspector Ghote trusts the heart   1972
Bats fly up for Inspector Ghote   1974
Filmi, filmi, Inspector Ghote   1976
Inspector Ghote draws a line   1979
Go west, Inspector Ghote   1981
The Sherriff of Bombay   1984
Under a monsoon cloud   1986
The body in the billiard room   1987
(Published by Collins.)
Inspector Ghote: his life and crimes   Hutchinson
   1989
The iciest sin   Hutchinson   1990
Cheating death   Hutchinson   1992

The rich detective   Macmillan   1993

Now read
James Melville.

Melville, James

British. His real name is Peter Martin, and he was born in London in 1931. He studied philosophy at the universities of London and Tubingen, and made his career in public service. He was a teacher, a lecturer in adult education, a local government officer and a cultural diplomat with the British Council for 23 years. It was while he was serving in Japan that he conceived the idea of writing detective stories with a Japanese setting. Their success has enabled him to become a full-time writer, though he is also in demand as a lecturer and critic.

He knows the Japanese way of life and their philosophy well, which adds authenticity to his descriptions and plots. Most of the books are set in Tokyo, the base of Superintendent Tetsuo Otani. Many of the plots concern foreigners in Japan, though crime among the Japanese is also featured. He paints a vivid picture of the

Japanese character, cosmopolitan and influenced by the West, but still tied to the old traditions. He has written one historical novel about Japan, and is at work on another.

Publications

SUPERINTENDENT OTANI

The wages of Zen   1978
The chrysanthemum chain   1980
A sort of Samurai   1981
The ninth netsuke   1982
Sayonara, sweet Amaryllis   1983
Death of a Diamyo   1984
The death ceremony   1985
Go gently Gaijin   1986
Kimono for a corpse   1987
The reluctant ronin   1988
(Published by Secker & Warburg.)
A Haiku for Hanae   Headline   1989
Bogus Buddha   Headline   1990
The body wore brocade   Little Brown   1992

Imperial way   Deutsch   1986
Tarnished phoenix   Barrie and Jenkins   1990

Now read
H. R. F. Keating.

Murari, R. N.

Indian. He was born in Madras in 1941 and educated in India. After leaving university he went to England, where he worked as a freelance journalist, contributing regularly to *The Observer*, *The Sunday Times*, and the *Guardian*. He writes stage plays and television documentaries, is married, and divides his time between London, Madras and New York.

His novels are highly acclaimed pictures of Indian life and customs. They vary from the contemporary to the historical. *Taj*, for example, is a fictional account of the life of the Shah Jahan, and the building of the Taj Mahal. *Imperial Agent* and *Last victory* are sequels to Kipling's *Kim*, continuing the adventures of Kim as a man.

Publications

> *Lovers are not people*   Methuen   1978
> *Field of honour*   Methuen   1982
> *The marriage*   Macmillan   1983
> *The shooter*   NEL   1984
> *Taj*   NEL   1985
> *Imperial agent*   NEL   1987
> *Last victory*   NEL   1988

Now read
Ruth Prawer Jhabvala, Shiva Naipaul.

Naipaul, Shiva

West Indian. He was born in Trinidad in 1945, and educated there and at University College, Oxford, where he read classical Chinese. His home is in London, but he has travelled widely in India, Africa, the Caribbean and the United States, where he was a Guggenheim Fellow.

He is one of the most respected young West Indian novelists, and has been the recipient of many literary prizes. He writes well and convincingly about daily life and social conditions in the countries he knows well – India and the Caribbean – and achieves the distinction of being eminently readable as well as 'literary'. He won the Jock Campbell *New Statesman* Award, the John Llewellyn Rhys Memorial Prize and the Winifred Holtby Memorial Prize with his first novel, *Fireflies* in 1970, and the Whitbread Prize for *The chip-chip gatherers* in 1973.

Publications

> *Fireflies* H. Hamilton 1970
> *The chip-chip gatherers* Deutsch 1973
> *Black and white* H. Hamilton 1980
> *A hot country* H. Hamilton 1983
> *Beyond the dragon's mouth* (stories) H. Hamilton
> 1984

Now read
Ruth Prawer Jhabvala.

Pearce, Michael

British. He writes well and convincingly about Egypt in the early years of the century. The books are a sort of detective story, in which the principal character is the Mamur Zapt, the Chief of Police in the British Consular Service, which was then still responsible for law and order in Egypt, in liaison with the local Khedive.

The plots are intricate and full of local knowledge, giving a great deal of insight into the character and temperament of the native Egyptian. The settings are absolutely authentic, depicting life in Cairo and along the Nile in a realistic way. The somewhat sensitive relationship which existed at that time between the British and Egyptian governments is described with credibility, and there are frequent touches of humour.

Publications

> *The Mamur Zapt and the return of the carpet* 1988
> *The Mamur Zapt and the night of the dog* 1989
> *The Mamur Zapt and the donkey-vous* 1990
> *The Mamur Zapt and the men behind* 1991
> *The Mamur Zapt and the girl in the Nile* 1992
> *The Mamur Zapt and the spoils of Egypt* 1993
> (All published by Collins.)

Now read
H. R. F. Keating, James Melville.

GLITZ

A comparatively new genre, but rapidly expanding and extremely popular with women readers. It is derived from the 'bodice-ripper', historical novels in which the heroine undergoes a variety of trials: abduction, rape and slavery, to name but a few, before finding true love. The 'glitz' stories are similar in vein, full of sex, violence and greed, and usually set in the world of big business, the media or the film industry. Like the innocuous romances published by Mills and Boon, these novels are written to a formula predetermined by the publishers and literary editors, and many are subjected to a considerable amount of publishing 'hype' to ensure sales. They are usually published in paperback format very soon after the hardback version appears, or sometimes before. Certain publishers, such as Bantam, Macdonald and Judy Piatkus, specialise in this particular genre.

The forerunner of the genre was Harold Robbins, who set the pattern for later authors like Judith Krantz and Jackie Collins. Although some are mere pot-boilers, others have a certain amount of literary merit and promote long waiting lists in public libraries. They are essentially escapist reading, found in airports and station bookstalls.

Booth, Pat

British, but she now lives in the United States for part of the time. She began her career as a top model, but soon moved into photo-journalism. She has had three exhibitions of her work, and has written several books on photography. She is married to a doctor and has two children.

She writes gritty, sexy novels about the world of the rich and famous. Many of the situations are based on her own experiences and acquaintances. Her plots are well-constructed and achieve realism as well as sensationalism. The style and characterisation are average for the genre.

Publications

Sparklers   Macdonald   1983
The big apple   Macdonald   1985
Palm Beach   Century   1986
Sisters   Century   1987
Beverly Hills   Century   1989
Malibu   Century   1990

Now read
Jackie Collins, Shirley Conran.

Bright, Freda

American. She specialises in novels about women in executive positions, ambitious and ruthless, and in direct competition with men. There is always a romantic theme, with some fairly steamy sex scenes, but the situations are well researched, and the characters have a certain amount of depth, although they are stereotyped in many cases.

Publications

Options   Pan   1982
Futures   Collins   1983

> *Decisions*   Collins   1984
> *Infidelities*   Deutsch   1987
> *A singular woman*   Michael Joseph   1988
> *Consuming passions*   Pan   1990

Now read
Ruth Harris, Judith Krantz.

Briskin, Jacqueline

Born in London, but grew up as an American in Beverly Hills, California, where she still lives. She writes lengthy books with many sub-plots and a fast pace, about the rich and powerful in the United States. The story line is well sustained, and the characters have depth. There is not as much overt sex and violence as in the books by other writers of this genre, but the formula is much the same.

Publications

> *Paloverde*   1975
> *Rich friends*   1976
> *Decade*   1981 (original title: *California generation*)
> *Onyx*   1982
> *Everything and more*   1984
> *Too much too soon*   1985
> (All published by Granada.)
> *The naked heart*   Bantam   1989

Now read
Freda Bright, Jackie Collins, Ruth Harris, Judith Krantz, June Flaum Singer.

Collins, Jackie

British. Born in the late 1930s, the younger sister of Joan Collins, the actress. Their father was a theatrical agent and intended both daughters to go into the theatre, which they did, but, while Joan became a successful film star, Jackie decided that her talents lay in writing. She achieved overnight success with her first novel, *The world is full of married men*, which was considered shocking when it was first published, because of its sexual content, and went on to write in the same vein for some years. Her last few novels have much greater depth of plot and characterisation, though the formula is still the same, and are well-constructed, drawing on her own and her sister's experiences in Hollywood for authenticity. The sex and violence are still there, but are closely woven into the plot, and the quality of her writing has improved.

Publications

> *The world is full of married men*   W. H. Allen   1968
> *The stud*   W. H. Allen   1969
> *Sunday Simmons and Charlie Brick*   W. H. Allen   1971   (retitled *Sinners*   Pan   1984)
> *Lovehead*   W. H. Allen   1974 (retitled *The love killers*   1989)
> *The world is full of divorced women*   W. H. Allen   1975
> *Lovers and gamblers*   W. H. Allen   1977
> *The bitch*   Pan   1979
> *Chances*   Collins   1981
> *Hollywood wives*   Collins   1984
> *Lucky*   Collins   1985
> *Hollywood husbands*   Heinemann   1986
> *Rock star*   Heinemann   1988
> *Lady boss*   Heinemann   1989
> *American star*   Heinemann   1993

Now read
Shirley Conran, Judith Krantz, June Flaum Singer, Harold Robbins.

Conran, Shirley

British. Born in 1932. Took a degree in Fabric Design, and went on to marry Terence Conran in 1955 and design for his textile firm. She later became a journalist, and wrote the *Superwoman* books, which led to another career in television. Her first novel, *Lace*, was published in 1982, with considerable hype, and became an immediate bestseller. It was later made into a television series. Her books are written in a racy style, full of sex and violence, but with glamorous settings and flamboyant characters. The plots are carefully researched and have authentic detail.

Publications

> *Lace*   1982
> *Lace 2*   1986
> *Savages*   1987
> *Crimson*   1992
> (All published by Sidgwick & Jackson.)

Now read
Jackie Collins, Judith Krantz, Harold Robbins.

Cooper, Jilly

British. She was born in Yorkshire, but now lives in Gloucestershire, with her husband, the publisher Leo Cooper, and an assortment of animals.

She started her career in journalism, and wrote observant and witty columns for *The Sunday Times* and *Mail on Sunday*, as well as contributing to a number of magazines. Her debut as a novelist was with a series of tongue-in-the-cheek romantic novels with lively heroines. She moved from that to long blockbusters, set in the world of the rich and famous.

The books are well-written, with lots of action and extremely shrewd characterisation. There are any amount of steamy sex scenes, but overlaid with her own particular brand of humour.

Publications

> *Emily*   1976
> *Bella*   1977
> *Harriet*   1977

Octavia 1978
Prudence 1978
Imogen 1979
Lisa & Co 1982
(All published by Corgi.)
Rivals Bantam 1988
Riders Bantam 1989
Polo Bantam 1991
The man who made husbands jealous Bantam 1993

Now read
Jackie Collins, Judith Krantz.

Cowie, Vera

British. She was born in County Durham, but lived and worked in London before moving to Bishop's Stortford to become a full-time writer. She has written since she was a child, and her first novel was published in 1978.

She has an easy, flowing style, with crisp dialogue. Her books are less concerned with sex and violence than those of some of her contemporaries, but the theme of power and ambition runs through her novels. Her plots are well-executed, and her characters sympathetic.

Publications

Amazon summer 1978
The rich and the mighty 1983
The bad and the beautiful 1985
Fortunes 1987
Secrets 1989
Face value 1990
(All published by Collins.)
A double life Heinemann 1992

Now read
Freda Bright, Julie Ellis, Ruth Harris, Judith Krantz.

Ellis, Julie

American. She lives in New York. She writes long novels about ambition and the power struggle. They are well-written, with enough sub-plot and depth of characterisation to sustain interest. The sex and violence is there, but does not form the main theme.

Publications

> *Maison Jennie*   Severn House   1990
> *Glorious morning*   Severn House   1991
> *The Hampton women*   Severn House   1992
> *The Hampton heritage*   Severn House   1992
> *The only sin*   Sidgwick & Jackson   1986
> *A daughter's promise*   Sidgwick & Jackson   1988
> *The velvet jungle*   Sidgwick & Jackson   1988
> *East wind*   Grafton   1988
> *Rich is best*   Sidgwick & Jackson   1989
> *Loyalties*   Grafton   1989
> *No greater love*   Grafton   1991
> *Trespassing hearts*   HarperCollins   1992

Now read
Vera Cowie, Ruth Harris, June Flaum Singer.

Harris, Ruth

American. She is an editor and freelance writer who lives in New York. She writes about wealth and ambition, with plots in which women are competing in a male-dominated business sphere. The books are better written than a lot of the genre, and have a reasonable literary style, with credible characters.

Publications

> *The last romantics*   Eyre   Methuen   1981
> *A self-made woman*   New English Library   1983
> *Decades*   Chivers   1984
> *The rich and the beautiful*   Chivers   1984
> *Husbands and lovers*   Piatkus   1986

Love and money   Michael Joseph   1988
Modern women   Macdonald   1991

Now read
Freda Bright, Judith Krantz, June Flaum Singer, Danielle Steel.

Krantz, Judith

American. Born in New York. She began her career as a fashion editor and writer of magazine articles. She now lives in Beverly Hills, California, with her husband, who is a film producer.

Her first novel, *Scruples*, was published in 1978, and was the subject of the biggest hype then known in the publishing trade. She has followed it with four more, each of which has had enormous publicity and press coverage before publication. Her books are often serialised and made into TV mini-series. The books are long, well-constructed and carefully researched, usually drawing on her own experience for their setting. The main characters are portrayed in some depth and developed throughout the book. Judith Krantz is probably the best writer of this particular genre.

Publications

Scruples   Weidenfeld & Nicolson   1978
Princess Daisy   Bantam   1980
Mistral's daughter   Sidgwick & Jackson   1983
I'll take Manhattan   Bantam   1986
Till we meet again   Bantam   1988
Dazzle   Bantam   1990
Scruples 2   Bantam   1993

Now read
Shirley Conran, Ruth Harris, June Flaum Singer, Danielle Steel.

Singer, June Flaum

American. Born in New Jersey, but now lives in Bel Air, Hollywood.

She writes mainly about the film industry and its power struggles, and the rich American jet set. Her characterisation is rather better than that of some writers in this genre, and the plots are slightly more credible.

Publications

> *The debutantes*   1983
> *Star dreams*   1984
> *The movie set*   1985
> (Published by Piatkus.)
> *The Markoff women*   1986
> *The president's women*   1988
> *Sex in the afternoon*   1990
> *Brilliant divorces*   1992
> (Published by Bantam.)

Now read
Jackie Collins, Ruth Harris, Judith Krantz, Danielle Steel.

Steel, Danielle

American. Born in New York, educated in Europe and at New York University. She started her career in public relations, helping to set up a firm in New York, but became a full-time writer in 1973.

She is undoubtedly the most popular writer in the genre, and the most prolific. Her stories are about rich and privileged women, whose characters are explored in some depth. However, they invariably tire of life in high society, and long for fulfilment in the creative arts. All suffer some dramatic experience or tragedy which changes their lifestyle and strengthens their character. Danielle Steel uses the same plot over and over again, changing the locations and the characters, but still manages to retain credibility. Her stories are more romantic than others of the genre, with very little explicit sex, and a hint of melodrama. She creates long waiting lists in public libraries, and her books are second in popularity only to Catherine Cookson.

Publications

> *Going home* 1973
> *Golden moments* 1977
> *The promise* 1978
> *Season of passion* 1979
> *The ring* 1980
> *Loving* 1981
> *To love again* Sphere 1981
> *Remembrance* Hodder 1982
> *Palomino* 1982
> *Summer's end* 1982
> *A perfect stranger* 1982
> *Once in a lifetime* 1983
> *Crossings* 1983
> *Thurston House* 1983
> *Now and forever* 1984
> *Family album* 1985
> *Wanderlust* 1986
> *Fine things* 1987
> *Kaleidoscope* 1988
> *Zoya* 1988
> *Star* Michael Joseph 1989
> *Daddy* Bantam 1989
> *Message from Nam* Bantam 1990
> *No greater love* Bantam 1991
> *Jewels* Bantam 1992
> *Mixed blessings* Bantam 1992
> (Published by Piatkus except where otherwise stated.)

Now read
Ruth Harris, June Flaum Singer; see also Family stories.

GOTHIC ROMANCES

This is a genre of particular appeal to women readers, in which the books are well-crafted, but are pure escapism, demanding little in the way of concentration, and ideal for picking up to read while travelling, or between jobs around the home. They are the female equivalent of the adventure stories of the Alistair MacLean type so popular with both men and women for much the same reasons.

The stories have a woman as the main character, and contain elements of adventure, mystery, love and the supernatural, often in an historical setting, and written in the first person. The heroines encounter danger and misunderstanding, and the enmity of jealous rivals, but there is invariably a happy ending. The favourite locations for this type of novel are Cornwall, the Yorkshire Moors and Scotland, or similar wild areas of the country, and often involve stately homes with mysterious owners. They are, obviously, derived from the 'gothick' novels of the nineteenth century, and particularly from the work of the Bronte sisters. The best modern example is Daphne Du Maurier's *Rebecca*.

The genre does overlap, to some extent, with the family story and with the historical novel, but certain authors, such as Victoria Holt and Mary Williams, while writing about family life in rural nineteenth-century England, typify the literary style and plot of this sort of novel.

Brent, Madeleine

British. Born in London, where her father was a journalist. She writes under a closely guarded pseudonym. She worked for a magazine publishing company, and then joined the forces, where she was a cipher clerk. Her first novel was published in 1971, with immediate success, and she went on to win the Romantic Novelists' Association Award in 1978, with *Merlin's Keep*.

The books are based in Victorian England, but in each case the heroine spends some time abroad, in locations as varied as Tibet and China. The main characters are far from typical of the Victorian woman, and pursue unusual careers, for instance, that of trapeze artist. They are also portrayed as strong, determined and resourceful, quite able to look after themselves without the help of the men whom they encounter. The plots are fast-moving, action-filled mysteries, with good dialogue and vivid geographical description. There is a good deal of love interest, and the men match the women in strength of character.

Publications

> *Tregaron's daughter*   1971
> *Moonraker's bride*   1973
> *Kirkby's changeling*   1975
> *Merlin's Keep*   1977
> *The Capricorn Stone*   1979
> *The long masquerade*   1981
> *Heritage of shadows*   1983
> *Stormswift*   1984
> *The golden urchin*   1986
> (All published by Souvenir Press.)

Now read
Victoria Holt, Sara Hylton.

Coffman, Virginia

American. Born in San Francisco in 1914. She studied at the

University of California, Berkeley, and graduated in 1938. She became a secretary at many of the film studios in Hollywood, and later worked in real estate, before becoming a full-time writer. Her output is enormous. Many of the books were published in America in the 1970s, and are being published in the UK by Piatkus Books and Severn House at regular intervals.

She writes in two styles; one is the traditional first-person historical gothic romance, the other is more a type of supernatural thriller. She has also recently written family sagas. The quality of writing varies with the type of book. Virginia Coffman says that she was influenced by the Brontes, and by Sheridan LeFanu, whose 'gothick' mysteries she read as a child. She does not regard herself as a great writer, because, she says, 'I am not too observant of people. But I feel that few writers can be as observant as I am when it comes to the atmosphere of places. I believe the one special thing that the reader will get out of my books is the atmosphere.'

Publications

> *Moura*   1959
> *The beckoning*   1965
> *The curse of the island pool*   1965   (Severn House 1986)
> *Castle Barra*   1966
> *Black heather*   1966
> *The high terrace*   1966   (published as *To love a dark stranger* by Hale   1969).
> *Castle at Witches Coven*   1966   (Piatkus   1988)
> *A haunted place*   1966   (Milton House   1975)
> *The demon tower*   1966   (Severn House   1986)
> *The devil vicar*   1966; revised as *The vicar of Moura* 1972
> *The shadow box*   1966
> *The small tawny cat*   1967; revised as *The stalking terror*   1977 (Piatkus   1983)
> *Richest girl in the world*   1967 (Severn House   1988)
> *The Chinese door*   1967   (Hale   1971)
> *The rest is silence*   1967   (Severn House   1985)
> *A few fiends to tea*   1967   (Severn House   1989)

The hounds of Hell   1967
One man too many   1968   (Severn House   1988)
The villa fountains   1968
The mist at darkness   1968
Call of the flesh   1968
The candidate's wife   1968   Severn House   1990
The dark gondola   1968; revised as *The dark
  beyond Moura*   1977
Of love and intrigue   1969
Voodoo widow   Hale   1970
The beach house   1970   (Piatkus   1982)
Masque by gaslight   1970   (Hale   1971)
The vampire of Moura   1970
The master of Blue Mire   1971 (Milton House   1975)
Night at Sea Abbey   1972   (Piatkus   1981)
The house on the moat   1972   (Piatkus   1990)
Mistress Devon   1972   (Piatkus   1983)
The cliffs of dread   1972   (Piatkus   1981)
The dark palazzo   1973   (Piatkus   1980)
Garden of shadows   1973
Legacy of fear   1973
The evil at Queen's Priory   1973   (Piatkus   1980)
Survivor of darkness   1973
The house at Sandalwood   1974   (Milton House
  1975)
Hyde Place   1974   (Severn House   1988)
The ice forest   1975
Veronique   1975   (Souvenir Press   1988)
Marsanne   1976   (Souvenir Press   1979)
The alpine coach   1976   (Souvenir Press   1980)
Careen   1977   (Piatkus   1989)
Enemy of love   1977   (Piatkus   1989)
Fire dawn   1977   (Piatkus   1979)
The Gaynor women   1978   (Souvenir Press   1981)
Looking glass   1979   (Piatkus   1984)
Dinah Faire   1979   (Souvenir Press   1982)
Pacific cavalcade   1980   (Severn House   1985)
The Lombard cavalcade   1982 (Severn House   1986)
The Lombard heiress   1984   (Severn House   1986)

LUCIFER COVE SERIES

The devil's mistress   1969   (Severn House   1987)
Priestess of the damned   1970   (Piatkus   1982)
The devil's virgin   1970   (Severn House   1987)
Masque of Satan   1971   (Severn House   1988)
Chalet of the devil   1971   (Severn House   1988)
From Satan, with love   1972   (Piatkus   1983)

Strange secrets   1984
The orchid tree   1985
Dark winds   1986
Tana Maguire   Severn House   1987
The jewelled darkness   Severn House   1989
Dark desire   Piatkus   1990
The Royles   Severn House   1992
Dangerous loyalties   Severn House   1993

Now read
Phyllis Whitney, Daoma Winston.

Gaskin, Catherine

Irish. Born in Dundalk in 1929. She was educated in Australia, but lived in London from 1948 to 1955, when she married and went to live in New York. She now lives in the Isle of Man.

The books fall into two categories. Some are stories with all the ingredients of the gothic romance – stately homes, mysterious landowners, and threatened heroines – but set in the present. Others are historical novels of family life, but with a certain atmosphere of suspense which qualifies their inclusion in the gothic genre. The books are well-crafted, with evidence of painstaking research into background. The locations move from Australia to Scotland, Spain, London and Yorkshire. The plots are often set around specific industries, such as glass-making, fashion or the wine trade, and these are described with authenticity. The main character is always a woman, portrayed as strong and resourceful, and providing a focal point around which the plot revolves.

Publications

        This other Eden   1947
        With every year   1949
        Dust in sunlight   1950
        All else is folly   1951
        Daughter of the house   1952
        Sara Dane   1954
        Blake's Reach   1958
        Corporation wife   1960
        I know my love   1962
        The Tilsit inheritance   1963
        The file on Devlin   1965
        Edge of glass   1967
        Fiona   1970
        A falcon for a queen   1972
        The property of a gentleman   1974
        The Lynmara legacy   1975
        The summer of the Spanish woman   1977
        Family affairs   1980
        Promises   1982
        The ambassador's woman   1985
        The charmed circle   1988
        (All published by Collins.)

Now read
Jane Aiken Hodge, Victoria Holt, Sara Hylton, Rona Randall.

Hodge, Jane Aiken

British, but born in Massachusetts. She is the daughter of Conrad Aiken, and sister of Joan Aiken, both writers. She was educated in England, and the United States, and took degrees at both Oxford University and Harvard. She worked in America for departments of the British government, then became a freelance reader and reviewer for publishers and film companies. She returned to England after the death of her husband in 1979.

    Her books could equally well be classified as historical novels, since many of them are family sagas set in eighteenth and nineteenth century America. Others, though, are contemporary gothic romances. She says that she prefers to think of herself as a romantic rather than a gothic writer, since she believes that the term 'gothic' conjures up visions of horror and violence. She has, she says, been much influenced by the work of Georgette Heyer and Mary Stewart, the former for her historical accuracy and the latter for her ability to create excitement without violence. The plots of her historical novels are full of atmosphere, without long descriptions and boring detail, and are set against real historical events, such as the Napoleonic Wars and the American War of Independence. The characters in all her books are vivid and likeable, and the heroines show strength and resource, as well as charm.

Publications

Maulever Hall   1964
The adventurers   1966
Watch the wall, my darling   1967
Here comes a candle   1967
The winding stair   1968
Marry in haste   1969
Greek wedding   1970
Savannah Purchase   1971
Strangers in company   1973
Shadow of a lady   1974
One way to Venice   1974
Rebel heiress   1975
Runaway bride   1976
Judas flowering   1976
Red sky at night   1979
Last act   1979
Wide is the water   1981
The lost garden   1982
The secret island   1985
Polonaise   1987
First night   1989
Leading lady   1990
Windover   1992
(All published by Hodder.)

Now read
Catherine Gaskin, Victoria Holt, Rona Randall.

Holt, Victoria

British. One of the several names used by Jean Plaidy, whose work appears in the section on historical novels. The books written as Victoria Holt are typical of the genre. They are set, for the most part, in the nineteenth century, and are told in the first person. The heroines are often employed as governesses or ladies' companions, and there is a great deal of love interest. They find themselves at the centre of a mystery, which leads them into danger before it is resolved with a happy ending. The heroines, while portrayed in depth, are not as strong and resourceful as those of other writers, and tend to rely on the leading male character for help. The books are extremely popular and, in spite of the author's prodigious output, are inventive and appealing.

Publications

> *Mistress of Mellyn*   1961
> *Kirkland revels*   1962
> *Bride of Pendorric*   1963
> *The legend of the seventh virgin*   1965
> *Menfreya*   1966
> *The king of the castle*   1967
> *The Queen's confession*   1968
> *The shivering sands*   1969
> *The secret woman*   1971
> *The shadow of the lynx*   1971
> *On the night of the seventh moon*   1973
> *The curse of the kings*   1973
> *The House of a Thousand Lanterns*   1974
> *Lord of the far island*   1975
> *The pride of the peacock*   1976
> *The devil on horseback*   1977
> *My enemy the Queen*   1978
> *The spring of the tiger*   1979

The mask of the enchantress   1980
The Judas kiss   1981
The demon lover   1982
The time of the hunter's moon   1983
The Landower legacy   1984
The road to Paradise Island   1985
The secret of the nightingale   1986
The silk vendetta   1987
The India fan   1988
The captive   1989
Snare of serpents   1990
Daughter of deceit   1991
Seven for a secret   1992
(All published by Collins.)

Now read
Madeleine Brent, Sara Hylton, Carola Salisbury, Mary Williams.

Hylton, Sara

British. She lives in Yorkshire, where many of her books are set. Her novels of romantic suspense are well-written, with skilfully constructed plots and rounded characters. The first five novels all followed the traditional gothic pattern; the later ones have been more in the tradition of the family story.

There is a strong element of mystery in the early novels, where the heroine sets out to discover the secret of a strange legacy, or searches for buried treasure. *The Talisman of Set* has an archaeological background, with supernatural events surrounding an ancient Egyptian artefact.

Publications

Caprice   Souvenir Press   1980
The Carradice chain   Souvenir Press   1982
The crimson falcon   Souvenir Press   1983
The Talisman of Set   Souvenir Press   1984
The whispering glade   Souvenir Press   1985

Glamara   1986
Tomorrow's rainbow   1987
My sister Clare   1988
Fragile heritage   1989
Summer of the flamingoes   1990
The chosen ones   1991
The last reunion   1992
(Published by Century.)

Now read
Madeleine Brent, Victoria Holt, Elizabeth Peters, Rona Randall.

Lorrimer, Claire

British. Born in Sussex in 1921. Her real name, under which she writes light romances, is Patricia Robins, and she is the daughter of Denise Robins, also a prolific author. She was educated privately in Sussex and at finishing schools in Europe, before joining the staff of *Woman's Illustrated* as a sub-editor. She served in the WAAF during the Second World War, and became a freelance writer on her return to civilian life. She says that it did not occur to her that she could write anything other than light romantic fiction until her agent persuaded her to try to improve the standard of her work, under another name. She tries to ensure that the actions and dialogue of her characters are compatible with real-life situations, thus bringing realism to her stories.

Her books, like those of other writers in the genre, fall equally well into the category of historical or family novels, but they all contain elements of the gothic.

Publications

A voice in the dark   Souvenir Press   1967
The shadow falls   Avon, NY   1974
The secret of Quarry House   Avon, NY   1976
Mavreen   1976
Tamarisk   1978
Relentless storm   Arlington   1979

Chantal 1980
The chatelaine 1981
The wilderling 1982
Frost in the sun 1986
(All published by Arlington Press.)
Ortolans Bantam 1990
The spinning wheel Bantam 1991
The silver link Bantam 1993

Now read
Catherine Gaskin, Jane Aiken Hodge, Rona Randall.

Michaels, Barbara

American. Born in Illinois in 1921. Her real name is Barbara Mertz, and she also writes under the name of Elizabeth Peters (see under Adventure stories).

The books written as Barbara Michaels are either historical gothics, or are set in the present, with a strong element of the supernatural, rooted in legend. They feature a strong female character, an action-filled plot, and a good sprinkling of humour.

Publications

The Master of Blacktower Jenkins 1967
   (reprinted by Souvenir Press in 1987)
Sons of the wolf Jenkins 1968
Ammie, come home Jenkins 1969
Prince of darkness Hodder 1971 (reprinted by
   Souvenir Press in 1985)
The dark on the other side 1973
The crying child 1973
Greygallows 1974
Witch 1975
House of many shadows 1976
The Sea-King's daughter 1977
Patriot's dream 1978
Wings of the falcon 1979

Wait for what will come   1980
The walker in shadows   1981
The wizard's daughter   1982
Someone in the house   1983
Black rainbow   1984
Here I stay   1985
Be buried in the rain   1986
Grey beginning   1986
Shattered silk   1987
(All published by Souvenir Press.)
Search the shadows   Piatkus   1988
Smoke and mirrors   Piatkus   1989
Into the darkness   Piatkus   1990
Vanish with the rose   Piatkus   1992

Now read
Virginia Coffman, Victoria Holt, Carola Salisbury, Daoma Winston.

Randall, Rona

British. Born in Birkenhead, and educated there and at Pitman's College, London. She worked in theatre repertory companies for three years, then became a journalist. She started writing novels in 1942, and produced a considerable number of light romances between then and 1967, when she turned to the gothic romance. She uses the traditional formula of stately homes, remote locations and imperilled heroines, but her plots are fresh and well-constructed, and her style is full of interest, with strong characterisation and smooth action. Her later novels have reflected her interest in the theatre, and have been family novels rather than true gothics.

Publications

Knight's Keep   Collins   1967
Glenrannoch   Collins   1973
Dragonmede   Collins   1974
Watchman's stone   Collins   1975
The eagle at the gate   H. Hamilton   1978

The mating dance   H. Hamilton   1979
The ladies of Hanover Square   H. Hamilton   1981
Curtain call   H. Hamilton   1983
The Drayton legacy   H. Hamilton   1985
The potter's niece   H. Hamilton   1987
Mountain of fear   Severn House   1989
The rival potters   Hamish Hamilton   1990
Lyonhurst   Severn House   1990

Now read
Victoria Holt, Sara Hylton, Claire Lorrimer, Mary Williams.

Salisbury, Carola

British. A pseudonym for Michael Butterworth, a writer of thrillers under his own name, and of detective stories under the name of Sarah Kemp. He was born in 1924, and served in the Royal Navy before making his career in art, first as a tutor at Nottingham College of Art and then as Art Director, and later Managing Editor of Fleetway Publications.

He started writing gothic romance in 1975. The stories are of the traditional type, but the author's experience of thriller writing is displayed by the atmosphere of suspense, and the tension in the plots. He writes convincingly about women, and the first person narratives show an insight into women's thoughts and feelings. The stories are full of action and intrigue, and are among the highest rank of gothics.

Publications

Mallion's pride   1975
Dark inheritance   1976
The 'Dolphin' summer   1977
The winter bride   1978
The shadowed spring   1980
Count Vronsky's daughter   1981
Autumn in Araby   1983
Daisy Friday   1984

A certain splendour   1985
(All published by Collins.)

Now read
Madeleine Brent, Victoria Holt, Rona Randall, Phyllis Whitney,
Mary Williams.

Whitney, Phyllis A.

American. She was born in Japan in 1903, and educated there and in
America. She graduated from high school in Chicago in 1924 and
married in 1925. She became Children's Book Editor on the Chicago
Sun, and went on to lecture in Juvenile Fiction Writing at North
Western University in Illinois, and later at New York University. She
is a past president of the Mystery Writers of America.

Her books are a combination of gothic romance and thriller, full of
suspense, but with a strong romantic interest, and with a woman as
the main character. She has also written many children's books and
several short stories for magazines.

Her books were all originally published in America, but have now
appeared in Britain, some originally in paperback and later in
hardback.

Publications

> *The red carnelian*   1943   Coronet   1976
> *The quicksilver pool*   1955   Coronet   1973
> *The trembling hills*   1956   Coronet   1974
> *Skye Cameron*   1957   Hurst & Blackett   1959
> *The mask and the moonflower*   1958   Hurst &
>   Blackett   1960
> *Thunder heights*   1960   Coronet   1973
> *Blue fire*   1961   Hodder   1962
> *Window on the square*   1962   Coronet   1969
> *Seven tears for Apollo*   1963   Coronet   1969
> *Black amber*   Hale   1965
> *Sea jade*   Hale   1966
> *Columbella*   Hale   1967

Silverhill   Heinemann   1968
Hunter's Green   Heinemann   1969
The winter people   Heinemann   1970
Lost island   Heinemann   1971
Listen for the whisperer   Heinemann   1972
Snowfire   Heinemann   1973
The turquoise mask   Heinemann   1975
Spindrift   Heinemann   1975
The golden unicorn   Heinemann   1977
The stone bull   Heinemann   1977
The glass flame   Heinemann   1979
Domino   Heinemann   1980
Poinciana   Heinemann   1980
Vermilion   Heinemann   1982
Emerald   Heinemann   1983
Rainsong   Heinemann   1984
Dream of orchids   Hodder   1985
The flaming tree   Hodder   1986
Silversword   Hodder   1987
Feather on the moon   Hodder   1988
Rainbow in the mist   Hodder   1989
The singing stones   Hodder   1990
Woman without a past   Hodder   1991

Now read
Virginia Coffman, Barbara Michaels, Daoma Winston.

Williams, Mary

British. She has lived in Cornwall since 1947, and is married to a Welshman. She says that she has an affinity with Celtic lands and especially loves sea and mountains. She wrote a regular column for the *St. Ives Times*, and wrote and illustrated children's programmes for BBC Wales for six years. She now concentrates on writing novels, plays and television scripts, with the occasional art exhibition.

Most of her novels are set in Cornwall, with the occasional one in Wales, and are all in the classic gothic style. She writes with authority about her Cornish backgrounds, and her books, though fairly light, are fast-moving and full of character.

She has also written a series of collections of ghost stories and writes historical 'bodice-rippers' under the name of Marianne Harvey.

Publications

Carnecrane   1979
Trenhawk   1980
Heronsmere   1980
Return to Carnecrane   1981
Louise   1981
The granite king   1982
The Tregallis inheritance   1982
The Stuart affair   1983
Forest heritage   1983
Castle Carnack   1983
Merlake Towers   1984
Mistress of Blackstone   1984
Tarnefell   1985
Folly's end   1985
Portrait of a girl   1986
Destiny's daughter   1987
Stormy heritage   1987
Dark flame   1988
The secret tower   1988
(Published by Kimber.)
Tangled roots   Piatkus   1990
Duke's gold   Piatkus   1992

GHOST STORIES

Haunted waters
The haunted garden
Chill company
The dark land
The dark god
Ghostly carnival
The haunted valley

159

They walk at twilight
Unseen footsteps
Where no birds sing
Where phantoms stir
Whisper in the night
(All published by Kimber, 1978–88.)

Now read
Victoria Holt, Sara Hylton, Rona Randall, Carola Salisbury.

Winston, Daoma

American. Born in Washington DC, where she still lives, in 1922. She was educated at George Washington University. Like other authors in the genre, she writes a mixture of gothic mysteries and family stories with a gothic element. Her main female characters are always strong and resourceful, and deal with complex family problems or solve mysteries equally well. The plots are original and exciting, and the tension is built up to the climax. In the longer, family novels, the characters are drawn in detail, and there are several interwoven themes in the plot.

All the books were originally published in America, but most have appeared in Britain; details are given for British editions.

Publications

Tormented lovers   1962
Love her, she's yours   1963
The secrets of Cromwell Crossing   1965   Piatkus
   1984
Sinister stone   1966   Piatkus   1985
The Wakefield witches   1966   Piatkus   1987
The mansion of smiling masks   1967   Piatkus   1993
Shadow of an unknown woman   1967
The castle of closing doors   1967
The Carnaby curse   1967   Piatkus   1991
Shadow on Mercer Mountain   1967   Piatkus   1988
Pity my love   1967   Severn House   1988

The Traficante treasure   1968   Severn House   1990
The Moderns   1968   Severn House   1988
The long and living shadow   1968
Bracken's world   1969
Mrs. Berrigan's dirty book   1970
Beach generation   1970
Wild country   1970
Dennison Hill   1970   Piatkus   1988
House of mirror images   1970   Piatkus   1984
Sound stage   1970
The love of Lucifer   1970   Severn House   1986
The vampire curse   1971   Piatkus   1993
Flight of a fallen angel   1971   Piatkus   1982
The devil's daughter   1971   Piatkus   1989
The devil's princess   1971   Piatkus   1980
Seminar in evil   1972
The victim   1972   Severn House   1985
The return   1972
The inheritance   1972
Kingdom's Castle   1972   Piatkus   1981
Skeleton key   1972   Piatkus   1980
Moorhaven   1973   Severn House 1989
The trap   1973   Piatkus   1989
The unforgotten   1973
The Haversham legacy   1973   Futura   1977
Mills of the gods   1974   Macdonald   1980
Emerald Station   1974   Futura   1977
The golden valley   1975   Futura   1978
Death watch   1975   Severn House   1986
A visit after dark   1975   Piatkus   1983
Walk around the square   1975   Piatkus   1984
Gallow's way   1976   Macdonald   1978
The dream killers   1976
The adventuress   1978   Macdonald   1979
The lotteries   Macdonald   1980
A sweet familiarity   1981   Piatkus   1983
Mira   Piatkus   1982
Family of strangers   Piatkus   1983
Hands of death   Severn House   1984

Now read on

A double life   Severn House   1991
Hannah's Gate   Piatkus   1992
The curse of Hannah's Gate   Piatkus   1992

Now read
Virginia Coffman, Phyllis Whitney.

HISTORICAL NOVELS

This is a genre which is closely related to both the saga and the gothic romance, but is distinguished from both by the breadth of its scope, and its emphasis on historical events as they affect the nation, rather than a particular family. They often use a central character or family as a mirror through which events are reflected, but the global view is of greater importance. The depth of research and wealth of detail in many of these novels make them a valuable adjunct to historical biography and textbooks for the student.

Historical novels are written at many levels, from the academic to the frivolous, but all have a valid point to make. Georgette Heyer, for example, wrote light, witty romances set in the Regency period, but they are, in fact, an excellent source of information about the costume, social customs and forms of speech of that era. Irving Stone's long, detailed novels about the lives of great artists like Michaelangelo can almost be classed as biography, except that they have dialogue.

A great number of historical writers are so well known as to need no introduction to the reader. Some of them have been listed, with others who may not be as widely recognised.

Anand, Valerie

British. She was born in London, but grew up in Kent and Surrey. She started writing at the age of six, and has continued ever since. She became a journalist in her twenties, and still works part-time in journalism. She lives with her husband in Surrey.

She writes about early medieval England, from the eleventh century onwards, and has a great depth of feeling for this period of history. Her locations, customs and social life of the time are meticulously researched and vividly portrayed. She gets beneath the skin of her characters, whom she presents as products of their time, influenced by the events happening around them.

Crown of Roses is a perceptive and sympathetic chronicle of the Wars of the Roses, seen through the eyes of a lady-in-waiting to the Nevilles.

Publications

Gildenford   Chatto   1977
The Norman pretender   Chatto   1980
Disputed crown   Chatto   1982
To a native shore   Piatkus   1985
King of the wood   Headline   1988
Crown of Roses   Headline   1989

BRIDGES OVER TIME

Proud villeins   Headline   1990
The ruthless yeoman   Headline   1991
Women of Ashdon   Headline   1992
The faithful lovers   Headline   1993

Now read
Pamela Belle, Annette Motley, Jean Plaidy, Carol Wensby-Scott.

Auel, Jean M.

American, she lives in Oregon. Her novels are sweeping panoramic sagas about prehistoric Europe, describing the life and times of the early tribesmen. A great deal of research into the known areas of pre-historic civilisations has been done, and an element of fantasy added to lend excitement and adventure. The books are very long, extremely detailed, with vivid description and rounded characters. The sequence is titled Earth's Children.

Publications

EARTH'S CHILDREN

Clan of the cave bear   1980
The valley of horses   1983
The mammoth hunters   1985
Plains of passage   1990
(All published by Hodder.)

Now read
James Clavell, Dorothy Dunnett, William Horwood.

Belle, Pamela

British. She was born in Suffolk, and was a teacher before she gave up her job to become a full-time writer. She writes well and convincingly about seventeenth-century England, with painstaking research into the social and political conditions of the age. She paints a descriptive picture of life in a country household, weaving her plot and characters around contemporary events. Her novels are long and detailed, but the plot moves quickly and the dialogue is good: an enjoyable read for anyone interested in that period of history.

Publications

Moon in the water   Pan   1983   reprinted   Severn
   House   1989
Chains of fate   Bodley Head   1984
Alathea   Pan   1985   reprinted   Bodley Head   1988
The lodestar   Bodley Head   1987
Wintercombe   Bodley Head   1988
Herald of joy   Bodley Head   1989

Falling star   Century   1990
Treason's gift   Century   1992

Now read
Dorothy Dunnett, Rosalind Laker, Annette Motley, Sharon Penman,
E. V. Thompson, Sarah Woodhouse.

Cordell, Alexander

British. He was educated mainly in China, and joined the army in
1932. He served in France during the Second World War, and then
became a civil servant, working in Hong Kong. During this time, he
wrote fiction with a Chinese theme. He has also written for children.
   He is best known for his sequence of novels about Wales in the
Industrial Revolution. His backgrounds are detailed studies of the
social and economic conditions of the period, in relation to the lives
of the people. His characters are strong and courageous, prepared to
fight the establishment to make a better life for their families. The
plots are intricate, and the style holds the reader's interest.

Publications

A thought of honour   Museum Press   1954
Race of the tiger   Gollancz   1963
The sinews of love   Gollancz   1965
The bright Cantonese   Gollancz   1967
The dream and the destiny   Hodder   1975
To slay the dreamer   Hodder   1981
Rogue's march   Hodder   1981
Peerless Jim   Hodder   1984
Tunnel tigers   Weidenfeld & Nicolson   1986
Requiem for a patriot   Weidenfeld & Nicolson   1988

WELSH SEQUENCE

Rape of the fair country   Weidenfeld & Nicolson
   1966
The Hosts of Rebecca   Weidenfeld & Nicolson   1968

Song of the earth   Weidenfeld & Nicolson   1969
The fire people   Weidenfeld & Nicolson   1972
This sweet and bitter earth   Weidenfeld & Nicolson
   1977
Land of my fathers   Weidenfeld & Nicolson   1983
This proud and savage land (prelude to the series)
   Weidenfeld & Nicolson   1987
Beloved exile   Piatkus   1993

Moll   Weidenfeld & Nicolson   1990

Now read
Catherine Gavin, Edith Pargeter, E. V. Thompson.

Dunnett, Dorothy

British. Born in Dunfermline, Scotland, in 1923. She was educated
in Edinburgh, and at both Edinburgh and Glasgow Colleges of Art.
She worked in the Public Relations Department of the Secretary of
State for Scotland, and in the Research Department of the Board of
Trade in Glasgow from 1940 to 1956. She is a professional portrait
painter, exhibiting at the Royal Scottish Academy, and is also a
Director of Scottish Television. She is married to Alistair Dunnett, a
fellow writer. She writes detective stories under her maiden name,
Dorothy Halliday.
   Her major work is a sequence of six novels set in sixteenth
century Europe, in which the chief character is Francis Crawford of
Lymond, younger son of a noble house. The action ranges from
Scotland (at the court of Mary, Queen of Scots), to France, Malta (in
the headquarters of the Knights of St. John of Jerusalem), Turkey (at
the court of Suleiman the Magnificent), Russia (at the time of Ivan
the Terrible) and back to Scotland for the climax of the series. The
research is meticulous, the detail exhaustive, and the prose vivid and
descriptive, obviously influenced by a painter's eye. The books are
long and the plots intricate, but the pace is hectic, and the action
gripping. The novels require the reader's full attention, to keep track
of the many threads in the plot, but make compulsive reading, and
are enormously informative about European history of the period.

She has moved on to a new series, set in fifteenth-century Italy, about a young merchant venturer, and has also written one single volume, *King hereafter*, about Macbeth.

Publications

CRAWFORD OF LYMOND

The game of kings   1962
Queen's play   1964
The disorderly knights   1966
Pawn in frankincense   1969
The ringed castle   1971
Checkmate   1975
(Published by Cassell.)

THE HOUSE OF NICCOLO

Niccolo rising   1986
The Spring of the Ram   1987
Race of scorpions   1989
Scales of gold   1991

King hereafter   1982
(Published by Michael Joseph.)

as Dorothy Halliday

THE DOLLY SERIES

Dolly and the singing bird   1968   (*Tropical issue*)
Dolly and the cookie bird   1970   (*Rum affair*)
Dolly and the doctor bird   1971   (*Ibiza surprise*)
Dolly and the starry bird   1973   (*Operation Nassau*)
Dolly and the nanny bird   1976   (*Roman nights*)
(Published by Cassell.)
Dolly and the bird of paradise   Michael Joseph   1983
   (*Split code*)
Moroccan traffic   Chatto   1991

Now read
Pamela Belle, Annette Motley, Sharon Penman, Nigel Tranter.

Gavin, Catherine

British. Born in Aberdeen in 1907. She gained an MA in 1928 and a PhD in 1931 from the University of Aberdeen, and lectured in History there and at the University of Glasgow. She became a journalist in 1943, acting as War Correspondent for Kemsley Newspapers, and then Middle East correspondent for the *Daily Express*. She was on the staff of *Time* in New York, 1950–52, before becoming a full-time writer.

She writes novels which are linked by theme rather than characters. They are historically accurate, with great attention to detail, and evoke the atmosphere of place and time in a remarkable way. The 'Second Empire Quartet' concerns the revolutionary struggles which took place in the nineteenth century, in France, Italy, Finland and Mexico, and mix fictional characters with historical personalities. The First World War and Second World War novels are about the pressures of war on the people involved in it, and she succeeds in capturing the atmosphere and events of both wars without provoking criticism from those who were actively engaged in them. Although all her books are based on solid fact, the blend of fact and fiction, and the pace of the plots, make them attractive to the reader.

Publications

> *Clyde Valley*　Barker　1938
> *The hostile shore*　Methuen　1940
> *The black milestone*　Methuen　1941
> *The mountain of light*　Methuen　1944

> THE SECOND EMPIRE QUARTET
>
> *Madeleine*　Macmillan　1958
> *The cactus and the crown*　1962
> *The fortress*　1964
> *The moon into blood*　1966

> FIRST WORLD WAR
>
> *The devil in harbour*　1968

The House of War   1970
Give me the daggers   1972
The snow mountain   1973

SECOND WORLD WAR

Traitor's Gate   1976
None dare call it treason   1978
Now sleep the brave   1980
(All published by Hodder, except where stated.)

A light woman   1986
The glory road   1987
A dawn of splendour   1989
(Published by Grafton.)

Now read
Pamela Hill, Jean Plaidy, Sarah Woodhouse.

Heaven, Constance

British. Born in Middlesex in 1911, and educated in Essex and at King's College, London, where she gained a BA(Hons) in 1931. She is also a Licentiate of the Royal College of Music. She became an actress in 1939, after her marriage, and managed theatre companies with her husband, William Heaven, until his death in 1958. She became a writer in 1966, and says that a lifelong interest in history prompted her first novels – fictional biographies of the Ralegh family. These, and three other books, were written under her maiden name of Constance Fecher.

She fits equally well into the Gothic romance category, since some of her novels are essentially of that type. However the attention to historical detail is apparent, even when the characters and plots are romanticised. She writes about places which have fired her imagination: Tsarist Russia, the Camargue area of France, and the Fens. She researches their history first, then invents a plot to fit the setting, which she does very well. Her books are immensely popular, on both levels.

Now read on

Publications

as Constance Fecher

THE RALEGHS

Queen's delight   1966
Traitor's son   1967
King's legacy   1967

Player queen   1968
Lion of Trevarrock   1969
The night of the wolf   1972
(Published by Hale.)

as Constance Heaven

KURAGIN SERIES

The House of Kuragin   1972
The Astrov inheritance   1973
Heir to Kuragin   1978

AYLSHAM FAMILY

Lord of Ravensley   1980
The Ravensley touch   1982
The fire still burns   Collins   1989

Castle of eagles   1974
The place of stones   1975
The fires of Glenlochy   1976
The queen and the gypsy   1977
The Wildcliffe bird   1981
Castle of doves   1984
Larksghyll   1986
The raging fire   1987
The wind from the sea   1991
(All published by Heinemann.)

Now read
Pamela Hill, Rosalind Laker, Philippa Wiat.

172

Hill, Pamela

Born in Nairobi in 1920, of a Scottish mother and Australian father. She was educated in Scotland, and became a teacher, which she disliked very much. Her first novel was a success, and it enabled her to leave teaching and buy a remote cottage in Galloway, where she lived for many years, writing, breeding dogs and mink farming. She now lives in London.

She writes about real historical characters in a light, easily absorbed way. Many of her books are set in seventeenth- and eighteenth-century Scotland, and concern the aristocracy of the period. Her plots are imaginative and fast-moving, her settings are authentic, and her facts, while unobtrusively presented, are accurate. The main characters are usually women, with strength of purpose and resolution. Her recent books have tended towards the light historical romance, still in an authentic setting, but much lighter in tone, and with imaginary characters.

Publications

> *Flaming Janet*   1954
> *Shadow of palaces: the story of Francoise d'Aubigny*
>   1955
> *Marjorie of Scotland*   1956
> *Here lies Margot*   1957
> (Published by Chatto & Windus.)
> *Maddalena*   1963
> *Forget not Ariadne*   1965
> *Julia*   1967
> (Published by Cassell.)
> *The Devil of Aske*   1972
> *The Malvie inheritance*   1973
> *The incumbent*   1974
> *Whitton's Folly*   1975
> *Norah Stroyan*   1976
> *The green salamander*   1977
> (Published by Hodder.)
> *Tsar's woman*   1977
> *Stranger's forest*   1978

Daneclere   1979
Homage to a rose   1979
Daughter of midnight   1979
Fire opal   1980
Knock at a star   1981
A place of ravens   1981
This rough beginning   1981
The House of Cray   1982
The fairest one of all   1982
Duchess Cain   1983
Bride of Ae   1983
The copper-haired marshal   1983
Still blooms the rose   1984
Children of Lucifer   1984
The governess   1985
Sable for the count   1985
My Lady Glamis   1985
Venables   1986
The sisters   1986
Digby   1987
Fenfallow   1987
Jeannie Urquhart   1988
The Sutburys   1988
The woman in the cloak   1988
Artemisia   1989
Trevithick   1989
Widow's veil   1989
Vollands 1990
The brocken   1990
The sword and the flame   1991
Mercer   1992
The silver runaways   1992
Aunt Lucy   1993
(Published by Hale.)

Now read
Constance Heaven, Maureen Peters, Philippa Wiat.

Laker, Rosalind

American. A pseudonym for Barbara Ovstedal, who also writes thrillers as Barbara Paul. She is another writer who spills over into the Gothic romance and Family stories genres. Her first novels were fairly lightweight gothics, her next a trilogy set in Eastbourne. Since then she has used real settings and characters in her books.

The novels are long and detailed, with intricate plots and good characterisation. She uses unusual backgrounds as a setting for her characters: a racing stable in nineteenth-century Newmarket, a dressmaker's shop in Louis Napoleon's Paris, a silversmith's workshop in nineteenth-century London. *Gilded splendour* was a fictional biography of Thomas Chippendale. In each case the locations and industries were carefully researched, adding authenticity to the story.

Publications

> *Sovereign's key*   1969
> *Far seeks the heart*   1970
> *Sail a jewelled ship*   1971
> *The Shripney lady*   1972   reprinted Firecrest
>   1989
> *The smuggler's bride*   1976
> *Ride the Blue Riband*   1978
> (Published by Hale.)

> THE WARWYCKS

> *Warwyck's woman*   1979
> *Claudine's daughter*   1979
> *The Warwycks of Easthampton*   1980
> (Published by Eyre Methuen.)

> *Banners of silk*   1981
> *Gilded splendour*   1982
> *Jewelled path*   1983
> *What the heart keeps*   1984
> *This shining land*   1985

Tree of gold   1986
The silver touch   1987
To dance with kings   1988
(Published by Methuen.)
The golden tulip   Doubleday   1991
The Venetian mask   Doubleday   1992

Now read
Constance Heaven, Joanna Trollope, Sarah Woodhouse.

Motley, Annette

Lives in Ireland. She writes long, detailed, meticulously researched novels. Some, like *The Quickenberry tree*, which is about the English Civil War are family stories set against an important historical event; others are about real historical personalities, as is *Men on white horses,* about Catherine the Great.

The plots are intricate and full of action, and the dialogue matches the period. The characters are drawn in depth, and relationships are explored with insight.

Publications

My lady's crusade   1981
The Quickenberry tree   1983
Sins of the lion   1985
Green dragon, white tiger   1986
Men on white horses   1988
(Published by Macdonald.)

Now read
Dorothy Dunnett, Sharon Penman, Jean Plaidy, Carol Wensby-Scott.

Pargeter, Edith

British. Born in Shropshire in 1913, where she still lives. She was educated at Coalbrookdale High School for Girls, then worked as a chemist's assistant. She served in the WRNS in the Second World War, and was awarded the BEM in 1944. She also writes detective stories under the name of Ellis Peters.

She has been writing novels since 1936. The early ones are little known, but she achieved success with her trilogy about medieval Wales, published 1961–63. She writes with convincing detail about the twelfth and thirteenth centuries, her favourite period, and builds character and suspense as the plot unfolds. She has been accused of glossing over the unpleasant side of medieval life, but her stories provide realism without gratuitous violence.

As Ellis Peters, she wrote a series in the 1960s about Chief Inspector George Felse, but turned in 1977 to a new detective, a twelfth-century monk living in Shrewsbury, Brother Cadfael. This series enables her to write about her beloved twelfth century, while retaining her interest in the mystery story, and her native Shropshire. Again, the historical detail is accurate, and the stories have a gentleness and simplicity in keeping with the religious life of the hero.

Publications

Hortensius, friend of Nero   Lovat Dickson   1936
Iron-bound   Lovat Dickson   1936
The city lies four-square   1939
Ordinary people   1941
She goes to war   1942

The eighth champion of Christendom   1945
Reluctant Odyssey   1946
Warfare accomplished   1947
(The above form a trilogy.)

The fair young phoenix   1948
By firelight   1948
Holiday with violence   1952
This rough magic   1953
Most loving mere folly   1953
The soldier at the door   1954
A means of grace   1956

WELSH TRILOGY

The heaven tree   1961
The green branch   1962
The scarlet seed   1963
(All published by Heinemann unless otherwise
  listed.)

A bloody field by Shrewsbury   1971
(reprinted   Headline   1989)

THE BROTHERS OF GWYNEDD

Sunrise in the West   1974
Dragon at noonday   1975
Hounds at sunset   1976
Afterglow and nightfall   1977
The marriage of Meggotta   1979
(All published by Macmillan.)

BROTHER CADFAEL (as Ellis Peters)

A morbid taste for bones   1977
One corpse too many   1979
Monks' wood   1980
Saint Peter's Fair   1981
The leper of St. Giles   1981
The virgin in the ice   1982
The sanctuary sparrow   1983
The devil's novice   1983
Dead man's ransom   1984
The pilgrim of hate   1985
An excellent mystery   1985
Raven in the foregate   1986
The rose rent   1986
(Published by Macmillan.)
The hermit of Eyton Forest   Headline   1987
The confession of Brother Haluin   Headline   1988
The potter's field   Headline   1989

The summer of the Danes   Headline   1991
The holy thief   Headline   1992

Now read
Pamela Hill, Jean Plaidy, Nigel Tranter.

Penman, Sharon

American. Of Anglo-Irish parentage, she lives in New Jersey. She is another comparative newcomer to the field of historical novels, and practised as a lawyer until her first book was published.

She writes with great authority and attention to detail. Her books are very long (some run to 900 pages), minutely observed, and meticulously researched. Her characters are so well drawn that the reader can almost believe they are real, and she has a remarkable sense of feeling for life in the English Middle Ages, creating an authentic atmosphere.

Publications

The sunne in splendour   1984
Here be dragons   1986
Falls the shadow   1988
(Published by Michael Joseph.)

Now read
Pamela Belle, Dorothy Dunnett, Annette Motley, Carol Wensby-Scott.

Peters, Maureen

British. Born in Caernarvon, Wales, in 1935. She was educated at Caernarvon Grammar School and University College, Bangor, where she gained a BA and a Dip.Ed. She still lives in Caernarvon. She is a very prolific writer, under several names, using Veronica Black and Levanah Lloyd for gothic romance, and Catherine Darby and Sharon Whitby for other historical novels.

Now read on

She writes almost exclusively for Hale and, as with the majority of their historical authors, her books are short, and easy to read. Those written under her own name are factual, based on the lives of real people, but romanticised to please the undiscriminating reader. This does not imply that she does not write well, but merely that there is not the same depth to her work as in that of other historical novelists. She instils a good sense of atmosphere into her books, and her plots are well-crafted, but there is no detailed picture of the background, and her characters are likeable but, again, without a lot of depth. Her books are extremely popular, however, particularly those written under her own name, and that of Catherine Darby, which are historical family sagas.

Publications

Elizabeth the beloved   1965
Katheryn, the wanton Queen   1967
Mary, the infamous Queen   1968
Bride for King James   1968
Joan of the lilies   1969
The Rose of Hever   1969
Flower of the Greys   1969
Princess of desire   1970
Struggle for a crown   1970
Shadow of a Tudor   1971
Seven for St. Crispin's Day   1971
The cloistered flame   1971
Jewel of the Greys   1972
The Woodville wench   1972
The Peacock Queen   1972
The gallows herd   1973
The Maid of Judah   1973
Flawed enchantress   1974
So fair and foul a queen   1974
The willow maid   1974
Curse of the Greys   1974
The queenmaker   1975
Kate Alanna   1975
A child called Freedom   1976

Beggar maid, queen 1980
I the maid 1980
The snow blossom 1980
Night of the willow 1981
Ravenscar 1981
Song for a strolling player 1981
Frost on the rose 1982
The dragon and the rose 1982
Red Queen, White Queen 1982
My lady Troubador 1983
Imperial harlot 1983
Lackland's bride 1983
Alianor 1984
My Philippa 1984
Isabella and the she-wolf 1985
The vinegar seed 1986
The luck bride 1987
The vinegar tree 1987
Lady for a chevalier 1987
The noonday queen 1988
Incredible, fierce desire 1988
My Catalina 1988
Mistress to a Valois 1989
Witch Queen 1990
Much suspected of me 1990
Proud Bess 1990
The flower of Martinique 1991
England's mistress 1991
A masque of Brontes 1991

as Catherine Darby

FALCON SERIES

Falcon for a witch 1975
A game of Falcons 1976
Fortune for a Falcon 1976
Season of the Falcon 1976
A pride of Falcons 1977

Falcon tree   1977
The Falcon and the moon   1978
Falcon rising   1978
Falcon sunset   1978
Seed of the Falcon   1981
Falcon's claw   1982
Falcon to the lure   1982

MOON SERIES

Whisper down the moon   1978
Frost on the moon   1979
The flaunting moon   1979
Sing me a moon   1980
Cobweb across the moon   1980
Moon in Pisces   1981

ROWAN SERIES

Rowan Garth   1982
Rowan for a queen   1983
Circle of rowan   1983
Scent of rowan   1983
Rowan maid   1984
Song of the rowan   1984

SABRE SERIES

Sabre   1985
Silken Sabre   1985
Sabre's child   1985
House of Sabre   1986
Breed of Sabres   1987
Morning of a Sabre   1987
Fruit of the Sabre   1988
Gentle Sabre   1988

OTHERS

A dream of fair serpents   1981
Child of the flesh   1982

Heart of flame 1986
Pilgrim in the wind 1988
The love knot 1989
(All published by Hale.)

Now read
Pamela Hill, Philippa Wiat.

Plaidy, Jean

British. Born in London in 1906. The best known pseudonym of
Eleanor Hibbert. As Jean Plaidy, she writes serious historical novels,
soundly based on facts, deeply researched, and about famous
historical personalities, largely royalty. She presents history in a very
readable manner. She is an extremely well-known writer, continually
in demand, and she is included here to serve as a comparison with
other authors. The books are not too long, and, though they demand
some concentration and an interest in the subject, they are easy to
read. There is, obviously, some licence taken with the characters, but
their actions are based on known facts. The novels are all published
by Hale, but are far more academic than their usual historical novels.
Jean Plaidy died at the end of 1992.

Publications

Beyond the blue mountains 1948
Murder most royal 1949
The goldsmith's wife 1950

CATHERINE DE MEDICI

Madame Serpent 1951
The Italian woman 1952
Queen Jezebel 1953

Daughter of Satan 1952
The sixth wife 1953
The Spanish bridegroom 1954

St Thomas's Eve   1954
Gay Lord Robert   1955
Royal road to Fotheringay   1955

CHARLES II

The wandering prince   1956
A health unto His Majesty   1956
Here lies our sovereign lord   1957

Flaunting, extravagant Queen   1957

LUCREZIA BORGIA

Madonna of the Seven Hills   1958
Light on Lucrezia   1958

Louis the wellbeloved   1959
The road to Compiegne   1959

ISABELLA AND FERDINAND

Castile for Isabella   1960
Spain for the sovereigns   1960
Daughters of Spain   1961

KATHARINE OF ARAGON

Katharine, the virgin widow   1961
The shadow of the pomegranate   1962
The King's secret matter   1962

The captive Queen of Scots   1963
The thistle and the rose   1963
Mary, Queen of France   1964
The murder in the tower   1964
Evergreen gallant   1965

THE LAST OF THE STUARTS

The three crowns   1965

The haunted sisters   1966
The Queen's favourites   1966

GEORGIAN SAGA

Queen in waiting   1967
The Princess of Celle   1967
The Prince and the Quakeress   1968
Caroline, the Queen   1968
The third George   1969
Perdita's prince   1969
Sweet lass of Richmond Hill   1970
Indiscretions of the queen   1970
The regent's daughter   1971
The goddess of the green room   1971

VICTORIAN SAGA

The captive of Kensington Palace   1972
Victoria in the wings   1972
The Queen and Lord M   1973
The Queen's husband   1973
The widow of Windsor   1974

NORMAN TRILOGY

The Bastard King   1974
The Lion of Justice   1975
The passionate enemies   1976

PLANTAGENET SAGA

The Plantagenet prelude   1976
The revolt of the eaglets   1977
The heart of the lion   1977
The Prince of Darkness   1978
The battle of the Queens   1978
The Queen from Provence   1979
Edward Longshanks   1979
The follies of the king   1980
The vow on the heron   1980

Passage to Pontefract 1981
The star of Lancaster 1981
Epitaph for three women 1981
Red Rose of Anjou 1982
The sun in splendour 1982

Hammer of the Scots 1981
Myself my enemy 1983
Uneasy lies the head 1984
Queen of this realm 1984
Victoria victorious 1985
Lady in the tower 1986
Courts of love 1987
In the shadow of the crown 1988
The Queen's secret 1989
The pleasures of love 1991
William's wife 1992

Now read
Edith Pargeter, Nigel Tranter.

Thompson, E. V.

British. He was born in London, and spent nine years in the navy before joining the Bristol police force, where he worked with the Vice Squad. He became an investigator with BOAC, worked with the Narcotics Bureau in Hong Kong, and became Chief Security Officer in Rhodesia's Department of Civil Aviation. While he was in Rhodesia, he had a number of short stories published, and returned to England determined to become a full-time writer. After supporting himself by doing a variety of jobs, he moved to Bodmin Moor, where he wrote *Chase the wind*. He now lives in Mevagissey, overlooking the sea.

He writes mainly about the Cornwall he knows and loves, with great authority and a remarkable sense of period. His stories are about the main concerns in Cornwall in the eighteenth and nineteenth centuries: tin mining and fishing. The plots are fast-moving, and carry the reader along as the story unfolds, with cleverly interwoven sub-plots to add to the interest. There is a wealth of detail about locations and traditions, and authentic events in the county's history. The characters are memorable and entirely credible. There are two sagas, and some individual novels. In some of the Retallick saga, the action takes place in South Africa, which reflects his own knowledge of the country. In *Becky*, set in the Bristol slums, his knowledge of police activities against vice is displayed.

Publications

RETALLICK FAMILY

Chase the wind   1977
Harvest of the sun   1978
Ben Retallick   1980
Singing spears   1982
The stricken land   1986
Lottie Trago   1990

NATHAN JAGO

The restless sea   1983
Polrudden   1985

The music makers   1979
The dream traders   1981
Becky   1988
God's highlander   1989
Cassie   1991
Wychwood   1992
(Published by Macmillan.)

Homeland (as James Monro)   Simon & Schuster
   1991
Blue dress girl   Headline   1992

Now read
Alexander Cordell, Catherine Gavin, Carol Wensby- Scott.

Tranter, Nigel

British. Born in Glasgow in 1909, and educated in Edinburgh. He joined the family insurance firm in 1929 and then served in the Royal Artillery in the Second World War. He became a full-time writer in 1946, and has published a prodigious number of novels about Scottish history.

He started by writing fairly lightweight novels, with a theme of historical adventure, rather like those of Rafael Sabatini or John Buchan, but moved on to fictional accounts of the major protagonists in Scottish history. His research is exhaustive, and his locations authentic. The historical detail is accurate, and most of the books are based on journals and letters of the period. The plots move fast enough to hold the reader's interest, without sacrificing authenticity. He holds a unique position as a chronicler of Scottish history and fictional biography. He has also written a number of travel books about Scotland, some children's books, and Westerns, as Nye Tredgold.

Publications

>
> *Trespass*   Moray Press   1937
> *Mammon's daughter*   1939
> *Harsh heritage*   1939
> *Eagle's feather*   1941
> *Watershed*   1941
> *The gilded fleece*   1942
> *Delayed action*   1944
> *Tinker's pride*   1945
> *Man's estate*   1946
> *Flight of Dutchmen*   1947
> *Island twilight*   1947
> *Root and branch*   1948
> *Colours flying*   1948
> *The chosen course*   1949
> *Fair game*   1950
> *High spirits*   1950
> *The freebooters*   1950
> *Tidewrack*   1951

Fast and loose 1951
Bridal path 1952
Cheviot Chase 1952
Ducks and drakes 1953
The Queen's Grace 1953
Rum week 1954
The night riders 1954
There are worse jungles 1955
Rio d'Oro 1955
The long coffin 1956
(All published by Ward Lock.)
MacGregor's gathering 1957
The enduring flame 1957
Balefire 1958
The stone 1958
The man behind the curtain 1959
The clansman 1959
Spanish galleon 1960
The flockmasters 1960
Kettle of fish 1961
The Master of Gray 1961
Drug on the market 1962
Gold for Prince Charlie 1962
The courtesan 1963
Chain of destiny 1964
Past master 1965
A stake in the kingdom 1966
Lion let loose 1967
Cable from Kabul 1968
Black Douglas 1968

ROBERT THE BRUCE

The steps to the empty throne 1969
The path of the hero king 1970
The price of the king's peace 1971

JAMES GRAHAM, EARL OF MONTROSE

The young Montrose 1972

Montrose, the Captain General   1973

The wisest fool   1974
The Wallace   1975

THE HOUSE OF STEWART

Lords of misrule   1976
A folly of princes   1977
The captive crown   1977

Macbeth the King   1978
Margaret the Queen   1979
David the Prince   1980
True Thomas   1981
The patriot   1982
Lord of the Isles   1983

JAMES V

The riven realm   1984
James, by the grace of God   1985
Rough wooing   1986

Unicorn rampant   1984
Columba   1987
Flowers of chivalry   1988
Mail royal   1988
Warden of the Queen's March   1989
Kenneth   1990
Crusader   1991
Children of the mist   1992
Druid sacrifice   1993
(All published by Hodder.)

Now read
Pamela Belle, Dorothy Dunnett, Sharon Penman, Jean Plaidy.

Trollope, Joanna

British. Born in 1943. Her real name is Joanna Potter, and she also writes family novels as Caroline Harvey. She was awarded an MA at St. Hugh's College, Oxford, and became a teacher before turning to writing.

She researches her novels deeply, and says that she does twice as much research as is really necessary for each book, because she wants to give a sense of life as it really was in the past, and so needs to familiarise herself with the period. Her books are set in the nineteenth century, and her characters are closely concerned with some important event in the history of the period: the Battle of Waterloo, the Crimean War, the India of Warren Hastings. Her characters are engaging and life-like, the plots well-constructed and fast flowing, and the locations and period details convincing. She won the Romantic Novelists' Association Major Award in 1980 with *Parson Harding's daughter*. A recent novel, *The choir*, is set in contemporary England, but has a sense of history in that it is about a great cathedral. She might now, however, equally well be placed in the section on Perceptive women's novels, since her later novels have all had contemporary settings, which explore current issues with depth and insight. A change of publisher obviously led to a shift in emphasis in her books. *A village affair* dealt with a lesbian relationship in a small village; *The rector's wife* explored the problems encountered by the families of the present-day clergy; while *A passionate man* described love in middle age.

Publications

> *Eliza Stanhope*   1978
> *Parson Harding's daughter*   1979
> *Leaves from the valley*   1980
> *The city of gems*   1981
> *Steps of the sun*   1983
> *Taverner's Place*   1986
> *The choir*   1988
> (All published by Hutchinson.)
> *A village affair*   Bloomsbury   1989
> *A passionate man*   Bloomsbury   1990

191

The rector's wife   Bloomsbury   1991
The men and the girls   Bloomsbury   1992
A Spanish lover   Bloomsbury   1993

Now read
Catherine Gavin, Constance Heaven, Rosalind Laker, Sarah Woodhouse.

Wensby-Scott, Carol

British. Born in Brighton, and educated in Devon. She ran an antiquarian bookshop in Brighton before becoming a full-time writer. She now lives in Northumberland, where most of her books are set.

She writes meticulously-researched family history, based on fact. Her plots are intricately woven, and her characters strongly drawn and convincing. She evokes the atmosphere of the Northumberland countryside in a vivid and graphic way, whether it is in the fifteenth century of Harry Hotspur, or the late Victorian period of *Coal baron*.

Publications

Proud conquest   Michael Joseph   1979

THE PERCY TRILOGY

Lion of Alnwick   1980
Lion dormant   1983
Lion invincible   1984

Coal baron   1988
Rich beyond our dreams   1991
(All published by Macdonald.)

Now read
Catherine Gavin, Rosalind Laker, Annette Motley, Jean Plaidy, Sarah Woodhouse.

Wiat, Philippa

British. She was born in Wimbledon, but has spent most of her adult life in Sussex. She left school, by choice, at fifteen, and worked in insurance and as a nurse, before she married and had three daughters. For some years she was an editor of *The Law List*.

She had no ambition to become a writer until she started to research her family history and, in particular, Sir Thomas Wyatt, the Elizabethan poet and lover of Anne Boleyn. The research turned into a full-blown novel, to be followed by some thirty more. Although they are historically accurate, her books are easy to read, and have a strong romantic interest. They tend to be part of long family sagas, and often have an element of the supernatural.

Publications

THE WYATT SAGA

Master of Blandeston Hall　1973
The heir of Allington　1973
Sound now the passing bell　1973
Knight of Allington　1974
Rebel of Allington　1977
My lute be still　1977

THE HOWARD SAGA

Maid of gold　1971
Like as the roaring waves　1972
The Queen's fourth husband　1976
Lion without claws　1976
Yet a lion　1978
Wear a green kirtle　1987

THE BLACK BOAR SAGA

Lord of the Black Boar　1975
Sword of Woden　1975
Tree of Vortigern　1976
The Atheling　1977

Raven in the wind   1978
Westerfalca   1979
Lord of the wolf   1980

THE WILMINGTON NOVELS

The fourposter   1979
Shadow of Samain   1980

CHARLTON MEAD

The mistletoe bough   1981
Bride of darkness   1982
Wychwood   1982

THE GREY FAMILY

Five gold rings   1982
Children of the Spring   1983

EDWARD III TRILOGY

Queen-gold   1985
The grey goose-wing   1985
The Whyte swan   1986

The golden chariot   1974
The King's vengeance   1981
Cartismandua   1984
Prince of the White Rose   1984
Fair Rosamund   1985
The cloister and the flame   1988
Phantasmagoria   1988
The kingmaker's daughter   1989
Child bride   1990
The Lady Editha   1992
The hammer and the sword: a novel of Wat Tyler   1992
(All published by Hale.)

Now read

Pamela Hill, Maureen Peters.

Woodhouse, Sarah

British. She lives in Norfolk, and writes about East Anglia. Her novels are historically accurate, and deeply researched, but with enough love interest and family detail to prevent them from becoming dull. Her narrative style is in the mould of Jane Austen and Anthony Trollope, and her settings are the rural areas of East Anglia in the eighteenth and nineteenth centuries.

Publications

> *A season of mists*   1984
> *The Indian widow*   1985
> *Daughter of the sea*   1986
> *The peacock's feather*   1988
> *Native air*   1990
> (Published by Century.)

Now read
Catherine Gavin, Constance Heaven, Edith Pargeter, E. V. Thompson, Joanna Trollope.

HORROR STORIES

This is an ever-increasing genre, constantly gaining in popularity among its readers. It seems to appeal to all sorts of people, without regard to age or sex. The main criterion is that it should be both frightening and repulsive, with elements of horror, fantasy and the supernatural. Most of the writers in the genre are men, though some women, notably Virginia Andrews and Mary Higgins Clark, write gothic romance/horror.

There is enormous variation in the quality of writing. Much of it is paperback pulp fiction, of little literary merit. Some, however, is well-crafted, with a good literary style and an inventive plot. We have tried to choose those authors who are creative in style and plot, and who can build up tension and horror without lapsing into the merely sensational.

Campbell, Ramsey

British. He was born in Liverpool in 1946, and now lives in the Wirral. He worked in the Civil Service and in public libraries, before becoming a full-time writer in 1973. He says that he particularly enjoys reading his stories to a live audience.

He is, with James Herbert, the most respected British writer of horror stories. His plots are inventive, and he is a master of the gradual build-up of tension towards a shattering climax. He writes both full-length novels and short stories, some of which have only been published in the US.

Publications

The inhabitants of the lake (short stories)
Demons by daylight (short stories)
The doll who ate his mother   Hutchinson   1978
The height of the scream (short stories)   Hutchinson   1978
The face that must die
The parasite
The nameless
Incarnate   Century   1984
Obsession   Century   1985
Dark companions (short stories)   1986
Cold print (short stories)   Grafton   1986
The hungry moon   Century   1987
The influence   Century   1988
Ancient images   Century   1989
Scared stiff   Macdonald   1989
Midnight sun   Macdonald   1990
Needing ghosts   Legend   1990
The face that must die   Macdonald   1991
The count of eleven   Macdonald   1991
Waking nightmares   Little, Brown   1992
(Publishers and dates are those published in UK.)

Now read
James Herbert, Stephen King, Graham Masterton.

Farris, John

American. He lives in Puerto Rico. His stories are essentially about evil, and supernatural possession. The themes are similar in each, but the plots differ, and the tension is sustained.

Publications

> *The captors*   New English Library   1970
> *Sharp practice*   Weidenfeld & Nicolson   1975
> *The fury*   Macdonald   1976
> *Shatter*   W. H. Allen   1980
> *Catacombs*   Hodder   1981
> *The uninvited*   Hodder   1983
> *Minotaur*   NEL   1985
> *Son of the endless night*   Hodder   1985
> *All heads turn as the hunt goes by*   Macdonald
>   1986
> *Wildwood*   Hodder   1987
> *Hellfire*   Hodder   1987
> *Nightfall*   Severn House   1988
> *Scare tactics*   Hodder   1989
> *Bad blood*   Gollancz   1989
> *The axeman cometh*   Hodder   1990
> *Fiends*   Grafton   1991

Now read
Graham Masterton, John Saul.

Gallagher, Stephen

British. He lives and works in the Ribble valley.

He writes tense, suspenseful stories about horror as experienced by ordinary people. The plots are chillingly credible, without the contrived supernatural experiences encountered in many of the books in this genre. The style is literate and flowing, with good description and convincing dialogue. The books have a pervasive sense of evil.

Publications

> *Valley of lights*   NEL   1987
> *October*   NEL   1988
> *Down river*   NEL   1989
> *Rain*   NEL   1990
> *Chimera*   NEL   1990
> *The boat house*   NEL   1991
> *Nightmare with angel*   NEL   1992

Now read
Peter James, Stephen King, Peter Straub.

Herbert, James

British. He has been writing horror stories, with great success, since 1974, and is the best known of the British exponents of the genre.

He writes eerie, atmospheric novels about hauntings. Some of his most chilling books concern rats. His plots are inventive and well-constructed, his style is literate and descriptive, and there is a horrible air of reality about his characters.

Publications

> RATS TRILOGY
>
> *The rats*   1974
> *Lair*   1979
> *Domain*   1984
>
> *The fog*   1975
> *The survivor*   1976
> *Fluke*   1977
> *The spear*   1978
> *The dark*   1980
> *The Jonah*   1981
> *Shrine*   1983
> *Moon*   1985
> (All published by New English Library.)

The magic cottage Hodder 1986
Sepulchre Hodder 1987
Haunted Hodder 1988
Creed Hodder 1990
Portent Hodder 1992

Now read
Stephen King, Richard Laymon, Peter Straub.

James, Peter

British. He was born in 1948, and educated at Charterhouse. He lived in the United States for some years, where he was involved in the film industry. He returned home to become a writer. He lives in Sussex with his wife, their Hungarian sheepdog, and the ghost of a Roman centurion, and lists research into the supernatural as one of his major interests.

He is acclaimed as one of the most important new writers of the genre, and has been compared to Stephen King. He claims that all his work is based on his own supernatural experiences. The novels are well researched, very readable, and extremely well constructed. The plots are full of suspense, and the tension mounts to a shocking climax.

Publications

Possession Sphere 1989
Dreamer Sphere 1990
Sweet heart Gollancz 1990
Twilight Gollancz 1991
Prophecy Gollancz 1992

Now read
Stephen Gallagher, Stephen King, Peter Straub.

King, Stephen

American. Born in 1947. He is reputed to be the most successful novelist, in the commercial sense, in the history of American publishing.

He writes with imagination and vigour about the supernatural in everyday life. The stories are mostly set in New England, and he uses graphic descriptions both for location and for horrifying situations. His plots are well-constructed, with good characterisation and a gradual build-up of tension. He appeals to all ages and types of reader, and many of his books have been filmed.

Publications

The dead zone   1972
Carrie   1974
Salem's lot   1976
The shining   1977
Night shift (short stories)   1978
The stand   1979
(All published by New English Library.)
Firestarter   Hodder   1980
Danse macabre   Macdonald   1981
Cujo   Macdonald   1982
Different seasons   Macdonald   1982
Christine   Hodder   1984
Pet Sematery   Hodder   1984
Skeleton crew (short stories)   Guild   1985
It   Hodder   1986
Misery   Hodder   1987
Eyes of the dragon   Macdonald   1987
The Tommyknockers   Hodder   1988
Dark visions   Gollancz   1989
The dark half   Hodder   1989
Four past midnight   Hodder   1990
Needful things   Hodder   1991
Gerald's game   Hodder   1992
Dolores Claiborne   Hodder   1993

As Richard Bachmann
Thinner   New English Library   1985
The Bachmann Books   NEL   1988

DARK TOWER

The dark tower   Sphere   1988
The drawing of the three   Sphere   1989
The wasteland   Sphere   1992
(These are fantasies with supernatural overtones.)

Now read
James Herbert, Richard Laymon, Dean Koontz.

Koontz, Dean R.

American. He lives in California. He writes better-than-average stories about possession and evil. Some are collections of short stories with a linked theme, others full-length novels. The atmosphere and tension in the books is handled well, and the climax, while horrifying, is not quite as violent as in some of the other writers in the genre.

Publications

Demon seed   Corgi   1973
Night chills   1977   reprinted by Headline   1991
Whispers   1981
Phantoms   1983   reprinted by Headline   1990
Darkness comes   1984
Shattered   1984
Chase   1985
Strangers   1986   reprinted by Headline   1991
Twilight eyes   1987   reprinted by Headline   1991
(All published by W. H. Allen.)
Watchers   Headline   1987
The vision   Headline   1988
Lightning   Headline   1988
The mask   Headline   1989
Night fears   Headline   1989
Midnight   Headline   1989
The bad place   Headline   1990

> *Cold fire*   Headline   1990
> *Hideaway*   Headline   1992
> *The voice of the night*   W. H. Allen   1989

Now read
Stephen King, Richard Laymon.

Laymon, Richard

American. He lives in Los Angeles. His novels are well-written with inventive plots and tense description, but are chillingly repulsive in theme. They are very popular, and he is considered to be among the best of the genre.

Publications

> *The cellar*   W. H. Allen   1980
> *Out are the lights*   New English Library   1982
> *Beware*   NEL   1985
> *The beast house*   NEL   1986
> *All Hallow's Eve*   NEL   1986
> *Flesh*   W. H. Allen   1987
> *Resurrection dreams*   W. H. Allen   1988
> *Funland*   W. H. Allen   1989
> *Stake*   Headline   1990
> *One rainy night*   Headline   1991
> *Darkness, tell us*   Headline   1991
> *Blood games*   Headline   1992
> *Savage*   Headline   1992
> *Alarums*   Headline   1993
> *Out are the lights and other tales*   Headline   1993

Now read
James Herbert, Stephen King, Whitley Strieber.

Lumley, Brian

British. Born in the North East, but now lives in Devon with his wife/agent, and cat. He has been writing fantasy/horror stories for over twenty years.

The books are exciting and entertaining, and mix science fiction with horror. The plots move quickly, and the supernatural incidents are vivid and, often, ghastly. Many of the books are in paperback, and form part of series. This is not great literature, but is easy to read, and very popular, particularly among younger readers.

Publications

Psychomech   Grafton   1984
Psychosphere   Grafton   1985
Psychamok!   Grafton   1985
The complete crow   Grafton   1987
Hero of dreams   Granada   1988
The ship of dreams   Headline   1989
Mad moon of dreams   Headline   1989
The clock of dreams   Headline   1992
Khai of ancient Khem   Grafton   1990
The House of Cthulhu   Headline   1991
The transition of Titus Crow   Headline   1991
House of doors   Grafton   1991
Sorcery in Shad   Headline   1991
Spawn of the winds   Headline   1992
In the moons of Borea   Headline   1993
Elysia   Grafton   1993
Fruiting bodies   Penguin   1993

NECROSCOPE

Necroscope   Grafton   1986
Wamphyri!   Grafton   1988
The source   Grafton   1989
Deadspeak   Grafton   1990
Deadspawn   Grafton   1991

Now read
Graham Masterton.

Masterton, Graham

British. He lives in Kent. He writes in two completely different styles, but unlike many authors, does not use a pseudonym. Most of his books are horror stories, but he also writes long, historical family novels. He has achieved considerable success in both genres, though it has to be said that his horror stories appear to be mere pot-boilers at the side of the others.

His stories, though equally inventive and gruesome, do not have the depth of those by authors like James Herbert and Stephen King. He writes prolifically, and, possibly, repetitively, about demons and monsters.

Publications

> *The Manitou*   Spearman   1976
> *Charnel House*   W. H. Allen   1979
> *Djinn*   W. H. Allen   1982
> *The devils of D-Day*   Chivers   1983
> *The plague*   W. H. Allen   1983
> *Ikon*   W. H. Allen   1983
> *The heirloom*   W. H. Allen   1984
> *Pariah*   W. H. Allen   1984
> *Tengu*   W. H. Allen   1984
> *The wells of Hell*   Chivers   1984
> *Revenge of the Manitou*   Piatkus   1984
> *Hell candidate*   Piatkus   1985
> *Sacrifice*   Piatkus   1985
> *Family portrait*   Severn House   1986
> *Death trance*   Severn House   1987
> *Night warriors*   Severn House   1987
> *Mirror*   Severn House   1988
> *Ritual*   Severn House   1988
> *Death dream*   Severn House   1989
> *Walkers*   Severn House   1990
> *The Sweetman curve*   (1979)   Severn House   1990
> *Night plague*   Severn House   1991
> *The hymn*   Macdonald   1991
> *Black angel*   Severn House   1991

Prey   Severn House   1992
Burial   Heinemann   1992

Now read
John Farris, John Saul.

McCammon, Robert

American. He was born and still lives in Birmingham, Alabama. His work appears regularly on the best-seller lists in America, where he is ranked as one of the world's finest writers of horror fiction. He was joint winner of the Bram Stoker Award in 1988.

  The books are well-written, with carefully executed plots, and credible characters.

Publications

Baal   Sphere   1990
The night boat   Kinnell   1990
Usher's passing   Severn House   1989
Swan song   Kinnell   1987
Stinger   Grafton   1989
Blue world   Grafton   1990
The wolf's hour   Grafton   1989
They thirst   Kinnell   1990
Mine   Grafton   1991
Boy's life   Joseph   1992
Gone south   Joseph   1993

Now read
Stephen King, Richard Laymon.

Rice, Anne

American. She was born in New Orleans in 1941, into an Irish Catholic family. She lived in San Francisco for many years, but has now returned to New Orleans, with her husband, the poet Stan Rice.

These are very literary horror stories, in the classic Gothick tradition. They concern, for the most part, vampires, and she has obviously made a deep study of all the vampire lore, before starting to write. The books are well-constructed, with intricate plots and convincing dialogue. They are not for the reader who wants an easy-to-read spine-chiller, but are, nevertheless, extremely popular.

Publications

THE VAMPIRE CHRONICLES

Interview with the vampire   1985
The vampire Lestat   1987
The Queen of the damned   1989
The tale of the body thief   1993
The mummy   1992
(All published by Chatto & Windus.)

Now read
Whitley Streiber.

Saul, John

American. He writes about good and evil, particularly in relation to children possessed by some diabolic force. The books are competently written, without great literary merit, but with some style and atmosphere.

Publications

Suffer the children   Hodder   1979
Comes the blind fury   Hodder   1981
All fall down   1983
When the wind blows   1983
Cry for the strangers   1984
Punish the sinners   1984
(All published by Severn House.)
Nathaniel   1985

Brainchild   1986
The unloved   1987   reprinted Severn House   1989
The unwanted   1988
(All published by Century.)
Second child   Inner Circle   1991
Shadows   Inner Circle   1993

Now read
John Farris, Graham Masterton.

Straub, Peter

American. He was born in Milwaukee, Wisconsin in 1943, spent ten years in Britain and Ireland, and now lives in Connecticut, though he writes in New York.

He writes fantasy/horror stories, with some straightforward ghost stories, and has also written one or two 'straight' novels and collections of poetry. His plots are deep and complex, and his characters rounded and credible. The pace is fast, and the action gripping, with terrifying dénouements. He won the 1983 British Fantasy Award with *Floating dragon*.

Publications

Julia   Cape   1976
If you could see me now   Cape   1977
Ghost story   Cape   1979
Shadowland   Collins   1981
Floating dragon   Collins   1983
The Talisman (with Stephen King)   Penguin   1986
Koko   Viking   1988
Houses without doors: short stories   Grafton   1990

Now read
James Herbert, Stephen King, Richard Laymon.

Strieber, Whitley

American. He writes in the true Gothick horror tradition, with black magic and the occult as his theme. The stories are well-crafted, tense and have a horrifying climax.

Publications

> *Wolfen*   Hodder   1978
> *Hunger*   Bodley Head   1981
> *Night church*   Severn House   1986
> *Black magic*   Severn House   1987
> *Catmagic*   Grafton   1987
> *Billy*   Macdonald   1991
> *The wild*   Macdonald   1991
> *Unholy fire*   Macdonald   1992

Now read
Ramsey Campbell, John Farris, Graham Masterton.

HUMOROUS NOVELS

It is rather difficult to find contemporary novelists who specialise in humorous novels. There are many writers who inject a great deal of humour into their books, and others who write a funny novel as a 'one-off', but very few who set out to make the reader laugh out loud, as did P. G. Wodehouse and Caryl Brahms and S. J. Simon, in the 1920s and 1930s, and Kingsley Amis and Richard Gordon in the 1950s and 1960s. This can perhaps be explained by the fact that people's tastes in humour change, and that television comedies tend to be rewritten in book form, filling the gap to some extent. Black comedies are plentiful, but do not quite fall into the genre.

The genre itself is difficult to define, since humour is a very personal thing, but we have tried to select novels which set out to entertain, by appealing to the reader's sense of the ridiculous, and by the use of comic description and witty dialogue.

Adams, Douglas

British. Born in 1952. He writes science fiction spoofs, originally conceived for radio, but soon translated to book form. In his first series, his hero, Arthur Dent, avoids the destruction of Earth to make way for a hyper-space bypass, by stowing away on an alien spacecraft, in company with Ford Prefect. The situations and characters which he encounters are inventive, hilarious and very cleverly conceived. The second series concerns Dirk Gently, a sort of zany, space-age private eye, in the mould of Raymond Chandler.

Publications

THE HITCHHIKER'S GUIDE

The hitchhiker's guide to the galaxy   1979
The restaurant at the end of the universe   1980
Life, the universe and everything   1982
So long, and thanks for all the fish   1984
Mostly harmless   1992

DIRK GENTLY

Dirk Gently's Holistic Detective Agency   1987
The long, dark tea-time of the soul   1988
(Published by Heinemann.)

Now read
Tom Holt, Terry Pratchett.

De Vries, Peter

American. Born in Chicago in 1910, and educated at Calvin College, Michigan, and North-Western University; he died in September 1993. He was a former journalist, working on community newspapers and magazines, before joining the staff of the *New Yorker*. His novels are satires about the life-styles of the upwardly-mobile surburbanites who work in New York and commute to Long

Island or Connecticut. He has an acute ear for the pretentious and the ridiculous, and his dialogue is witty and acid.

Publications

> *No, but I saw the movie*   1952
> *The tunnel of love*   1954
> *Comfort me with apples*   1956
> *The mackerel plaza*   1958
> *The tents of wickedness*   1959
> *Through the fields of clover*   1961
> *Reuben, Reuben*   1964
> *Let me count the ways*   1965
> *The cat's pajamas* (short stories)   1968
> *Mrs. Wallop*   1970
> *Into your tent I'll creep*   1971
> *Without a stitch in time*   1972
> *Forever panting*   1973
> *The glory of the humming-bird*   1975
> *I hear America swinging*   1976
> *Madder music*   1978
> *Consenting adults*   1981
> *Sauce for the goose*   1982
> *Slouching toward Kalamazoo*   1983
> *The prick of noon*   1986
> *Peckham's marbles*   1987
> (All published by Cape.)

Now read
David Nobbs, Tom Sharpe.

Holt, Tom

British. Born in Scotland in 1962. A real find. He started by writing follow-ups to E. L. Benson's 'Lucia' novels, but has recently written hilarious fantasies based on mythology. The first is a very funny, updated version of the Siegfried idyll, and the second about Norsemen playing out the Eddas in contemporary England. He has recently dealt with the legend of the Flying Dutchman, the Gods on Olympus, and the concept of time-slips. The novels in his 'Walled orchard' trilogy are more serious in concept, set in Ancient Greece, but there are still flashes of humour. The plots are fast-moving and very inventive, and the dialogue crisp and full of wit.

Publications

Lucia in wartime   Macmillan   1985
Lucia triumphant   Macmillan   1986
Expecting someone taller   Macmillan   1987
Who's afraid of Beowulf?   Macmillan   1988
Flying Dutch   Macdonald   1991
Ye Gods!   Orbit   1992
Overtime   Orbit   1993
Here comes the sun   Orbit   1993

THE WALLED ORCHARD

Goatsong   1989
Walled orchard   1990
(Published by Macmillan.)

Now read
Douglas Adams, Terry Pratchett.

Hood, Christopher

British. He was born in Lancashire in 1943, and now lives in Swansea, writing novels and screenplays. He is an anarchic satirist of middle-class and media life-styles, with over-the-top characters, but acute observations of real situations.

Publications

The Mutterthorpe thing   1971
The other side of the mountain   1979
Banana cat   1985

217

Dropping in   1989
(Published by Michael Joseph.)

Now read
Kingsley Amis, Peter De Vries, Tom Sharpe.

Nobbs, David

British. Born in Orpington, Kent. He was educated at Marlborough
College, and St. John's College, Cambridge, and served in the Royal
Corps of Signals. He spent eighteen months as a reporter on the
Sheffield Star, then moved to London as a television scriptwriter and
unpublished playwright. He began to write novels in the 1960s, and
achieved real fame when his books about Reginald Perrin were
adapted for television. He lives in Herefordshire with his wife and
three step-children.

The books are all genuinely funny, but there is an underlying
pathos in them, which arouses sympathy as well as laughter in the
reader. The characterisation is deep and rounded, and the dialogue is
crisp and witty. The plots are constructed around situations which
are encountered in everyday life, and spiced with humour.

Publications

A piece of the sky is missing   1966
The itinerant lodger   1967
Ostrich country   1968
A bit of a do   1986
Fair do's   1990

Second from last in the sack race   Methuen   1983
Pratt of the 'Argus' (sequel)   Methuen   1988
The death of Reginald Perrin   Gollancz   1975
The return of Reginald Perrin   Gollancz   1977
The better world of Reginald Perrin   Gollancz   1978

Now read
Peter Tinniswood, Keith Waterhouse.

Pratchett, Terry

British. He was born in 1948. He has received considerable critical acclaim, and has been compared in inventive humour to P. G. Wodehouse. He is basically a writer of fantasy, but has written a number of spoof fantasies, in the manner of Douglas Adams. His plots are inventive, his situations comic and his dialogue sparkles. He has created an imaginary flat, circular planet, 'Discworld', carried through space on the back of four elephants and a giant turtle, the great Atuin, and inhabited by a collection of eccentrics. The books go from strength to strength, and have now achieved cult status.

Publications

> *The carpet people*   C. Smythe   1971
> *The dark side of the moon*   C. Smythe   1971
> *Strata*   NEL   1982
>
> DISCWORLD
>
> *The colour of magic*   C. Smythe   1983
> *Light fantastic*   C. Smythe   1986
> *Equal rites*   Gollancz   1987
> *Mort*   Gollancz/ Smythe   1987
> *Sourcery*   Gollancz   1988
> *The Wyrd sisters*   Gollancz   1988
> *Pyramids*   Gollancz/ Corgi   1989
> *Guards! Guards!*   Gollancz   1989
> *Eric*   Gollancz   1990
> *Moving pictures*   Gollancz   1990
> *Reaper man*   Gollancz   1991
> *Witches abroad*   Gollancz   1991
> *Small gods*   Gollancz   1992
> *Lords and ladies*   Gollancz   1992
>
> *Good omens* (with Neil Gaiman)   Gollancz   1990

Now read
Douglas Adams, Tom Holt.

Sharpe, Tom

British. Born in 1928 and educated at Lancing College and Pembroke College, Cambridge, where he gained an MA. He did his National Service in the Royal Marines, and then became, in succession, a social worker, a teacher and a photographer in South Africa, from where he was deported because of his opposition to apartheid. He lectured in history at Cambridge College of Art and Technology, 1963–71, before becoming a full-time writer.

He writes sharply observed, satirical novels about the eccentricities and pretensions of the middle classes. His wit can be cruel at times, but his characters are everyday people, portrayed as much larger than life. His plots and situations are often pure farce, and his dialogue captures the tone of the book. His first two books were biting satires about the South African security forces.

Publications

> *Riotous assembly*   1971
> *Indecent exposure*   1973
> *Porterhouse Blue*   1974
> *Blott on the landscape*   1975
> *The great pursuit*   1977
> *The throwback*   1978
> *Ancestral vices*   1980
> *Vintage stuff*   1982
>
> WILT
>
> *Wilt*   1976
> *The Wilt alternative*   1979
> *Wilt on high*   1984
> (Published by Secker & Warburg.)

Now read
Peter De Vries, Evelyn Waugh.

Tinniswood, Peter

British. He was born in Liverpool, and now lives in Wiltshire with his wife, actress Liz Goulding, and their four children. He, too, started his career as a journalist, and worked for some time for Sheffield newspapers, which gave him the background for many of his novels. He began to write comedy sketches for television programmes like 'That Was The Week That Was', and moved on to situation comedy and radio plays.

He has a good ear for the dry humour and witty dialogue of the South Yorkshire people. He bases his plots on real-life situations, with added humour, and peoples them with a wealth of hilarious eccentrics. There is, however, a seriousness beneath the humour, and a touch of pathos. He also writes very funny short stories about cricket, featuring a character called the Brigadier.

Publications

THE BRANDON FAMILY

A touch of Daniel   1969
I didn't know you cared   1973
Except you're a bird   1974
Call it a canary   1985
Uncle Mort's North Country   1986
Uncle Mort's South country   Arrow   1990

THE BRIGADIER

Tales from a long room   1981
More tales from a long room   1982
The Brigadier down under   1983
The Brigadier in season   1984
The Brigadier's collection   1986
Tales from Witney Scrotum   1987

Mog   1972
The Stirk of Stirk   1975
(All published by Hodder except where stated.)

Shemerelda   Hodder   1981
The home front   Hodder   1983
Hayballs   Hutchinson   1989
Winston   Hutchinson   1991

Now read
David Nobbs, Keith Waterhouse.

Waterhouse, Keith

British. Born in Leeds in 1929, and educated there. He has been a freelance journalist for many years, writing regular columns for the *Daily Mirror* and *Punch*. He has also written many plays and film scripts, often with Willis Hall, and now writes adaptations of novels for television.

Some of his novels are outright comedies; others are serious novels with a certain amount of humour injected. His plots are inventive, and his main characters explored in depth. His fertile imagination leads him to invent unlikely settings and situations for his characters, which all seem quite credible as the plot unfolds. Again, there is a touch of sadness in many of the books, particularly when he is writing about the elderly.

Publications

There is a happy land   1957
Billy Liar   1959
Jubb   1963
The bucket shop   1968
Billy Liar on the Moon   1975
Office life   1978
Maggie Muggins   1981
In the mood   1983
Mrs. Pooter's diary   1983
Thinks   1984
Our song   1989
(Published by Michael Joseph.)

Bimbo   Hodder   1990
Unsweet charity   Hodder   1992

Now read
David Nobbs, Peter Tinniswood.

'PERCEPTIVE' WOMEN'S NOVELS

This is a rapidly increasing genre which lies somewhere between the family chronicle and the feminist novel. The books mainly deal with situations with which most women can identify, whether in a personal or family setting, and are written with discernment and humour. The characters are for the most part closely observed, developed in depth, and seen in a close domestic or work environment, as opposed to the long family sagas which have a broad range of characters and settings. Their appeal is mainly to women readers, though the more sensitive man will also enjoy them. They are closely linked with the literary novel in style and construction, but are easier to read, and thus have a wider appeal.

Billington, Rachel

British. She was born in 1942, and is a daughter of the Earl of Longford. She took a BA in English at London University, married Kevin Billington, the film and television director, in 1967, and is the mother of four children. Her first novel was published in 1969. She has also written four books for children.

She writes about family situations and their effect on one particular individual. This may be a parent, a child, or someone close to the family. The plots are convincing and the characters totally credible. The relationships between parents and children are particularly well portrayed. Her style is literary without being precious, and the books are an enjoyable read, popular with many women.

Publications

> All things nice   1969
> The Big Dipper   1970
> Lilacs out of the dead land   1971
> Cock Robin   1973
> Beautiful   1974
> A painted devil   1975
> A woman's age   1979
> Occasion of sin   1982
> The garish day   1985
> Loving attitudes   1987
> (Published by Hamish Hamilton.)
> Theo and Matilda   Macmillan   1990
> Bodily harm   Macmillan   1992

Now read
Jennifer Chapman, Penelope Lively, Deborah Moggach, Elizabeth North, Teresa Waugh.

Brookner, Anita

British. She was born in 1928, and was educated at King's College, University of London, and the Courtauld Institute, where she became a Reader. She has lectured in Fine Art at Cambridge and Reading Universities, and is a Fellow of New Hall, Cambridge. She published several books on art before she began to write novels. She was awarded the Booker Prize for *Hotel du Lac* in 1984.

Her books are written in a witty, economical and very stylish manner, and concern middle-aged, middle-class, well-educated women. They have absorbing and successful careers, but all have a common factor – loneliness. The novels are character studies of women who lead a bleak existence without any emotional support. The events leading to this situation are a major factor in the plot, and sometimes a solution is offered, though often the woman is left to face a future without much hope of warmth.

Publications

> *A start in life*   1981
> *Providence*   1982
> *Look at me*   1983
> *Hotel du Lac*   1984
> *Family and friends*   1985
> *A misalliance*   1986
> *A friend from England*   1987
> *Latecomers*   1988
> *Lewis Percy*   1989
> *A closed eye*   1991
> *Fraud*   1992
> *A family romance*   1993
> (All published by Cape.)

Now read
Rachel Billington, Penelope Lively, Elizabeth North, Teresa Waugh.

Chapman, Jennifer

British. She lives in Cambridgeshire, where she runs her own public relations agency, in addition to writing novels. She writes about marriage in a witty and penetrating way. Her settings are the world of the middle class and upwardly mobile, subject to contemporary social pressures. Her characterisation is shrewd and perceptive, and the reader can readily identify with the women who occupy the central role in her novels.

Publications

> *The long weekend* 1984
> *Mysterious ways* 1985
> *Not playing the game* 1986
> *Regretting it* 1987
> (Published by Century.)
> *Victor Ludorum* Hale 1991

Now read
Rachel Billington, Anabel Donald, Penelope Lively, Deborah Moggach, Teresa Waugh, Mary Wells.

Christie, Anne

Scottish, though she is half-Swedish. She studied Drawing and painting at Edinburgh College of Art, but married Jack Ronder, the late television writer, halfway through her studies. She has lived in London since 1972, where she has been a successful portrait painter for many years. She began to write after the death of her husband.

Her novels are based on her own experiences as a wife and mother, and three of them, *First act*, *My secret gorilla* and *A time to weep* form a trilogy. She writes vividly, with an eye for detail and a real gift for dialogue. At times, especially in *My secret gorilla*, in which the harassed and child-ridden young mother invents a fantasy gorilla as a confidante and companion, the books become pure comedy, but there is always an underlying seriousness and sensitivity. The last book in the trilogy, *A time to weep*, in which she nurses her husband through an agonising last illness, is almost unbearably poignant.

Publications

> *My secret gorilla* 1981

> *First act*   1983
> *An honest woman*   1985
> *A time to weep*   1987
> (All published by Piatkus.)

Now read
Anabel Donald, Penelope Lively, Dee Phillips, Mary Wesley.

Donald, Anabel

British, though she was born in India. She was educated at an English convent school, then at St. Anne's College, Oxford, where she took a degree in English. She is now Head of English at a girls' school near Banbury. Her first novel was published in 1985, and achieved critical acclaim.

Her heroines in each case are women who have extricated themselves from situations in which they feel they have been exploited and taken for granted; the first by divorce, the second by out-manoeuvring her teaching colleagues in the in-fighting attached to school life, the third by rejecting fame and publicity and her dominating mother. The books are witty, observant and unobtrusively feminist, and women readers will empathise with the characters.

Publications

> *Hannah at 35, or how to survive divorce*   1985
> *Poor, dear Charlotte*   1987
> *Smile, Honey!*   1988
> (Published by Hodder.)
> *An uncommon murder*   Macmillan   1992

Now read
Jennifer Chapman, Penelope Lively, Elizabeth North, Dee Phillips, Mary Wesley.

Friedman, Rosemary

British, of Jewish parentage. She has been writing for many years, originally under the name of Robert Tibber, when she wrote semi-humorous novels about the life of a doctor, rather in the style of the James Herriot books about vets.

The novels written under her own name are well-constructed, sensitive portraits of both men and women in the context of the family. She has a real feeling for characterisation and dialogue, and her situations are true to life. She writes about marriage in a perceptive and satisfying way, and evokes a sympathetic response from her readers. Her accounts of Jewish family life are authentic and convincing.

Publications

The life situation   Barrie & Jenkins   1977
The long hot summer   Hutchinson   1980
A loving mistress   Gollancz   1983
A second wife   Piatkus   1985
An eligible man   Piatkus   1989

ANGLO-JEWISH TRILOGY

Proofs of affection   Gollancz   1982
Rose of Jericho   Gollancz   1984
To live in peace   Piatkus   1987

as Robert Tibber
No white coat   Hodder   1958
Love on my list   Transworld   1959
We all fall down   1960
Patients of a saint   1961
The fraternity   1963
The commonplace day   1964
The general practice   1967
Practice makes perfect   1969
(All published by Hodder.)

Now read
Jennifer Chapman, Penelope Lively, Gillian Tindall, Teresa Waugh.

Hocking, Mary

British. She lives in Lewes, Sussex, and has been an established novelist for many years. She served in the WRNS in the Second World War, and then became a local government officer.

Her books are written with insight and subtlety, and explore the dark recesses of the human mind. Many of her characters are obsessives, totally immersed in their own concerns, and are drawn with a knowledge of human psychology. The books are not tragedies and, indeed, have a considerable amount of quiet humour. She has recently written a trilogy about a middle-class family during the Second World War.

Publications

> *Visitors to the Crescent*   reprinted Severn House 1975
> *The winter city*   reprinted Severn House   1985
> *The sparrow*   reprinted Severn House   1985
> *The young Spaniard*   1965
> *Ask no question*   1967
> *A time of war*   1968
> *Checkmate*   1969
> *The hopeful traveller*   1970
> *The climbing frame*   1971
> *Family circle*   1972
> *Daniel come to judgment*   1974
> *The bright day*   1975
> *The mind has mountains*   1976
> *Look, stranger!*   1979
> *He who plays the king*   1980
> *March House*   1981
>
> THE FAIRLEYS
>
> *Good daughters*   1984
> *Indifferent heroes*   1985
> *Welcome strangers*   1986

An irrelevant woman   1987
A particular place   1989
Letters from Constance   1991
The very dead of winter   1993
(All published by Chatto & Windus.)

Now read
Rachel Billington, Penelope Lively, Elizabeth North, Mary Wesley.

Lively, Penelope

British, though she was born in Cairo in 1933 and spent her childhood there until 1944. She went to school in Sussex, and then read Modern History at St. Anne's College, Oxford. She married Jack Lively, now Professor of Politics at Warwick University, has two children and lives partly in London and partly in Oxfordshire. She has written many books for children, as well as short stories and adult novels, and has won several awards: the Carnegie Medal for *The ghost of Thomas Kempe*, and the Whitbread Award for *A stitch in time* (both children's books). She was shortlisted for the Booker Prize in 1977 and 1984, and finally won it in 1987 with *Moon Tiger*.

Her novels are quiet and reflective, with well-constructed plots, and great depth of characterisation. Family relationships are carefully and credibly described, and most of the action in the books comes from the interplay of characters.

Publications

The road to Lichfield   1977
Nothing missing but the samovar (short stories)   1978
Treasures of time   1979
Judgment Day   1980
Next to nature, art   1982
Perfect happiness   1983
Corruption (short stories)   1984
According to Mark   1984
Pack of cards (short stories)   1986
(All published by Heinemann.)

> *Moon Tiger*   Deutsch   1987
> *Passing on*   Deutsch   1989
> *Cleopatra's sister*   Viking   1993

Now read
Rachel Billington, Anita Brookner, Deborah Moggach, Elizabeth North, Dee Phillips.

Lowe-Watson, Dawn

British. She lives in London and Norfolk, where she is a fiction reviewer for the *Eastern Daily Press*. She has been a journalist, and has also written many plays for radio and television. She has three sons, one of whom is a concert pianist. Her first novel won the Authors' Club Award for the most promising first novel of 1980, and was shortlisted for the *Yorkshire Post* First Novel award. Her second won the Mary Elgin Prize from Hodder & Stoughton.

Her books concern women coming to terms with illness or grief, and how they meet the challenge to accept a new way of life. The settings are carefully researched, and are accurate in detail. She spent some time in the Lake District before writing *The sound of water*, and has used her son's experiences to lend authenticity to *The black piano*. Her characters are rounded, and readers will identify with them.

Publications

> *The good morrow*   1980
> *The sound of water*   1983
> *The black piano*   1986
> (All published by Hodder.)

Now read
Anne Christie, Penelope Lively, Deborah Moggach, Dee Phillips, Mary Wesley.

Moggach, Deborah

British. Born in 1948. She is one of four sisters from a writing family, and lives in Camden Town, London. She writes with humour and insight into family problems, and is not afraid to tackle controversial issues such as incest and surrogacy. Her female characters are strong and rounded, and are matched in depth by their male protagonists. Her books are not always a comfortable read, but arouse feelings of sympathy in their readers.

Publications

> *You must be sisters*   Collins   1978
> *Close to home*   Collins   1979
> *A quiet drink*   Collins   1980
> *Hot water man*   Cape   1982
> *Porky*   Cape   1983
> *To have and to hold*   Viking   1986
> *Smile* (short stories)   Viking   1987
> *Driving in the dark*   H. Hamilton   1988
> *Stolen*   Heinemann   1990
> *The ex-wives*   Heinemann   1993

Now read
Rachel Billington, Jennifer Chapman, Penelope Lively, Dee Phillips, Teresa Waugh.

North, Elizabeth

British. She lives in Harrogate, Yorkshire. Her father was an Admiral in the Royal Navy, and the family lived in several countries during his foreign service.

She looks at the world with a sharp and satirical eye. Her characters are forceful, shrewd and very sure of themselves. The books all concern women as a catalyst for the situations surrounding them. The locations are varied, often in foreign countries, drawing on her own experiences. She writes with considerable wit and good dialogue.

Publications

> *The least and vilest things*   1971
> *Pelican rising*   1975
> *Enough blue sky*   1976
> *Everything in the garden*   1978
> *Florence Avenue*   1979
> (Published by Gollancz.)
> *Dames*   Cape   1981
> *Ancient enemies*   Cape   1982
> *Wordly goods*   Methuen   1987

Now read
Anita Brookner, Penelope Lively, Teresa Waugh.

Phillips, Dee

British. She is an artist and a practising child psychotherapist. She began her writing career by writing short stories for magazines and 'Woman's Hour', and went on to full-length novels.

She writes with wit and vigour. Her books are about women of all ages, from childhood, in *The coconut kiss*, to old age, in *Hollybush Row*. Her characters are drawn with deep insight, and her plots are convincing and satisfying. The family backgrounds are credible, and the dialogue crisp.

Publications

> *No, not I*   1980
> *The coconut kiss*   1982
> *Hollybush Row*   1983
> *Ella*   1986
> (All published by Hodder.)

Now read
Rachel Billington, Jennifer Chapman, Anabel Donald, Deborah Moggach.

Rivers, Caryl

American. She lives near Boston, Massachusetts, and is Professor of Journalism at Boston University. She has had a very wide experience as a journalist, and has written columns for *The New York Times*, *The Washington Post* and *The Los Angeles Times* among others.

Her novels are witty and irreverent, and often sexy. The plots are fast-moving and the dialogue crisp and racy. Her major characters are women, beset by problems to do with sex, religion and marriage. The many aspects of love are handled with sensitivity as well as humour, and the books make compelling reading.

Publications

> *Virgins* 1984
> *Girls forever brave and true* 1986
> *For better, for worse* no date
> *The mind stealers* no date
> *Intimate enemies* 1988
> (All published by Andre Deutsch.)

Now read
Anne Christie, Teresa Waugh.

Tindall, Gillian

British. Born in 1938. She was awarded a BA at Oxford, and has been a freelance journalist for many years, writing for, among others, *The Guardian*, the *Observer* and *The Times*. Her novels are perceptive and well-constructed, dealing mainly with the relationship between parents and children, and its interaction with life inside and outside the family. Characterisation is the all-important thing and the plots, while holding the reader's attention, do not have a great deal of action, though their locations are varied.

Publications

> *No name in the streets* Cassell 1959

> *The water and the sound* Cassell 1961
> *The edge of the paper* 1963
> *Someone else* 1969
> *Fly away home* 1971
> *Dance of death* (short stories) 1973
> *The traveller and his child* 1975
> *The intruder* 1979
> *The china egg* (short stories) 1981
> *Looking forward* 1983
> (All published by Hodder.)
> *To the city* Hutchinson 1987
> *Give them all my love* Hutchinson 1989
> *Journey of a lifetime* (stories) Hutchinson 1990
> *Spirit weddings* Hutchinson 1992

Now read
Rachel Billington, Anita Brookner, Penelope Lively, Deborah Moggach.

Tyler, Anne

American. She was born in Minneapolis in 1941, but grew up in North Carolina, and considers herself a Southerner. She graduated from Duke University, where she won the Anne Flexner Award for creative writing. She did post-graduate work in Russian studies at Columbia University, and worked as the Russian bibliographer at Duke University.

She writes witty, perceptive accounts of American family life. She has a keen ear for dialogue, and creates totally life-like characters. Her novels have won a good deal of critical acclaim, and she is now one of America's most respected women authors. She won the National Book Critics' Award for *The accidental tourist*.

Publications

> *The accidental tourist* Chatto 1985
> *Celestial navigation* Pan 1990
> *Searching for Caleb* Pan 1990

A tin can tree   Vintage   1990
A slipping down life   Vintage   1990
Morgan's passing   Vintage   1991
If morning ever comes   Vintage   1991
Saint maybe   Chatto   1991
Dinner at the homesick restaurant   Vintage   1992

Now read
Caryl Rivers, Mary Wesley.

Waugh, Teresa

British. She was born in 1940, a daughter of the Earl of Onslow, and was brought up in Surrey. She took a degree in French and Italian as a mature student at Exeter University. She is married to Auberon Waugh, has four children, lives in Somerset, and has translated several books, in addition to writing novels.

Her books are about the eccentricities of family life, and are full of revealing details. She has an acute sense of the absurd and ridiculous, which adds humour to her writing. Her characters, while often somewhat unusual, can be found in many real family situations, and are drawn with care and sympathy.

Publications

Painting water   1984
Waterloo, Waterloo   1986
An intolerable burden   1988
Song at twilight   1989
(All published by H. Hamilton.)

Now read
Rachel Billington, Anne Christie, Penelope Lively, Elizabeth North, Dee Phillips, Mary Wesley.

Wells, Mary

British. She was born and educated in London, but spent long periods abroad with her husband, who was in the RAF. She later trained as a teacher of English as a Foreign Language, and has written books on the subject. She is now widowed, and lives in Hampshire.

Her trilogy, while not autobiographical, is based on her local knowledge of the countries in which she has lived. It concerns the fortunes of the Aitkin family, first in Sudan before independence, later in South-East Asia, and finally in the Philippines. Her insight into the character of women under pressure is remarkable, although her male characters are equally strong. The books all have backgrounds of political unrest and its effect on the lives of expatriates. The interaction between natives and foreigners is explored in depth, and forms an integral part of the plot.

Publications

> *The expatriates*   1986
> *The silk king*   1987
> *The tycoon*   1988
> (All published by Severn House.)

Now read
Mary Hocking, Elizabeth North.

Wesley, Mary

British. Born in 1908. She lives in Devon, and devotes all her time to writing. She has written all her life, though not for publication, and describes herself as a solitary person. She wrote her first adult novel at the age of 70, 'to purge myself of the despair I felt', after the death of her husband. Her principal characters are women who find themselves in difficult situations and rely on their innate intuition and wit to extricate themselves. She writes with insight and sensitivity, but with great humour, as shown in her first novel, about a woman who is determined to commit suicide, but is continually prevented from doing so by other people's needs, and her third, about a widow who has to keep a home for her son, and does so by a mixture of sex and cookery, the only two things at which she excels.

The plots are inventive, her dialogue good, and her characters memorable. Sadly, her sixth novel lacked the sparkle of the others, but she regained her old vigour with her latest books. Three of the books have now been adapted for television, to which they have translated very well.

Publications

Jumping the queue   1983
The camomile lawn   1984
Harnessing peacocks   1985
The vacillations of Poppy Carew   1986
Not that kind of a girl   1987
Second fiddle   1988
(Published by Macmillan.)
A sensible life   Bantam   1990
A dubious legacy   Bantam   1992

Now read
Anita Brookner, Jennifer Chapman, Anne Christie, Anabel Donald, Penelope Lively, Elizabeth North, Teresa Waugh.

POLICE WORK

This is a genre which is very closely allied to the detective story; indeed it is hard to differentiate in some cases. The same criteria apply, but in the case of novels about police work the information about police methods and procedures is more detailed, there is less emphasis on the detective as an individual, more on his performance as a policeman. In the American novels, the police force is seen as a working unit, solving a number of crimes, and not just one, as in most of the detective stories. The stories tend to be less domestic than many of the classic detective novels, with tougher surroundings and corresponding dialogue and characterisation.

Blaisdell, Anne

American. Born in Illinois in 1921, and educated in California where she now lives. Her real name is Elizabeth Linington, and she uses several pseudonyms for her work.

The books are all set in California, and are about the exploits of one particular police precinct, in this case in Hollywood. Although they are written under different names, the books are all similar in theme; the author says that she tries to keep them authentic as far as police techniques are concerned, and to base the stories on real cases where possible. She also tries to add interest by writing about the personal life of the police officers, in relation to their job.

The police settings, and descriptions of Californian city life, are entirely credible, and the characters are drawn with care. The plots are fast-moving, and neatly dovetailed, and the dialogue is crisp and joky. Her novels have achieved great success and high praise on both sides of the Atlantic.

Publications

SGT. IVOR MADDOX AND WILCOX STREET PRECINCT

Greenmask   1965
No evil angel   1966
Date with death   1967
Something wrong   1968
Policeman's lot   1969
Practice to deceive   1971
Crime by chance   1974
Perchance of death   1978
No villain need be   1979
Consequence of death   1981
Skeleton in the closet   1983
Felony report   1985
Strange felony   1986
(All published by Gollancz.)

Now read
Lesley Egan, Dell Shannon, Ed McBain, Jan van de Wetering.

Butler, Gwendoline

British. Born in London around 1928, and educated at Haberdasher's Aske's Hatcham Girls' School, and Lady Margaret Hall, Oxford, where she took a BA in Modern History. She taught at Oxford for a while, but became a full-time writer in 1958. She now lives in Surrey. She received the Crime Writers' Association Silver Dagger Award in 1973 for *A coffin for Pandora*. She also writes as Jennie Melville.

Her novels, under each of her names, fall into two categories: the straightforward police procedural novel, and the gothic romance, but with a mystery attached. As Gwendoline Butler, her main character is Inspector John Coffin, a tough, uncompromising policeman, working in South London, who has a habit of becoming involved in rather bizarre cases, which he solves by a mixture of shrewd common sense and a working knowledge of criminal psychology. As Jennie Melville, she writes about Inspector Charmian Daniels, a woman detective operating in what is very much a man's world, who has to prove her ability to cope with tough situations, as well as solve a crime. Many of the novels featuring Charmian are psychological thrillers.

She writes well, with good use of language and dialogue, an injection of wit, and a lot of atmosphere. The sense of evil which she conjures up in some of her books is almost tangible. The police procedures are described with authenticity, and the Victorian settings in the gothics are realistic and historically accurate.

Publications

INSPECTOR WINTER SERIES

Receipt for murder   1956
Dead in a row   1957
The dull dead   1958 (introduces Sgt. Coffin)

INSPECTOR COFFIN

The murdering kind   1958
The interloper   1959
Death lives next door   1960

Make me a murder　1961
Coffin in Oxford　1962
Coffin for baby　1963
Coffin waiting　1964
Coffin in Malta　1964
A nameless Coffin　1966
Coffin following　1968
Coffin's dark number　1969
A Coffin from the past　1970
A Coffin for the canary　1974
(All published by Geoffrey Bles.)
Coffin on the water　1986
Coffin in fashion　1987
Coffin underground　1988
Coffin in the Black Museum　1989
Coffin on Murder Street　1991
Cracking open a Coffin　1992
(Published by Collins.)

GOTHICS

A coffin for Pandora　1973
The Vesey inheritance　1975
The Brides of Friedberg　1977
The red staircase　1980
(Published by Macmillan.)

as Jennie Melville

CHARMIAN DANIELS

Come home and be killed　1962
Burning is a substitute for loving　1963
Murderer's houses　1964
There lies your love　1965
Nell alone　1966
(Published by Michael Joseph.)
A different kind of summer　Hodder　1967
A new kind of killer, an old kind of death　Hodder
　1970

Murder wears a pretty face   Macmillan   1981
Windsor red   Macmillan   1987
Witching murder   Macmillan   1990
Footsteps in the blood   Macmillan   1990
Dead set   Macmillan   1992
Whoever has the heart   Macmillan   1993

GOTHICS

The hunter in the shadows   Hodder   1969
Ironwood   Hodder   1972
Nun's castle   Hodder   1974
Raven's Forge   1975
Dragon's eye   1977
Axwater   1978
The painted castle   1982
Hand of glass   1983
(Published by Macmillan.)

Now read
Reginald Hill, Alan Hunter, Roy Lewis, but see also Detective stories and Gothic romances.

Dexter, Colin

British. He lives in, and writes about, Oxford, which he knows intimately. He has a civil service and university background, which he applies with great success to his novels.

His novels fall equally well into the detective story category, but are listed here because Chief Inspector Morse, the detective who features in all the books, is first and foremost a policeman who uses all the procedures and modern techniques at his command. Morse is a complex character, a confirmed bachelor, brusque in manner and with a drink problem, but inwardly sensitive and easily wounded. His assistant, Sergeant Lewis, is a perfect foil: placid, happily married and without the intellectual weight of his superior. The stories are set in and around the Oxford colleges for the most part, and paint an accurate and colourful picture of life in a university town. The descriptions of police and forensic science procedures are authentic, and the plots are intricate and involved, with deep characterisation and a fair amount of psychology.

Publications

CHIEF INSPECTOR MORSE

Last bus to Woodstock   1975
Last seen wearing   1976
The silent world of Nicholas Quinn   1977
Service of all the dead   1979
The dead of Jericho   1981
The riddle of the third mile   1983
The secret of Annexe 3   1986
The wench is dead   1989
The jewel that was ours   1991
The way through the woods   1992
(All published by Macmillan.)

Now read
S. T. Haymon, Reginald Hill, Alan Hunter, P. D. James, Bill Knox.

Egan, Lesley

American. Another of the pseudonyms used by Elizabeth Linington. In this series, the stories are set in Los Angeles, and the characters are based at the Glendale Police Department. Some of the books concern the whole police force, others feature either Detective Vic Varallo or Jesse Falkenstein, a Jewish lawyer, friend and colleague of the police. Again, the police procedures are accurately described, and the characters developed as individuals as the series progresses.

Publications

GLENDALE POLICE DEPT.

A case for appeal   1962
Scenes of crime   1976

A dream apart 1978
Random death 1982
Crime for Christmas 1984
Chain of violence 1985

VIC VARALLO

The borrowed alibi 1962
Run to evil 1963
Detective's due 1965
The nameless ones 1967
The wine of violence 1970
Malicious mischief 1972
The hunters and the hunted 1980
A choice of crimes 1981

JESSE FALKENSTEIN

Against the evidence 1963
My name is death 1965
Some avenger, rise! 1967
A serious investigation 1969
In the death of a man 1970
Paper chase 1973
The blind search 1977
Look back on death 1979
Motive in shadow 1980
The miser 1982
Little boy lost 1984
(All published by Gollancz.)

Now read
Anne Blaisdell, Dell Shannon, Ed McBain, Jan van de Wetering.

Hart, Roy

British. He was born in Essex in 1930. He did National Service in
the RAF, and then entered the avionics industry. He later worked in
the electrical branch of civil engineering. He is married, with one

son, and now lives in Norwood, writing full-time. He lists his interests as photography and music, and indulging his insatiable curiosity. The novels are set in Dorset, and feature the CID team headed by Chief Inspector Roper. The plots are fast-moving, and well-constructed, and police procedures are described in accurate detail. Convincing dialogue and touches of humour make the books easy and enjoyable to read.

Publications

Seascape with dead figures   1987
A pretty place for a murder   1987
A fox in the night   1988
Remains to be seen   1989
Robbed blind   1990
Breach of promise   1990
Blood kin   1992
(All published by Macmillan.)
Final appointment   Little, Brown   1993

Now read
Gwendoline Butler, Alan Hunter, John Wainwright.

Harvey, John

British. He was born in London, but lived in Nottingham for many years. He has run Slow Dancer Press since 1977, editing and publishing *Slow Dancer* magazine, and numerous books and pamphlets. He has adapted several novels for television, including two of his own, and has dramatised a number of novels for Radio 4.

His novels are police procedurals, tough and uncompromising. They are set in Nottingham, and show his detailed knowledge of the city. The seamier side of police work is explored in detail; his policemen are not heroes, but cynical, hard-bitten men fighting a losing battle against crime. The chief character is Inspector Charlie Resnick, who never quite loses hope that things will improve, and is capable of pity for both criminal and victim. The plots are intricate, and the dialogue credible.

251

Publications

RESNICK

Lonely hearts 1989
Rough treatment 1990
Cutting edge 1991
Off minor 1992
Wasted years 1993
(All published by Viking.)

Now read
Reginald Hill, Bill James, Peter Turnbull, John Wainwright.

Hill, Reginald

British. Born in Hartlepool, Co. Durham, in 1936. He was educated at Carlisle Grammar School and St. Catherine's College, Oxford, where he gained a BA(Hons) in English after National Service in the Border Regiment. He worked briefly as a Student Officer for the British Council, and became a teacher in Essex in 1962. Since 1967, he has lectured at Doncaster College of Education, and lives in Doncaster. He also writes thrillers under the name of Patrick Ruell, and historical adventure as Charles Underhill.

The main characters in his police novels are Superintendent Andy Dalziel, a bluff, vulgar, somewhat Falstaffian figure, and Inspector Peter Pascoe, a complete contrast: introspective, intellectual and prone to questioning the validity of police methods from a liberal standpoint. The interaction between the two forms a substantial part of the plots, as Pascoe deplores the brashness of his boss, while admiring his shrewdness in solving crimes.

The books are extremely well-written, with accurate detail about police procedures, warts and all, and acutely observed descriptions of the social conditions of South Yorkshire, in which they are located. The plots are often topical, and are uncompromising in their approach to the sordid and brutal crimes which the police are called upon to solve. The books which do not concern Dalziel and Pascoe are psychological thrillers, often about corruption and revenge.

Publications

DALZIEL AND PASCOE

A clubbable woman   1971
Fell of dark   1971
An advancement of learning   1971
A fairly dangerous thing   1972
Ruling passion   1973
An April shroud   1975
A pinch of snuff   1978
Pascoe's ghost (short stories)   1979
A killing kindness   1980
Deadheads   1983
Exit lines   1984
Child's play   1986
Under world   1988
Bones and silence   1990
One small step: a novella   1990
Recalled to life   1992

A very good hater   1974
Another death in Venice   1976
Traitor's blood   1983
To guard a Prince   1985
Blood sympathy   1993
(All published by Collins.)

as Patrick Ruell
The castle of the demon   1971
Red Christmas   1972
Death takes the low road   1974
Urn burial   1975
The long kill   1986
Death of a dormouse   1988
The only game   1991

as Charles Underhill
Captain Fantom   1978
The forging of Fantom   1979
(All published by Hutchinson.)

Now read
Gwendoline Butler, Alan Hunter, Bill Knox, John Wainwright, but see also Detective stories, e.g. J. B. Hilton, Roy Lewis.

Hunter, Alan

British. Born in Norfolk in 1922, and has lived there ever since. He was a poultry farmer, 1936–40, then served as an aircraft electrician in the Royal Air Force Volunteer Reserve during the Second World War. After the war, he managed the antiquarian department of a Norwich bookshop, then bought his own bookshop in 1950. He writes regularly for the *Eastern Daily Press*, and is a Zen Buddhist.

All his novels are about a middle-aged Detective Chief Superintendent, George Gently, and most are set in Norfolk, though some of the recent ones have been set around the coast of Normandy. The character of Gently is an amalgam of several senior policemen, and the procedures which he follows are accurately described. He is based at Scotland Yard, and is called in to solve cases which have defeated the local police, this making his character the catalyst around which the action revolves. The novels are short and tautly written, with an economical use of dialogue and description. Alan Hunter says that he thinks of himself as a playwright, so that the time covered in his books is kept to the minimum, and the plot unfolds in a series of confrontations.

Publications

GENTLY

Gently does it   1955
Gently by the shore   1956
Gently down the stream   1957
Landed Gently   1958

Gently through the mill   1958
Gently in the sun   1959
Gently with the painters   1960
Gently to the summit   1960
Gently go man   1961
Gently where the roads go   1962
Gently floating   1963
Gently Sahib   1964
Gently with the ladies   1965
Gently northwest   1966
Gently continental   1968
Gently coloured   1969
Gently with the innocents   1970
Gently at a gallop   1971
Vivienne: Gently where she lay   1972
Gently French   1973
Gently in trees   1974
Gently with love   1975
Gently where the birds are   1976
Gently instrumental   1977
Gently to a sleep   1978
The Honfleur decision   1980
Gabrielle's way   1981
Fields of heather   1981
Gently between the tides   1982
Amorous Leander   1983
The unhung man   1983
Once a prostitute ...   1984
Goodnight, sweet prince   1986
Strangling man   1987
Traitor's end   1988
Gently with the millions   1989
Gently scandalous   1990
Gently to a kill   1991
Gently tragic   1992
(All published by Constable)

Now read
Gwendoline Butler, Douglas Clark, Reginald Hill, Sheila Radley.

James, Bill

British. He writes tough police procedurals, set in the world of seedy clubs and gang warfare. The policemen are authentic, presented as blunt, disillusioned and uncompromising. The books contain taut dialogue, with excellent characterisation and believable plots, enlivened with a sprinkling of humour. The leading character is Detective Chief Superintendent Colin Harpur.

Publications

DET. CHIEF SUPERINTENDENT HARPUR

You'd better believe it   1985
The Lolita man   1986
Halo parade   1987
Protection   1988
Come clean   1989
(Published by Constable.)
Take   Macmillan   1990
Club   Macmillan   1991
Astride a grave   Macmillan   1991

Now read
John Harvey, Reginald Hill, Peter Turnbull, John Wainwright.

Knox, Bill

British. Born in Glasgow in 1928, and educated there. He served in the Royal Naval Auxiliary, then became a journalist, working in various capacities on the Glasgow newspapers, before joining Scottish television as News Editor. He has been a freelance writer and broadcaster since 1962, and is well-known to Scottish viewers as writer and presenter of 'Crime Desk'. He also writes thrillers under the name of Robert MacLeod – listed in the appropriate chapter.

His police novels fall into two categories: those about Chief Inspector Colin Thane and Inspector Phil Moss, of the Glasgow CID, and those about a completely different type of police work, that of the Scottish Fishery Protection Service, as personified by Chief Officer Webb Carrick. In both series, details about police procedures are accurate and neatly woven into the plot. Thane and Moss complement each other in the same way as Dalziel and Pascoe do in the books by Reginald Hill. The books are full of action, with touches of humour, and vivid descriptions of locations. He won the *Police Review* award for the crime novel which gave the best portrayal of police procedures with *The crossfire killings*.

Publications

THANE AND MOSS

Deadline for a dream   1957
Death department   1958
Leave it to the hangman   1959
Little drops of blood   1960
Sanctuary Isle   1961
The man in the bottle   1962
Taste of proof   1965
Deep fall   1966
Justice on the rocks   1967
The tallyman   1969
Children of the mist   1970
To kill a witch   1971
Draw batons   1973
Rally to kill   1975
Pilot error   1976
Live bait   1978
A killing in antiques   1981
The hanging tree   1983
The crossfire killings   1986
The interface man   Century 1989

WEBB CARRICK

The scavengers   1964
Devilweed   1965
Black light   1966
The Klondyker   1968
Blueback   1969

Seafire 1970
Stormtide 1972
Whitewater 1974
Hellspout 1976
Witchrock 1977
Bombship 1979
Bloodtide 1982
Wavecrest 1985
Dead man's mooring 1987
The drowning nets 1991
(All published by Hutchinson.)

Now read
Reginald Hill, Peter Turnbull.

McBain, Ed

American. Born in New York in 1926, and educated there. This is a pseudonym for Evan Hunter, a respected writer of novels under his own name. He served in the United States Navy during the latter years of the Second World War, before completing his education, and became a full-time writer in the mid-1950s.

He has written a very long series of police procedural novels, set in the 87th Precinct, an imaginary district of a large city (New York). The district is sufficiently varied to attract most types of crime, and the officers of 87th Precinct work in teams to solve them. There is no one prominent character, though Steve Carella appears in most of the books. The books, while identical in setting, are nevertheless varied in the type of case and the action taken to solve it. There is a good deal of humour, and some well-drawn cameos among the non-police characters. A new series recounts the adventures of Matthew Hope, a private eye in the mould of Sam Spade and Philip Marlowe.

Publications

87TH PRECINCT

Cop hater 1956
The mugger 1956

The pusher   1956
The con man   1957
Killer's choice   1958
Killer's payoff   1958
Lady killer   1958
Killer's wedge   1959
'Til death   1959
King's ransom   1959
Give the boys a great big hand   1960
The heckler   1961
See them die   1961
Lady, lady I did it   1961
Like love   1962
The empty hours   1962
(All published by Boardman.)
Ten plus one   1963
Axe   1964
He who hesitates   1964
Doll   1965
Eighty million eyes   1966
Fuzz   1968
Shotgun   1969
Jigsaw   1970
Hail, hail the gang's all here   1971
Sadie when she died   1972
Let's hear it for the Deaf Man   1972
Hail to the Chief   1973
Bread   1974
Blood relatives   1975
So long as you both shall live   1976
Long time no see   1977
Calypso   1979
Ghosts   1980
Heat   1981
Ice   1983
Lightning   1984
Eight black horses   1985
Poison   1987
Tricks   1987

McBain's ladies: the women of the 87th Precinct 1988
Lullaby 1989
McBain's ladies, too 1990
(All published by Hamish Hamilton.)
Vespers Heinemann 1990
Widows Heinemann 1991
Kiss Heinemann 1992
Mischief Hodder & Stoughton 1993

Another part of the city (5th Precinct) H. Hamilton
1986
Downtown Heinemann 1989

MATTHEW HOPE

Goldilocks 1978
Rumpelstiltskin 1981
Beauty and the Beast 1982
Jack and the beanstalk 1984
Snow White and Rose Red 1985
Cinderella 1986
Puss in Boots 1987
The house that Jack built 1988
(Published by Hamish Hamilton.)
Three blind mice Heinemann 1991
Mary, Mary Heinemann 1992

Now read
Anne Blaisdell, Lesley Egan, Dell Shannon, Jan van de Wetering.

Robinson, Peter

British. He grew up in Leeds, but emigrated to Canada in 1974, where he attended university in Windsor, and York University, Toronto. He now lives in Toronto, and, as well as writing, he teaches occasionally at community colleges. His first novel, *Gallows view* was shortlisted for the John Creasey Award in Britain, and the Crime Writers of Canada first novel award.

The books are all set in the Yorkshire Dales, a part of the country which he clearly knew well as a young man. His fictional town of Eastvale is Richmond, and most of the action takes place around the villages of Swaledale. The novels relate the cause and effect of murder on a rural community. Village life is accurately described, and the characters ring true. The police team is headed by Detective Inspector Banks, who has recently moved to Yorkshire from London, to escape the violence and corruption of police work in a large city. His struggle for acceptance among the dour northerners, and the integration of his family, form an integral part of the plots.

Publications

> *Gallows view* 1988
> *A dedicated man* 1989
> *A necessary end* 1989
> *The hanging valley* 1990
> *Past reason hated* 1991
> (All published by Viking.)

Now read
S. T. Haymon, Reginald Hill, J. B. Hilton, Barbara Whitehead.

Shannon, Dell

American. The third pseudonym of Elizabeth Linington (for more details see Anne Blaisdell in this section). This series, set in Los Angeles, is about Lieutenant Luis Mendoza, of Mexican descent. He is a scholarly type of policeman, who abhors violence in his cases, and applies reason to their solutions. There is rather more personal detail in Mendoza's character than in the detectives in her other series; he drives fast, expensive sports cars, and keeps exotic breeds of cats, indulgences made possible by a substantial inheritance. The police procedures are, however, equally factual and authentic.

Publications

> LT. LUIS MENDOZA
>
> *Case pending* Gollancz 1960

Extra kill   1962
Ace of spades   1963
Knave of hearts   1963
Death of a busybody   1963
Double bluff   1964
(Published by Oldbourne Press.)
Mark of murder   1965
Root of all evil   1966
The death-bringers   1966
Death by inches   1967
Coffin corner   1967
With a vengeance   1968
Chance to kill   1969
Rain with violence   1969
Kill with kindness   1969
Schooled to kill   1970
Crime on their hands   1970
Unexpected death   1971
Whim to kill   1971
The ringer   1972
Murder with love   1972
With intent to kill   1973
No holiday for crime   1974
Spring of violence   1974
Crime file   1975
Deuces wild   1976
Streets of death   1977
Cold trail   1978
Felony at random   1979
Felony file   1980
Murder most strange   1981
The motive on record   1982
Exploit of death   1983
Destiny of death   1985
Chaos of crime   1986
Blood count   1987
(All published by Gollancz.)

The Manson curse   Gollancz   1991

Now read
Anne Blaisdell, Lesley Egan, Ed McBain.

Turnbull, Peter

British. Born in Scotland, and was a member of the Glasgow CID. He writes taut, authentic novels, set in Glasgow, about the members of P Division. The plots are inventive and well-constructed, with credible dialogue and a lot of atmosphere. The police are portrayed as hard-working officers, doing their best to contain crime in a violent city.

Publications

> *Deep and crisp and even*   1981
> *Dead knock*   1982
> *Fair Friday*   1983
> *Big money*   1984
> *Two way cut*   1988
> *Condition purple*   1989
> *And did murder him*   1991
> *Long day Monday*   1992
> (All published by Collins.)

Now read
Lesley Egan, Reginald Hill, Bill Knox, Ed McBain, Jan van de Wetering, John Wainwright.

Wainwright, John

British. Born in Leeds in 1921. He was educated at local schools, and took an external degree of LLB from London University. He served as an Air Crew Gunner in the RAF during the Second World War, and then joined the West Riding Constabulary, in Yorkshire. He retired in 1969, having already had several books published, and devoted his time to writing novels and newspaper columns. He says that he does not think of himself as an author, but rather as someone doing a job of work, whose product is imagination. When asked what he would like to be if he was not an author his reply was 'Dead!' He lives near Ripon in North Yorkshire.

His novels are all set in Yorkshire, and feature a mixture of policemen as main characters. Detective Superintendent Lewis is a calculating and ruthless officer, dedicated to hunting down the criminals he despises, but equally hard on his own men. Divisional Superintendent Collins is his antithesis: a quiet man who enjoys his job, but not the violent aspects of it. Superintendent Ripley is their counterpart in the rural areas of the district, and his cases are more of the type encountered in the classic detective stories. The books are economically written, with tightly constructed plots and crisp dialogue. His own police background adds authenticity to his description of procedures and methods. A recurring element in his books is the fight of the police force against organised crime, and he does not hesitate to introduce violence and brutality to add reality to the stories.

Publications

Death in a sleeping city   1965
Ten steps to the gallows   1965
Evil intent   1966
The crystallised carbon pig   1966
Talent for murder   1967
The worms must wait   1967
Web of silence   1968
Edge of extinction   1968
The darkening glass   1968
The take-over men   1969
(Published by Collins.)
The big tickle   1968
Freeze thy blood less coldly   1970
Prynter's devil   1970
The last buccaneer   1971
Dig the grave and let him die   1971
Night is a time to die   1972
Requiem for a loser   1972
A pride of pigs   1973

High class kill   1973
A touch of malice   1973
Kill the girls and make them cry   1974
The hard hit   1974
Square dance   1974
Death of a big man   1975
Landscape with violence   1975
Coppers don't cry   1975
Acquittal   1976
Walther P.38   1976
Who goes next?   1976
The bastard   1976
Pool of tears   1977
A nest of rats   1977
The day of the peppercorn kill   1977
The jury people   1978
Thief of time   1978
Death certificate   1978
A ripple of murders   1978
Brainwash   1979
Tension   1979
Duty elsewhere   1979
Take murder   1979
The eye of the beholder   1980
Dominoes   1980
A kill of small consequences   1980
Venus fly trap   1980
The tainted man   1980
All on a summer's day   1981
An urge for justice   1981
Anatomy of a riot   1982
Blayde RIP   1982
Distaff factor   1982
Their evil ways   1983
Spiral staircase   1983
Heroes no more   1983
Cul-de-sac   1984
Ride   1984
The forest   1984

All through the night   1985
Clouds of guilt   1985
The forgotten murders   1987
A very parochial murder   1988
The man who wasn't there   1989
(All published by Macmillan.)
Hangman's Lane   Little, Brown   1992
Sabbath morn   Little, Brown   1993

Now read
Reginald Hill, Bill Knox, Ed McBain, Peter Turnbull, Jan van de Wetering.

Wetering, Jan Willem van de

Dutch. He served with the Amsterdam Police Force for seven years, but now lives in Maine, USA. He writes about the Amsterdam CID, with great attention to detail in police procedures. The main characters are Adjutant Grijpstra and Sergeant de Gier, but there are other recurring characters in the division, who appear in most of the books.

The policemen's characters are built up during the series, and their interests, behaviour and methods form the substance of the novels. Most of the books are actually set in central Amsterdam, but in one or two the police go outside the city to solve a case. The criminals are portrayed as victims of the pressures of society, rather than hardened villains, and a good deal of psychology is applied by the police in the solution of cases.

The novels are written with humour, in a distinctive style, and with a smattering of Zen philosophy.

Publications

AMSTERDAM COPS SERIES

Outsider in Amsterdam   1976
Tumbleweed   1976
Corpse on the dike   1977

Death of a hawker   1977
The Japanese corpse   1978
The blond baboon   1978
The Maine massacre   1979
The mind murders   1981
Streetbird   1984
Rattle-rat   1986
Hard rain   1987
The sergeant's cat (short stories)   1988
Seesaw millions   1989

The butterfly hunter   1983
(All published by Gollancz.)

Now read
Reginald Hill, Bill Knox, Ed McBain, Dell Shannon, Peter Turnbull,
John Wainwright.

Whitehead, Barbara

British. She was born in Sheffield, and educated at High Storrs
Grammar School and Sheffield College of Arts and Crafts. She has
had a variety of jobs; librarian, civil servant, genealogist, shopkeeper
and teacher. She is now married, with three sons, and lives at
Murton, near York, where she says her home life is dominated by her
Shetland sheep dogs. She still works as a part-time lecturer in adult
education, but devotes most of her time to writing fiction. She
published several books before turning to her chosen genre –
detective stories.

   She is writing a series with the overall title of *The York Cycle of
Mysteries*. All are set within the city of York, which is described in
meticulous detail. The novels are police procedurals, rather than pure
detective stories, and though the same characters recur, the whole
police force is involved in solving the various crimes. The plots are
well-crafted, and full of local interest. The first novel, *Playing God*,
is set around the performance of the York Mystery Plays, while the
third concerns the Dean and Chapter of the Minster.

Publications

YORK CYCLE OF MYSTERIES
Playing God   Quartet   1988
The girl with red suspenders   Constable   1990
The Dean it was that died   Constable   1991
Sweet death, come softly   Constable   1992

Now read
John Greenwood, S. T. Haymon, Roy Lewis, Peter Robinson, June Thomson.

Wingfield, R.D.

British. He lives in Basildon, Essex. He is a prolific writer of crime plays for radio, and of comedy scripts.

His first novel, *Frost at Christmas*, was first published in Canada in 1984, where it received favourable reviews, and was later published in England. It was quickly followed by two sequels, and all three were successfully adapted for television.

The novels are police procedurals set in a provincial town, with a police force constantly under stress through lack of manpower, and an unsympathetic Chief Superintendent. The major character is Detective Inspector Jack Frost, a sloppy, down at heel, sardonic officer, who masks his undoubted intelligence under a veneer of insolence. He is a constant thorn in the flesh of his superior officer, who tries hard not to put Frost in charge of a case, because of his behaviour. Frost however, is not only an excellent detective, but also holds the George Medal for bravery. The plots are well crafted, with humour and realism. The police are portrayed as ordinary, fallible people, and the other characters are entirely credible. The dialogue is crisp, and the books move along at a good pace.

Publications

DET. INSPECTOR JACK FROST
Frost at Christmas   1989

A touch of Frost　1990
Night Frost　1992
(All published by Constable.)

Now read
Reginald Hill, J. B. Hilton.

THE SAGA

This, as its name suggests, is the novel on an epic scale, long, detailed and packed with incident. A great deal of research is necessary to write a convincing saga, and its preparation involves the author in visits to the locations used in the book, hours of work in libraries and record offices, and the compilation of indexes of characters, settings and relationships.

The saga falls into two categories: those which deal with the history of an extended family over the centuries in several volumes, in which the settings are only relevant to the movements of that family, and in which external events are only recorded as they affect the lives of members of the family; and those which are published in one volume, and present a broad panorama of life in one particular era or place. In each category, the characters in the book are developed in some depth, and there are a number of sub-plots interwoven into the main theme. This type of novel has a vast following, especially among women, and they often become bestsellers immediately on publication.

Winston Graham is a good example of the first category, with his Poldark series, which spans several centuries in ten volumes. R. F. Delderfield was a master of the second category, with his panoramic novels of English life.

See also Family stories and Historical novels.

Barclay, Tessa

British. She lives in South-West London, and is a former publishing editor and journalist. She writes sagas about families who are in some way connected with the land. The first was set in the American Mid-West, about a family who gained in power and stature as the century progressed, and the second concerned a woman widowed and left to manage a vineyard in the Champagne area of France. The plots are flowing and full of interest, and the characters are developed throughout the series. The historical and agricultural details are accurate, and add realism to the stories.

Publications

CRAIGALLAN FAMILY

A sower went forth   1980
The stony places   1981
Harvest of thorns   1983
The good ground   1984

THE WINE WIDOW

The wine widow   1985
The Champagne girls   1986
The last heiress   1987

A web of dreams   1988
Broken threads   1989
The final pattern   1990
(All published by W. H. Allen.)
A professional woman   Headline   1991
Gleam of gold   Headline   1992

Now read
Judith Glover, Pamela Oldfield, Jessica Stirling, Janet Tanner.

Bradford, Barbara Taylor

British. She was born in Leeds, but has lived in New York for some years. She became a reporter on the *Yorkshire Evening Post* at the age of sixteen, and was fashion editor on *Woman's Own* by the time she was twenty. She worked on several Fleet Street newspapers before she left for America. She writes novels on the grand scale, with a multitude of characters revolving round a central one, in her case a strong, dominant woman. Her settings are usually North Yorkshire, in surroundings she knows well. The plots are detailed, with many interwoven strands, and are full of action and colour. All the books are instant bestsellers.

Publications

> *Voice of the heart*   1983
>
> EMMA HARTE
>
> *A woman of substance*   1979
> *Hold the dream*   1985
> *To be the best*   1988
>
> *Act of will*   1986
> *The women in his life*   1990
> *Remember*   1991
> *Angel*   1993
> (All published by Grafton.)

Now read
R. F. Delderfield, Iris Gower, Susan Howatch, Malcolm Macdonald, Pamela Oldfield.

Burton, Betty

British. She was born in Romsey, Hampshire, and now lives in Southsea with her husband Russ.

She has always been a writer, for television and radio, and she is a past winner of the Chichester Festival Theatre Award.

She writes family sagas, some historical, others set in the first half of the 20th century. Most are set in the West Country, which she knows and describes well. The books are full of incident, and the ups and downs of family life are depicted with realism. Her female characters are particularly strong, and the books revolve around them. In addition to her novels, she has produced an acclaimed collection of short stories, *Women are bloody marvellous!*.

Publications

> *Jude*   Grafton   1986
> *Jaen*   Grafton   1987
> *Women of no account*   Grafton   1988
> *Hard loves, easy riches*   Grafton   1989
> *The consequences of war*   Grafton   1990
> *Goodbye Piccadilly*   Collins   1991
> *Long, hot summer*   HarperCollins   1993

Now read
Judith Glover, Pamela Oldfield, Patricia Wendorf.

Carr, Philippa

British. Born in London in 1906, her real name is Eleanor Hibbert, but she is better known as Jean Plaidy.

She has written, under this name, a long family chronicle with the overall title of *The daughters of England*. It traces the history of the family from the sixteenth to the nineteenth centuries, and links the events in the story very closely with authentic episodes in English history. The extended family is described with care and detail, and each successive generation is fitted in with relation to the family background. The historical detail is well-researched, and the dialogue matches that of the period. Each of the volumes stands up well as a novel on its own.

Publications

THE DAUGHTERS OF ENGLAND

The miracle at St. Bruno's   1972
The lion triumphant   1974

The witch from the sea   1975
Saraband for two sisters   1976
Lament for a lost lover   1977
The lovechild   1978
Song of the siren   1980
The drop of the dice   1981
The adulteress   1982
Zipporah's daughter   1983
Voices in a haunted room   1984
The return of the gipsy   1985
Midsummer's Eve   1986
The pool of St. Branock   1987
The changeling   1989
Black swan   1990
A time for silence   1991
The gossamer cord   1992
(All published by Collins.)
We'll meet again   HarperCollins   1993

Now read
Winston Graham, Cynthia Harrod-Eagles, Anne Melville, Clare Rayner.

Cox, Josephine

British. She was born in Blackburn during the Second World War. She was one of ten children, brought up in the slums in dire poverty. Her mother worked in the cotton mills, and her father had a low paid job with the Corporation. Josephine used to tell stories to the children in the district for a penny each, to help provide money for the gas meter. She left school at fourteen to work in a warehouse, sticking labels on vinegar bottles. When the family broke up, she went south with her mother, and married at the age of sixteen. She has two sons.

She wrote stories from a very early age, and won her first prize at school at the age of eleven. She used to be a teacher, but now writes full time. Her stories are well-crafted, and set mainly in her native Lancashire. They deal with families struggling to overcome poverty, deprivation and misfortune. Her female characters are strong and earthy, fighting to raise themselves and their families from their depressing circumstances. The descriptions of life among the under-privileged is obviously drawn from her own experiences, and are quite harrowing at times. The books are immensely popular, though the reader cannot always look forward to a happy ending.

Publications

> *Her father's sins*   1989
> *Let loose the tigers*   1989
> *Angels cry sometimes*   1990
> *Take this woman*   1990
> *Whistledown woman*   1991
> *Outcast*   1990
> *Alley urchin*   1991
> *Vagabonds*   1992
> (All published by Macdonald.)
> *Don't cry alone*   Headline   1992
> *Jessica's girl*   Headline   1993

Now read
Catherine Cookson, Iris Gower, Marie Joseph, Lena Kennedy.

Dailey, Janet

American. She is a former farm girl from Iowa, but now lives with her husband in Missouri. She is America's best selling female novelist, and one of the top five world best sellers.

She writes long family sagas, sometimes in more than one volume, presenting a well-drawn picture of American life. Most of her novels are set in the mid-West, and are drawn from her own experiences of farming life. The characters are rounded and strongly drawn, and the story-lines hold the reader's interest to the end.

Publications

> *Touch the Wind*   Collins   1979

The rogue Collins 1979
Ride the thunder Macdonald 1980
Night way Macdonald 1981
This Calder sky Macdonald 1982
This Calder range Hodder 1983
Stands a Calder man Hodder 1983
Calder born Calder bred Hodder 1984
Silver wings, Santiago blue Hodder 1985
The pride of Hannah Wade Hodder 1985
The glory game Joseph 1985
The great alone Joseph 1986
Heiress Joseph 1988
Rivals Joseph 1989
Masquerade Joseph 1990
Aspen gold Joseph 1991
Tangled vines Joseph 1992

Now read
Betty Burton, Belva Plain.

Forrester, Helen

British. She was born in Hoylake, Cheshire, but her formative influence was Liverpool, a city which is featured in nearly all her work. For the past thirty years she has made her home in Edmonton, Alberta, though she has travelled extensively in Europe, India, the United States and Mexico.

She wrote four best selling volumes of autobiography about her life in Liverpool, and then began to write novels. She won the Writers' Guild of Alberta Award for the best novel of 1988, with *Yes, Mama*, and in the same year she was awarded an honorary D.Litt. by Liverpool University, in recognition of her achievements as an author.

Most of her books are set in Liverpool, and all deal with family life, and ordinary people struggling against adversity. She writes with style, and attention to detail. The plots are well-sustained and convincing, and the characterisation is excellent. The dialogue, too, is authentic.

Publications

AUTOBIOGRAPHY

Twopence to cross the Mersey   1974
Liverpool Miss   1979
By the waters of Liverpool   1981
Lime Street at two   1985
Minerva's stepchild   1986
(All published by Bodley Head.)

NOVELS

Thursday's child   Collins   1982
The latchkey kid   Collins   1984
Liverpool Daisy   Collins   1985
Three women of Liverpool   Collins   1986
The money-lenders of Shahpur   Collins   1987
Yes, Mama   Collins   1988
The lemon tree   Collins   1990
The Liverpool Basque   HarperCollins   1993

Now read
Audrey Howard, Marie Joseph, Anne Melville.

Fraser, Christine Marion

British. She was born in Glasgow just after the Second World War, and spent her early life in the tenements in Govan. She contracted a rare muscular disease at the age of ten, and has been confined to a wheelchair ever since. She now lives in Argyllshire with her husband.

She was always a keen reader and storyteller, and began writing at the age of five. She conceived the idea for her first novel whilst on holiday in the Hebrides, and the 'Rhanna' series was born. Her books are family sagas, which run into several volumes. 'Rhanna' is set on a small Hebridean island, and follows the fortunes of the islanders through several generations. 'King's' is about the Grant family, and is set in Glasgow and in rural Aberdeenshire. The series

279

are both carefully researched, and the historical detail is accurate. Her characters are developed in some depth throughout the books, and their actions and dialogue are consistent with life in rural Scotland. Both series are extremely popular.

Publications

RHANNA

Rhanna   1978
Rhanna at war   1979
Children of Rhanna   1984
Return to Rhanna   1984
A song of Rhanna   1985
Storm over Rhanna   1988
(All published by Macdonald.)
Stranger on Rhanna   HarperCollins   1992

KING'S

King's croft   1986
King's acre   1987
King's exile   1989
King's Close   1991
King's farewell   1992
(All published by HarperCollins.)

Now read
Tessa Barclay, Betty Burton, Jessica Stirling.

Glover, Judith

British. Born in the West Midlands, she began her writing career as a junior reporter on the *Wolverhampton Express and Star*. She moved to Tunbridge Wells, Kent in 1969, and became a freelance writer and reviewer. She has written several books about the history and placenames of Kent and Sussex. She started to write novels in 1982, and is writing a family chronicle set in nineteenth-century Sussex. The plot revolves round a farming family, and is full of authentic detail about rural life at that time. Her characterisation is good, the stories are fast moving, and the dialogue realistic.

Publications

> *The stallion man*   1982
> *Sisters and brothers*   1984
> *To everything a season*   1986
> *Birds in a gilded cage*   1987
> *The imagination of the heart*   1989
> *Tiger lilies*   1991
> *Mirabelle*   1992
> (All published by Hodder.)

Now read
Tessa Barclay, Pamela Oldfield, Jessica Stirling.

Gower, Iris

Welsh. She was born in Swansea, and all her novels are set there. She started to write full-time when her children were growing up.

She has often been called 'the Catherine Cookson of Wales'. This is a slight misnomer, because her novels, though compulsively readable, have greater depth than those of Catherine Cookson. A great deal of research has gone into her descriptions of the copper, coal and textile industries in Wales, and her characters are totally credible. The books are not about a single family, but deal with life in Swansea from the nineteenth century to the Second World War, and the same characters, from several families, appear in each book, with different degrees of importance. The same sub-plots run through each book, cleverly interwoven so that the reader does not lose track of any of the characters.

Publications

> *The copper cloud*   1976
> *Return to Tip Row*   1977
> Reprinted in one volume as *The loves of Caitlin*   1987

SWEYNESEYE

Copper kingdom 1983
Proud Mary 1984
Spinners Wharf 1985
Morgan's woman 1986
Fiddler's Ferry 1987
Black gold 1988
(All published by Century Hutchinson.)

CORDWAINERS

The shoemaker's daughter Bantam 1991
The oyster catchers Bantam 1992
Honey's farm Bantam 1993

Now read
Barbara Taylor Bradford, Susan Howatch, Michael Legat, Malcolm Macdonald, Jessica Stirling, Janet Tanner.

Harrod-Eagles, Cynthia

British. She took a degree in English and History, and lives in London. She won the Young Writers Award in 1972, with *The waiting game*. Since 1980, she has concentrated on writing the *Morland Dynasty*, about a Yorkshire family from the fifteenth century to the Second World War. The events which took place in English history are mirrored against the family background. The plots are well-constructed, and the details carefully researched. The dialogue matches the period, and the characters are fully developed in the course of the series.

Publications

THE MORLAND DYNASTY

The foundling 1980
Dark rose 1981
The princeling 1981

The oak apple   1982
The black pearl   1982
The long shadow   1983
The chevalier   1984
The maiden   1985
Floodtide   1986
The tangled thread   1987
The emperor   1988
The victory   1989
The regency   1990
Campaigners   1991
The reckoning   1992
(All published by Macdonald.)
The devil's horse   Little, Brown   1993

The orange-tree plot   Sidgwick & Jackson   1989

THE KIROV SAGA

Anna   1990
Fleur   1991
Emily   1992
(All published by Sidgwick & Jackson.)

Now read
Philippa Carr, Winston Graham, Anne Melville, Clare Rayner.

Howatch, Susan

British. Born in Leatherhead, Surrey in 1940. She took a LLB degree at King's College, London, in 1961, and became a law clerk and later a company secretary. She married in 1964, and went to live in America. She has written since she was a child, and had her first novel published when she was 25. She started by writing gothic romances: short, suspense novels, set in remote locations, and with an element of the supernatural. Six of these were published in quick succession, until she turned to the long, panoramic saga.

Penmarric, published in 1971, was an immediate success, and set the pattern for her future books. They are long, immensely detailed, and full of interest. She believes that locations should provide more than what she calls 'scenic glamour', but should form an integral part of the story, supporting both plot and atmosphere. Her characterisation is excellent, and the members of the extended family come to life with each generation. The books are often set in rural England, in great houses, and the families about whom she writes are wealthy and powerful. The stories, though spanning many years, are mainly completed in one volume, though there have been sequels to two of them.

Publications

GOTHICS

The dark shore   1965   H. Hamilton   1972
The waiting sands   1966   H. Hamilton   1972
Call in the night   1967   H. Hamilton   1972
The shrouded walls   1968   H. Hamilton   1972
April's grave   1969   H. Hamilton   1972
The devil on Lammas Night   H. Hamilton   1973

Penmarric   1971
Cashelmara   1974
The rich are different   1977
Sins of the fathers (sequel)   1980
(Published by H. Hamilton.)

The wheel of fortune   1984
Glittering images   1987
Glamorous powers (sequel)   1988
Ultimate powers (sequel)   1989
Scandalous risks (sequel)   1990
Mystical paths (sequel)   1992
(Published by Collins.)

Now read
Barbara Taylor Bradford, Iris Gower, Malcolm Macdonald, Pamela Oldfield.

Legat, Michael

British. He has spent most of his career in the publishing trade, and has written a standard guide for authors and publishers (1972). He became a full-time writer in 1978, and his first novel was published in 1980. Although he is a comparative newcomer to the genre, his books have achieved success and critical acclaim.

His books all concern family life, but in each case it is linked to a specific industry or trade. He researches his subjects in meticulous detail, paying great attention to processes and skills, and this adds to the interest and authenticity in his books. His locations are varied, ranging from the Californian vineyards to the diamond mines in South Africa and the iron-founding industry in Shropshire. All the books have historical settings. His characters are rounded and explored in depth, and he has a good grasp of the structure of family life in the nineteenth century.

Publications

> *Mario's vineyard*   1980
> *The silver fountain*   1982
> *The Shapiro diamond*   1984
> *The silk maker*   1985
> *The cast-iron man* (sequel)   1987
> (All published by Souvenir Press.)

Now read
Tessa Barclay, Iris Gower, Pamela Oldfield, Jessica Stirling.

Livingston, Nancy

British. She was born in Stockton-on-Tees, but now lives in an old house in Nottinghamshire.

She writes in two genres – detective stories and family sagas. Her sagas are set in the North-East at the turn of the century, and paint a compelling picture of family life as it was then. Her characters are drawn with sympathy and authenticity, and the plots have many threads carefully woven together to produce a satisfying whole.

Further details about Nancy Livingston may be found in the chapter on Detective stories.

Publications

THE McKIES

The far side of the hill   Macdonald   1987
Land of our dreams   Macdonald   1988
Never were such times   Macdonald   1990

Two sisters   Little, Brown   1992

Now read
Malcolm Macdonald, Jessica Stirling.

Macdonald, Malcolm

British. He was born in the West Country in 1932. His school education tended towards the scientific and medical, rather than literary; he decided to make art his career. He went to art college in Falmouth, and then, after service in the army, to the Slade School in London, where he obtained a diploma in painting. He has had a varied career as a teacher, an editor and a book designer, but decided to write novels in the early 1970s. He now lives in Ireland.

His books are long family chronicles, some in series, others in a single volume. They are well-written, with fast-moving plots, full of incident, and convincing pictures of family life in the nineteenth and early twentieth centuries. His scientific training is apparent in some of the novels, which concern engineering, canal building in *The silver highways* and cars in *The sky with diamonds*. The industrial scenes, though, are only a background to the development of the family.

Publications

THE STEVENSON FAMILY

The world from rough stones   1975

286

The rich are with you always   1977
Sons of fortune   1978
Abigail   1979

Goldeneye   1981
Tessa d'Arblay   1983
In love and war   1984
The silver highways   1987
The sky with diamonds   1988
His father's son   1989
The captain's wives   1991
(All published by Hodder.)

Now read
Barbara Taylor Bradford, R. F. Delderfield, Susan Howatch, Pamela Oldfield, Janet Tanner.

Melville, Anne

British. Her real name is Margaret Potter, and she is the daughter of Bernard Newman, the author and lecturer. She was born at Harrow, read Modern History at Oxford, and became a teacher. She has travelled widely in the Middle East, but now lives in Oxford.

She writes long family sagas, in multi-volume series. The Lorimer series is set in Bristol, and follows the fortunes of a family concerned with the shipping industry in the nineteenth and twentieth centuries. Her novels are lighter than some of the others in the genre, with less emphasis on contemporary events, but are still well-researched, with good characterisation. She also writes light romantic stories under the name of Anne Betteridge.

Publications

LORIMER SAGA

The Lorimer line   1977
Lorimer legacy   1979
Lorimers at war   1980
Lorimers in love   1981

The last of the Lorimers   1983
Lorimer loyalties   1984

THE HOUSE OF HARDIE

The House of Hardie   1987
Grace Hardie   1988

The Dangerfield diaries   1989
(All published by Grafton.)
Snapshots (stories)   Severn House   1989

Now read
Tessa Barclay, Judith Glover, Iris Gower, Pamela Oldfield, Jessica Stirling.

Mosco, Maisie

British. She is a Mancunian, of Jewish parentage. Her grandparents settled in Manchester in the late nineteenth century, having emigrated from, respectively, Russia and Vienna. She became a journalist, and was, at one time, News Editor of the *Manchester Jewish Gazette*. She is married to an accountant, has four children, and has been writing novels and plays since the 1960s.

Her Orthodox Jewish upbringing enables her to write with authority and sympathy about Jewish family life, and her characters, while in no way stereotypes, display many of the traditional attributes of the Jews. Her female characters are strong and resourceful, proud of their family traditions, and possessive of their children. The plot in many of the books revolves around the conflicts between the traditional Jewish parents and their children, who have become accustomed to less restrictive lives. The first series is set in Manchester, at the turn of the century, and has graphic descriptions of slum life in the inner city.

Publications

MANCUNIAN SERIES

Almonds and raisins   1979

Scattered seed   1980
Children's children   1981
Out of the ashes   1989

ALISON PLANTAINE

Between two worlds   1983
A sense of place
The price of fame   1985

The waiting game   1987
After the dream (sequel)   1988
(All published by NEL.)
For love and duty   Collins   1990
New beginnings   HarperCollins   1991

Now read
Michael Legat, Clare Rayner, Jessica Stirling.

Nicole, Christopher

British. He was born in 1930 in British Guiana, now Guyana, and educated there. He worked as a bank clerk from 1947 to 1956 and then became a full-time writer, and moved to Guernsey. He now lives in the Bahamas. He is a prolific writer in many genres and under many names. He writes light historical romance as Alison York, 'bodice-rippers' as Christina Nicholson, thrillers as Mark Logan and Andrew York, historical novels as Leslie Arlen and Peter Grange, and sagas under his own name.

He regards himself primarily as an historical novelist, and all his books are set in the past, in many countries. He has been listed under sagas because so many of his books are part of multi-volume series. He says that he aims to tell history as entertainingly as possible, and this is clearly reflected in his novels. The plots are fast and furious, with larger than life characters, plenty of sex and violence, and exotic locations. There is, however, an underlying seriousness, and a very genuine awareness of racial conflicts. His own upbringing as a white man in the West Indies gave him an insight into racial tension and inequality. Though his novels concern the excesses and injustices perpetrated by the white landowners, and are brutal in places, white supremacy is never condoned.

Publications

THE AMYOT FAMILY

Amyot's Cay   1963
Blood Amyot   1964
The Amyot crime   1965
(Published by Jarrolds.)

THE HILTON FAMILY

Caribee   1974
The devil's own   1975
Mistress of darkness   1976
Black dawn   1977
Sunset   1978
(Published by Cassell.)

HAGGARD

Haggard   1980
Haggard's inheritance   1981
The young Haggards   1982
(Published by Michael Joseph.)

BLACK MAJESTY

Seeds of rebellion   1984
Wild harvest   1985

CHINA TRILOGY

The crimson pagoda   1984
The scarlet princess   1985
Red dawn   1985

MCGANN FAMILY

Old Glory   1985
The sea and the sand   1986
Iron ships, iron men   1987
Wind of destiny   1987
Raging sea, searing sky   1988
The passion and the glory   1988

JAPANESE TRILOGY

The sun rises   1986
The sun and the dragon   1986
The sun on fire   1987
(All published by Severn House.)

KENYA SERIES

The high country   1988
The happy valley   1989

SINGAPORE

Pearl of the Orient   1988
Dragon's blood   1989

The regiment   1988
The command   1989
Sword of fortune   1990
Sword of Empire   1991
(All published by Century.)
Days of wine and roses   Severn House   1991
Resumption   Severn House   1992
The last battle   Severn House   1993

as Max Marlow
Growth   Severn House   1993

Now read
James Clavell, Kyle Onstott.

Oldfield, Pamela

British. She was born in London, spent most of the Second World War in Devon, and now lives in Kent. She taught for eleven years, and was a secretary for five, before devoting all her time to writing.

She writes about the places she knows best, Devon and Kent, though her most recent books have been set in America and the Southampton area. Her first books were a four-volume historical saga, set in Devon in the sixteenth century, tracing the fortunes of the Heron family. The next three were about a family of hop-growers in Kent, from 1900 to 1930, and the Londoners who travelled every year for the hop-picking. The more recent books have been one-volume sagas about the experiences of individual women. The novels have intricate, well-constructed plots with many interwoven strands, engrossing situations, and splendidly life-like characters. The central characters are developed in depth, but there are memorable cameos, often amusing, among the minor ones. Her research is comprehensive and her detail accurate, and the books move along at a satisfying pace, making engrossing reading.

Publications

THE HERON SAGA

The rich earth　1982
This ravished land　1982
After the storm　1982
White water　1983
(Published by Macdonald.)

THE FOXEARTH TRILOGY

Green harvest　1983
Summer song　1984
Golden tally　1985

The Gooding girl　1985
The stationmaster's daughter　1986
Lily Golightly　1987

The turn of the tide   1988
A dutiful wife   1989
(Published by Century.)
Sweet Sally Lunn   Joseph   1990
The Halliday girls   Joseph   1991
Long dark summer   Joseph   1992

Now read
Judith Glover, Iris Gower, Susan Howatch, Michael Legat, Malcolm Macdonald, Janet Tanner.

Rayner, Clare

British. Born in 1931. She trained as a nurse, and spent several years as a sister in obstetrics and paediatrics. She is married with three children. These experiences helped to further her new career in journalism in 1962. She became 'agony columnist' on *The Sun*, *Sunday Mirror* and *Woman's Own*, and combined this with frequent broadcasts on radio and television, where she is a popular presenter and guest on chat shows. She has written a number of books on family matters and medical care, and began to write novels in 1964. The first were gothic romances or novels about hospital life. She turned to the saga in 1973, with the publication of the first book in the 'The performers' series.

She writes with authority about medical history, and explores family life and relationships in depth. The performers is the story of a family concerned with either medicine or the theatre from the eighteenth century to the present, and the conflict between two such different ways of life is strongly presented. She has a real feeling for the period about which she is writing, and the historical detail and dialogue is carefully researched. Her characters are convincing and strongly developed over the course of the series, and the interaction between them is true to life. The plots are well-constructed, fast-moving and full of incident, and she has a good flowing style. Her new series is 'The poppy chronicles', set in Edwardian England, and she has also written some one-volume sagas in a contemporary setting.

Now read on

Publications

THE PERFORMERS

Gower Street   1973
Haymarket   1974
Paddington Green   1975
Soho Square   1976
Bedford Row   1977
Long Acre   1978
Charing Cross   1979
The Strand   1980
Chelsea Reach   1982
Shaftesbury Avenue   1983
Piccadilly   1985
Seven Dials   1986

THE POPPY CHRONICLES

Jubilee   1987
Flanders   1988
Flapper   1989
Blitz   1990
Festival   1991
Sixties   1992
(Published by Weidenfeld & Nicolson.)

Sisters   1978
The running years   1981
Family chorus   1984
Lunching at Laura's   1986
Maddie   1988
Postscripts   1991
Dangerous things   1993
(Published by Michael Joseph.)

Now read
Philippa Carr, Iris Gower, Winston Graham, Cynthia Harrod-Eagles, Malcolm Macdonald, Pamela Oldfield.

Stirling, Jessica

British. A pseudonym for Peggie Coghlan, who was born in Glasgow in 1920, and Hugh C. Rae, also born in Glasgow in 1935. Most of the actual research and writing appears to be done by Peggie Coghlan, with help and guidance from Hugh Rae, who is himself a full-time writer, under his own name, and that of Robert Crawford.

Peggie Coghlan says that she is trying to paint a picture with words, which is clearly borne out in her descriptive passages. The books are full of detail about the daily lives of her characters, and she can describe a setting in vivid prose. The books are all family sagas, but each is dominated by a strong female character, around whom the story revolves. The settings are mainly in the Scottish industrial communities, except for the Holly Beckman series, which is about life in the East End of London, and the antiques trade. The plots are well-constructed, with authenticity and credibility, and a good pace is maintained throughout the series.

Publications

THE STALKER FAMILY

The spoiled earth   1975
The hiring fair   1976
The dark pasture   1978

HOLLY BECKMAN

Deep well at noon   1979
Blue evening gone   1981
The gates of midnight   1983

THE PATTERSON FAMILY

Treasures on earth   1985
Creature comforts   1986
Hearts of gold   1987

NICHOLSON FAMILY

The good provider   1988
The asking price   1989
The wise child   1990
The welcome light   1991
Lantern for the dark   1992
(All published by Hodder.)

Now read
Judith Glover, Iris Gower, Malcolm Macdonald, Pamela Oldfield, Janet Tanner.

Tanner, Janet

British. She lives near Bath. She writes long, detailed family chronicles, set mainly in Somerset, and draws widely on her own knowledge of the Somerset countryside for the locations in her novels. The Hillsbridge novels are about the mining industry in the nineteenth century, and describe the life of a rural community. Her other novels are set in more exotic locations, and are one-volume sagas. Her plots are well-crafted and full of interest, and the characters are rounded and credible.

Publications

HILLSBRIDGE NOVELS

The Black Mountains   1984
The emerald valley   1985
The hills and the valley   1988

Oriental Hotel   1986
Women and war   1987
Inherit the skies   1989
Folly's child   1990
(All published by Century Hutchinson.)

Now read
Judith Glover, Susan Howatch, Malcolm Macdonald, Pamela
Oldfield, Jessica Stirling.

Wendorf, Patricia

British. She was born in Somerset, but now lives in Loughborough.
She is a widow, but has two sons and four grandchildren.

She wrote two short novels, perceptive studies of love and
marriage, and then embarked on a trilogy which is based on her own
family history. Set in Somerset in the nineteenth and twentieth
centuries, it traces the history of two interwoven families, one
involved in traditional farming, the other a gypsy family. The detail
and background of the novels make them almost pieces of social
history, but they are enlivened by engrossing plots, splendidly vivid
characters, and graphic descriptions of the everyday lives of people
of all classes in the period.

Publications

> *Peacefully in Berlin*   1983
> *Leo days*   1984
>
> THE PATTERAN TRILOGY
>
> *Larksleve*   1985
> *Blanche*   1986
> *Bye bye blackbird*   1987
>
> *Double wedding ring*   1989
> (Published by Hamish Hamilton.)
> *Lives of transition*   Viking   1992

Now read
Iris Gower, Michael Legat, Maisie Mosco, Jessica Stirling.

SCIENCE FICTION

This is a genre which has been written about at great length and by many people, some of them leading exponents of the genre, such as Brian Aldiss and Isaac Asimov, and others such as Kingsley Amis, who are eminent in other fields of literature.

It has therefore proved difficult to choose authors who are not already listed in other sources, and to find something fresh to say about the genre. The authors listed are British and American and some are comparative newcomers. Others are well-known without being household names, apart from Frank Herbert, who has been included as a sort of yardstick. The other great figures – Aldiss, Asimov, Ray Bradbury, Robert Silverberg, Cordwainer Smith and their like – have been omitted because they have already received so much critical attention.

Science fiction overlaps to some degree with fantasy, but the stories, while being imaginative, are more concerned with spaceships and interplanetary flight than with the heroic quest and 'sword and sorcery' adventures which are the hallmark of the writer of fantasy.

Bear, Greg

American. He was born in 1951. His style is mystical and poetic, yet full of action and interest. The plots are imaginative, and sometimes derived from the myths of ancient cultures. He uses a recurrent theme of apocalypse and transmutation. He is considered to be among the best of current writers of science fiction.

Publications

Corona Chivers 1985
Eon 1985
Blood music 1986
The forge of God 1987
Hegira 1987
The strength of stones 1988
(Published by Gollancz.)
The infinity concerto Legend 1988
The serpent mage (sequel) Legend 1988
Eternity Gollancz 1989
Beyond heaven's river Severn House 1989
Tangents (stories) Gollancz 1989
Heads Legend 1990
Queen of angels Gollancz 1990
Anvil of stars Legend 1992
The venging Legend 1992
Psychlone Severn House 1992

Now read
Michael Coney, Gary Kilworth, Kate Wilhelm.

Benford, Gregory

American. He was born in 1941. He writes convincingly about the far future, where humans are threatened by intelligent machines and cybernauts. He is particularly sound on technical detail about scientific research, but also has perceptive characterisation.

Publications

> The stars in shroud   Gollancz   1978
> In the ocean of night   Sidgwick & Jackson   1978
> If the stars are gods   (with Gordon Eklund)
>   Gollancz   1978
> Timescape   Gollancz   1980
> Shiva descending   (with William Rotsler)   Sphere
>   1980
> Against infinity   Gollancz   1983
> Find the changeling   (with Gordon Eklund)
>   Sphere   1983
> Across the sea of suns   Macdonald   1984
> Heart of the comet   Bantam   1986
> Artifact   Bantam   1986
> In alien flesh   Gollancz   1988
> Great sky river   Gollancz   1988
> Tides of light (sequel)   Gollancz   1989
> Against the fall of night, and Beyond the fall of night
>   (with Arthur C. Clarke)   Gollancz   1991

Now read
Octavia Butler, Michael Coney, Frank Herbert.

Bova, Ben

American. He was born in 1932. He is perhaps best known as editor of the science fiction magazines, *Analog* and *Omni*, and is thus a seminal influence on modern science fiction.

His plots are in the traditional science fiction mould, with high technology and interplanetary flight.

Publications

> The weathermakers   Dobson   1969
> As on a darkling plain   1972   Methuen   1981
> Star watchman   Dobson   1973
> The multiple man   Gollancz   1977

Colony Methuen 1979
Maxwell's demons Thorsons 1979
Kinsman Sidgwick & Jackson 1980
The starcrossed Magnum 1980
Voyagers Methuen 1982
Privateers Methuen 1983
Test of fire Severn House 1984
The exiles trilogy Methuen 1984
Orion Severn House 1985
The alien within Severn House 1987
Voyagers II Methuen 1987
Escape plus Methuen 1988
Millennium Methuen 1988
The vengeance of Orion Severn House 1988
The winds of Altair Severn House 1989
Cyberbooks Severn House 1990
Star brothers (Voyagers 3) Methuen 1990
Orion in the dying time Methuen 1991
Peacekeepers Severn House 1992
Sam Gunn, unlimited Methuen 1992

Now read
Frank Herbert, Bob Shaw.

Butler, Octavia

American. She lives in Los Angeles, and is one of the few black authors of science fiction. She won the Hugo Award for *Speech sounds* in 1984, and the Hugo and Nebula Awards for *Bloodchild* in 1985.

She writes about the far future, with thought-provoking plots. Her style is elegant, with vivid descriptions and sound characterisation.

Publications

Patternmasker Sphere 1978
Survivor Sidgwick & Jackson 1978
Mind of my mind Sidgwick & Jackson 1978

Wild seed   Sidgwick & Jackson   1980
Clay's Ark   Arrow   1985
Kindred   Women's Press   1988

XENOGENESIS

Dawn   1987
Adulthood rites   1988
Imago   1989
(Published by Gollancz.)

Now read
Greg Bear, Michael Coney, Kate Wilhelm.

Card, Orson Scott

American. He was born in 1951. He writes with real credibility about the society of the future. His books are imaginative and witty, and are strong on both technical detail and characterisation. Most are straightforward science fiction, but his *Tales of Alvin Maker* are fantasies.

Publications

Capitol (stories)   Thorsons   1979
Hot sleep   Thorsons   1979
Unaccompanied sonata (stories)   Macdonald
   1983
Ender's game   Century   1985
Speaker for the dead (sequel)   Century   1986
Hart's hope   Unwin   1986
Wyrms   Century   1988
The abyss   Century   1989

TALES OF ALVIN MAKER

Seventh son   Century   1987
Red prophet   Century   1988
Prentice Alvin   Legend   1989

Folk of the fringe　Legend　1990
Maps in a mirror　Century　1991
The Worthing saga　Century　1991
Xenocide　Legend　1991
The memory of earth　Century　1992
The call of earth　Legend　1993

Now read
Greg Bear, Octavia Butler, Richard Cowper.

Coney, Michael

British. He began to write in the 1970s, and was instantly acclaimed as a writer of promise. He won the British SF Award in 1975 with *Brontomek!* He writes about the far future, taking as his theme the effects of genetic engineering on human and animal life. His plots are well-constructed, with great imagination and convincing descriptions.

Publications

Syzygy　Elmfield Press　1973
Mirror image　Gollancz　1973
Hero of Downways　Futura　1974
Friends come in boxes　Gollancz　1974
Winter's children　Gollancz　1974
Girl with a symphony in her fingers　Elmfield Press
　1975
Charisma　Gollancz　1975
Hello summer, goodbye　Gollancz　1975
Brontomek!　Gollancz　1976
The ultimate jungle　Millington　1979
Cat Karina　Gollancz　1982
The celestial steam locomotive　Futura　1984
Gods of the greataway (sequel)　Futura　1986
Fang the gnome　Futura　1988

Now read
Gregory Benford, Octavia Butler, Orson Scott Card.

Cowper, Richard

British. Born in 1926, his real name is Colin Murry. He is one of the foremost British exponents of the genre. His books overlap to a large extent with the fantasy genre. His best known work is the 'Bird of kinship' saga, which tells the story of Europe after the Drowning, a global catastrophe which melted the icecaps, and divided Britain into seven islands. He writes with great assurance and style. His plots are thoughtful, with lyrical description and deft characterisation.

Publications

Breakthrough   1967
Phoenix   1968
Domino   1971
(Published by Dobson.)
Kuldesak   1972
Clone   1972
Time out of mind   1973
The twilight of Briareus   1974
Worlds apart   1974
The custodians (stories)   1976
Profundis   1979
The web of the Magi (stories)   1980
The Tithonian factor (stories)   1984
(Published by Gollancz.)
Shades of darkness   Kerosina   1986

BIRD OF KINSHIP SAGA

Piper at the gates of dawn   1976
The road to Corlay   1978
A dream of Kinship   1981
A tapestry of time   1982
(Published by Gollancz.)

Now read
Ray Bradbury, G. G. Kay, Ian Watson, Kate Wilhelm.

Herbert, Frank

American. He was born in 1920 and died in 1986. Before becoming a full-time writer, he was a journalist, holding a senior position on a San Francisco newspaper. He had also worked as a radio newscaster, an oyster diver and an instructor in jungle survival. He divided his time before his death between homes in the Pacific Northwest and Hawaii, which he ran in accordance with his conservationist beliefs, using wind and solar power for energy.

He was a doyen of the science fiction genre, respected and popular. His series about the planet Dune is a classic. His books were concerned with the effects of civilisation on the environment, and their plots deal with the destructive effects of human life forms on planets. The stories are exciting, with graphic descriptions and well-constructed plots. Some of the books have been filmed.

Publications

The dragon in the sea   Gollancz   1960
Destination: void   Penguin   1967
Santaroga barrier   Rapp & Whiting   1970
Whipping star   NEL   1972
Soul catcher   NEL   1973
The green brain   NEL   1973
The god makers   NEL   1973
Hellstrom's hive   NEL   1974
The eyes of Heisenberg   NEL   1975
The best of Frank Herbert   Sidgwick & Jackson   1975
The heaven makers   NEL   1976
The Jesus incident (with Bill Ransom)   Gollancz   1979
The priests of Psi   Gollancz   1980
The white plague   Gollancz   1983
The Lazarus effect (with Bill Ransom)   Gollancz   1983
Eye   Gollancz   1986
Man of two worlds   Gollancz   1986
The Ascension factor (with Bill Ransom)   Gollancz   1988

DUNE

Dune   1966
Dune Messiah   1971
Children of Dune   1981
God Emperor of Dune   1981
Heretics of Dune   1984
Chapterhouse Dune   1985
(Published by Gollancz.)

Now read
Isaac Asimov, Gregory Benford, Michael Coney, Robert Silverberg.

Kilworth, Gary

British. He was born in York in 1941, and spent eighteen years in the RAF as a cryptographer, stationed all over the world. Since then he has worked for Cable and Wireless, in London and the Caribbean. He studied English at King's College, London, and became a full-time writer in 1982. He lives in Essex with his wife, and has two grown-up children.

He writes short novels, tautly constructed, with fast-moving plots and dialogue, and graphic descriptions. His books are not the easiest of reads, but are worth pursuing because of the style and imagery. Some, like *Witchwater country*, and *Hunter's moon*, are not really science fiction.

Publications

In solitary   Faber   1977
The night of Kadar   Faber   1978
Split second   Penguin   1981
Gemini God   Faber   1981
Theatre of Timesmiths   Gollancz   1983
The songbirds of pain   Gollancz   1984
Witchwater country   Bodley Head   1986
Spiral winds   Bodley Head   1987
Tree Messiah   Unwin   1987

Cloudrock   Unwin   1988
Abandonati   Unwin   1988
Hunter's moon   Unwin   1989
In the hollow of the deep sea wave   Unwin   1989
Midnight's sun: a story of wolves   Unwin Hyman
   1990
Frost dancers: a story of hares   HarperCollins   1992
In the country of tattooed men (stories)   Grafton   1993
Angel   Gollancz   1993

Now read
Richard Cowper, Ian Watson.

Rowley, Christopher

American. He was born in Massachusetts in 1948, and had an English mother. He was educated mainly in England, but also in Canada and the United States. He became a journalist in London in the 1970s, but moved to New York in 1977, where he began his first novel, *War for eternity*, which won him the Compton Crook/Stephen Tall Memorial Award in 1983.

He writes traditional science fiction about spaceships and interplanetary conquests. The plots are well-constructed, with action, tension and credible characters transposed to a setting in the future. He shows breadth of imagination in location and incident, and the imagery of his language.

Publications

War for eternity   1986
The black ship   1987
Starhammer   1987
Golden sunlands   1988
The Vang: the military form   1989
(Published by Century.)

Now read
Ben Bova, Bob Shaw.

Russ, Joanna

American. She was born in New York in 1937. She is Associate Professor of English at the University of Washington, Seattle, and has written critical works as well as her output of science fiction.

She writes science fiction for and about women, presenting a feminist view of the future. Her descriptions are stylish, her settings imaginative, and her plots thought-provoking and at times provocative as she describes the behaviour and conflict between the sexes. Some of her books are collections of short stories, originally published in science fiction magazines; others, like *We who are about to...*, are full-length novels. She has been a winner of both Hugo and Nebula Awards.

Publications

> *Picnic in paradise*   Macdonald   1969
> *The adventures of Alyx*   1985
> *The female man*   1985
> *Extra(ordinary) people*   1985
> *The two of them*   1986
> *We who are about to...*   1987
> *The hidden side of the moon*   1989
> (Published by Women's Press.)

Now read
Octavia Butler, Kate Wilhelm.

Shaw, Bob

Irish. He was born in 1931. He is considered to be in the top flight of contemporary science fiction writers, and has been widely praised by the critics.

He has been writing consistently for twenty years, producing well-crafted novels in the traditional science fiction mould. His stories are exciting and fast-moving, with good plots and convincing locations, well written in an easy flowing style.

Publications

> *The two timers* 1969
> *Shadow of heaven* NEL 1970
> *Palace of eternity* 1970
> *One million tomorrows* 1971
> *Tomorrow lies in ambush* 1973
> *Other days, other eyes* 1974
> *Orbitsville* 1975
> *Ground zero man* Corgi 1976
> *Night walk* 1976
> *Cosmic kaleidoscope* 1976
> *A wreath of stars* 1976
> *Medusa's children* 1977
> *Who goes here* 1977
> *Ship of strangers* 1978
> *Vertigo* 1978
> *Dagger of the mind* 1979
> *The Ceres solution* 1981
> *A better mantrap* 1982
> *Orbitsville departure* 1983
> *Fire pattern* 1984
> *The peace machine* 1985
> *The ragged astronauts* 1986
> *The wooden spaceships* (sequel) 1988
> *The fugitive worlds* (sequel) 1989
> *Dark night in Toyland* 1989
> *Orbitsville judgement* 1990
> *Terminal velocity* 1991
> (All published by Gollancz, except where stated.)

Now read
Gregory Benford, Ben Bova, Christopher Rowley.

Watson, Ian

British. He was born on Tyneside in 1943. He studied English at
Balliol College, Oxford, then lectured in Japan for three years. His

first short story was published in 1969, and his first novel in 1973. He won the British Science Fiction Award with *The Jonah kit* in 1975, and has been a full-time writer since 1976. He was writer in residence in Northamptonshire Libraries in 1986.

He, too, writes in the traditional science fiction style. His books are set on imaginary planets, and concern space travel, but his prose has a lyrical quality, and his work is very stylish. He is one of the major British exponents of the genre.

Publications

> *The embedding*   1973
> *The Jonah kit*   1975
> *The Martian Inca*   1977
> *Alien embassy*   1977
> *Miracle visitors*   1978
> *The very slow time machine*   1979
> *God's world*   1979
> *The gardens of delight*   1980
> *Under heaven's bridge* (with Michael Bishop)   1981
> *Death hunter*   1981
> *Sunstroke*   1982
> *Chekhov's journey*   1983
> *Converts*   1984
> *The book of the river*   1984
> *The book of the stars* (sequel)   1984
> *The book of being*   1985
> *Slow birds*   1985
> *Queenmagic, Kingmagic*   1986
> *Evil water*   1987
> *The fire worm*   1988
> *Salvage rights*   1989
> *Stalin's teardrops and other stories*   1991
> *Lucky's harvest*   1993
> (All published by Gollancz.)

Now read
Michael Coney, Gary Kilworth, Bob Shaw.

Wilhelm, Kate

American. Her books are versatile and stylish. They are not necessarily science fiction of an interplanetary nature, but are very much concerned with environmental problems, biological research and stories of the future from a scientific point of view. She has also recently written detective stories.

Publications

Let the fire fall   Jenkins   1969
Fault line   Hutchinson   1978
Where late the sweet birds sang   Arrow   1978
The Clewiston test   Hutchinson   1979
Somerset dreams (stories)   Hutchinson   1979
Juniper time   Hutchinson   1980
City of Cain   Gollancz   1982
Listen, listen   Gollancz   1984
Welcome, chaos   Gollancz   1986
Huysman's pets   Gollancz   1986
Children of the wind   Hale   1991
Cambio Bay   Hale   1991

THRILLERS

Oh! Susannah   Houghton 1983
The Hamlet trap   Gollancz 1988
Smart house   Gollancz 1989

Now read
Greg Bear, Michael Coney, Octavia Butler, Joanna Russ.

SEA STORIES

This is a genre which falls into two distinct categories; novels about naval forces in the eighteenth and nineteenth centuries, often centred around the period of the Napoleonic Wars, and adventure or war stories in a contemporary setting, in which ships and the sea play a major role. They are equally popular, and both lend themselves to long series of novels about the same characters. They are invariably written by men, many of whom have served in the Royal Navy, or who have a special interest in ships and naval history. Two authors against whom many of the others can be measured are C. S. Forester, creator of the Hornblower novels, and Nicholas Monsarrat, who wrote widely about action at sea in the Second World War and after.

Callison, Brian

British. Born in Manchester in 1934. He was educated at Dundee High School before joining the Merchant Navy as a Midshipman with the Blue Funnel Line in 1950. He sailed mainly on cargo vessels to the Far East and Australia. After leaving the sea, he studied at Dundee College of Art, then went into management, in companies which included construction and entertainment. He served for some years in the Territorial Army, and maintains his links with the sea as Head of Unit, Royal Naval Auxiliary Service.

His novels are stories of adventure at sea. Some are set in the Second World War, and deal with Atlantic convoys, others are set at a later date, and concern shipwreck, salvage and treasure hunts. His first novel was an enormous success, repeated with the subsequent ones. His plots are fast-moving and exciting, and the details about naval life accurate.

Publications

A flock of ships   1970
A plague of sailors   1971
The dawn attack   1972
A web of salvage   1974
A ship is dying   1976
A frenzy of merchantmen   1977
The Judas ship   1978
The Auriga madness   1980
The sextant   1981
Spearfish   1983
The bone collectors   1984
A thunder of crude   1986
Trojan hearse   1990

CAPT. EDWARD TRAPP

Trapp's war   1973
Trapp's peace   1979
Trapp and World War III   1988
Crocodile Trapp   1993
(All published by Collins.)

Now read
Philip McCutchan, Douglas Reeman, Anthony Trew.

Draper, Alfred

British. He was born in 1924. He served as a Lieutenant in the Royal Navy during World War II, and survived two sinkings, one on D-Day, and one in the Atlantic. He served in the Far East and Borneo, before leaving the service. He became a journalist after the war, working at home and abroad as a specialist crime reporter. He is now a full-time writer, contributing to newspapers and magazines, as well as writing novels. He lives in Hertfordshire.

He writes about the Navy in World War II, with authenticity and conviction, obviously drawing on his own experiences. The stories are gripping and full of action. The main character is Crispin Paton, Commander of the submarine 'Grey Seal'. Naval life in wartime is pictured with accuracy, and the battle scenes are full of grim realism.

Publications

GREY SEAL

Grey Seal   1982
The restless waves   1983
The raging deep   1985
Storm over Singapore   1986
The great avenging day   1988
(All published by Macdonald.)
The crimson splendour   Piatkus   1991
Operation Midas   Piatkus   1993

Now read
Brian Callison, Alan Evans, Alexander Fullerton, Douglas Reeman.

Evans, Alan

British. He was born in Sunderland in 1930. He was a member of the

Royal Artillery Volunteers for many years, serving at home and abroad as a gunner, and later as Survey Sergeant. He is married, and lives in Walton on Thames.

He started his writing career with thrillers, but turned to sea stories in 1979. He writes about the navy at war, and paints a convincing picture of ships and men under stress. The battle scenes are authentic, and he brings his knowledge of gunnery to bear in his descriptions. The plots are action packed, moving quickly to a climax. The major character in the novels is Commander Smith, a shrewd and courageous leader.

Publications

> *Thunder at dawn*   1979
> *Ship of force*   1979
> *Dauntless*   1980
> *Audacity*   1981
> *Seek out and destroy*   1982
> *Deed of glory*   1985
> *Eagle at Taranto*   1987
> *Orphans of the storm*   1990
> *Sink or capture!*   1993
> (All published by Hodder.)

Now read
Alexander Fullerton, Philip McCutchan, Douglas Reeman.

Fullerton, Alexander

British. He was educated at the Royal Naval College, Dartmouth, and joined the Royal Navy in 1941, serving in the Mediterranean and in the Far East as a submariner, being mentioned in despatches for distinguished service. He studied Russian at Cambridge and worked for a while with Red Army units in Germany before returning to the Navy. He was released in 1949, and worked in South Africa as an insurance clerk in a Swedish shipping agency, and also as a publisher's representative. His first novel was published in 1953, based on his own experiences in submarines. He returned to

Britain in 1959 to work in the publishing industry, but decided to become a full-time writer in 1967.

His novels are primarily sea stories, but with a strong element of adventure, and are usually set in wartime. He draws on his own experiences of naval life to add authenticity and detail to his plots, and combines a strong story-line with a build-up of atmosphere and tension. He has written a long series about Nick Everard, a Naval Officer in the Second World War, and a later series about the exploits of the Special Boat Service. A few of his novels do not concern the sea, but are about industry and publishing, based, again, on his own experiences.

Publications

Surface   1953
Bury the past   1954
Old Moke   1954
No man's mistress   1957
A Wren called Smith   1957
The white men sang   1960
Soldier from the sea   1962
The waiting game   1961
(Published by Peter Davies.)
The thunder and the flame   Hodder   1964
Lionheart   Hodder   1965
Regenesis   Michael Joseph   1983

NICK EVERARD

Sixty minutes for St. George   1975
The blooding of the guns   1976
Patrol to the Golden Horn   1978
Storm force to Narvik   1979
Last lift from Crete   1980
All the drowning seas   1981
A share of honour   1982
The torch bearers   1983
The gatecrashers   1984
(Published by Michael Joseph.)

SPECIAL BOAT SERVICE

Special deliverance   1986
Special dynamic   1987
Special deception   1988
(Published by Macmillan.)
Look to the wolves   Little, Brown   1992

Now read
Brian Callison, Philip McCutchan, Douglas Reeman, Anthony Trew, John Wingate.

Kent, Alexander

British. A pseudonym for Douglas Reeman, who appears later in this section. Kent is among the best-known modern writers of historical naval adventure, and his books about Richard Bolitho are enormously popular, so much so that the publishers issue a regular newsletter about the life and times of Bolitho.

He says that he has always been fascinated by sailing ships and the men in the eighteenth- and nineteenth-century navy, and has spent a lifetime studying them. This is apparent in the meticulous detail and colourful atmosphere of his books. The stories are high adventure, with vivid descriptions of battles, and sub-plots about treason, smuggling and slaving, as well as accurate information about the progress of the Napoleonic Wars. The character of Richard Bolitho grows in stature as the series progresses, and the minor characters are well-drawn and historically credible.

Publications

RICHARD BOLITHO (arranged in the author's
  chronological order)

Richard Bolitho – Midshipman   1966
Midshipman Bolitho and the 'Avenger'   1971
Stand into danger   1980
In gallant company   1977

Sloop of war   1972
To glory we steer   1967
Command a King's ship   1973
Passage to mutiny   1976
With all despatch   1988
Form line of battle   1969
Enemy in sight   1970
The Flag-Captain   1971
Signal – close action   1974
Inshore squadron   1978
A tradition of victory   1981
Success to the brave   1983
Colours aloft   1986
Honour this day   1987
The only victor   1990
Beyond the reef   1992
(All published by Heinemann.)

Now read
Patrick O'Brian, C. N. Parkinson, Dudley Pope, Showell Styles, Richard Woodman.

Llewellyn, Sam

British. He was born in the Isles of Scilly in 1948, and now lives with his family in Herefordshire. He is a keen and experienced sailor. He is a comparative newcomer to the field of sea stories, though he has written non-fiction about sailing, and children's books. He writes thrillers with a nautical setting, drawing on his detailed knowledge of ships and the sea, in particular yachts, to add authenticity to his work. The books are full of action and adventure, with tight-knit plots, and credible characterisation.

Publications

GURNEY

Gurney's revenge   1977

Gurney's reward   1978
Gurney's release   1979

Dead reckoning   1987
Great circle   1987
Hell Bay   1988
Blood orange   1988
Death roll   1989
Blood knot   1991
Riptide   1992
Clawhammer   1993
(All published by Michael Joseph.)

Now read
Anthony Trew, John Wingate.

McCutchan, Philip

British. He joined the Royal Navy as a signalman in 1939, but transferred to the seaman branch on being recommended for a commission. He served in every type of warship during the Second World War, and ended as a Lieutenant RNVR. He is interested in naval and military history, up to 1946. He is a prolific writer, with over sixty novels to his credit, and two books about sailing ships. He divides his output of novels between sea stories and thrillers, and also appears in the section devoted to Spy stories. He has also written military novels as Duncan McNeil.

The sea stories are in two major series: about Lieutenant St. Vincent Halfhyde, RN, an officer serving in the Royal Navy in the nineteenth century, after the Napoleonic War, and about Donald Cameron, serving during the Second World War. A new series features Commodore John Mason Kemp, commander of Atlantic convoys. They are all meticulously researched, and the naval details are described with accuracy and atmosphere. The battle scenes are vivid and enthralling, and the plots are fast-moving. The main characters develop throughout the series. The foreign locations are authentic, and reflect the author's own knowledge of service in the Far East and in the Atlantic.

Now read on

Publications

LIEUT. HALFHYDE

Beware, beware the Bight of Benin 1974
Halfhyde's island 1975
The guns of arrest 1976
Halfhyde to the narrows 1977
Halfhyde for the Queen 1978
Halfhyde ordered south 1979
Halfhyde and the Flag Captain 1980
Halfhyde on the Yangtze 1981
Halfhyde on Zanatu 1982
Halfhyde outward bound 1983
The Halfhyde line 1984
Halfhyde and the chain-gang 1985
Halfhyde goes to war 1986
Halfhyde on the Amazon 1987
Halfhyde and the Admiral 1990
Halfhyde and the Fleet review 1991

DONALD CAMERON

Cameron, Ordinary Seaman 1979
Cameron comes through 1980
Cameron of the 'Castle Bay' 1981
Lt. Cameron, RNVR 1981
Cameron's convoy 1982
Cameron in the gap 1982
Orders for Cameron 1983
Cameron in command 1983
Cameron and the Kaiserhof 1984
Cameron's raid 1985
Cameron's chase 1986
Cameron's troop lift 1987
Cameron's commitment 1988
Cameron's crossing 1993

COMMODORE JOHN MASON KEMP

The convoy Commodore 1986

Convoy north   1987
Convoy south   1988
Convoy east   1989
Convoy of fear   1990
Convoy homeward   1992

The last farewell   1991
A lady of the line   1992
(All published by Weidenfeld & Nicolson.)

Now read
Brian Callison, Alexander Fullerton, Dudley Pope, Douglas Reeman, Anthony Trew, Richard Woodman.

O'Brian, Patrick

British. The pseudonym of Geoffrey Jenkins, whose work appears in Adventure stories.

He writes with skill and humour about life in the Royal Navy in Napoleonic times. The novels are not so much adventure stories as an evocation of the life of a ship, with insight into the characters and feelings of the men serving in it. The events of the period are cleverly woven into the narrative, and the dialogue is realistic and authentic. The main character is Jack Aubrey.

Publications

JACK AUBREY

Master and Commander   1969
Post Captain   1972
HMS Surprise   1973
The Mauritius command   1977
Desolation island   1978
Fortune of war   1979
The surgeon's mate   1980
The Ionian mission   1982
Treason's harbour   1983
The far side of the world   1985

Reverse of the medal 1986
Letter of marque 1988
The thirteen gun salute 1989
Nutmeg of consolation 1990
Clarissa Oakes 1992
(Published by Collins.)
The wine-dark sea HarperCollins 1993

Now read
Alexander Kent, C. N. Parkinson, Dudley Pope, Showell Styles, Richard Woodman.

Parkinson, C. N.

British. Born 1909, and educated at St. Peter's School, York, and Emmanuel College, Cambridge. He taught history in Devon before joining the army with the rank of Captain in 1939. He has had a distinguished career as Professor of History at universities both in Britain and abroad, and has published many books on economic history, though he is perhaps best known as the author of 'Parkinson's Law'. He has had a life-long interest in naval warfare in Napoleonic times, and his series of novels about Richard Delancey reflects this. He lived in Guernsey until his death in 1989.

His novels are deeply researched and contain detailed descriptions of ships and seamen of the period. They are enlivened with fast-moving plots, vivid descriptions of naval battles, and lively characterisation.

Publications

RICHARD DELANCEY

Devil to pay 1973
Fireship 1974
Touch and go 1977
Dead reckoning 1978
So near, so far 1981
The Guernseyman 1982
(All published by John Murray.)

Now read
Alexander Kent, Patrick O'Brian, Dudley Pope, Showell Styles, Richard Woodman.

Pope, Dudley

British. Born in 1925. He served in the Merchant Navy, and was torpedoed in the Battle of the Atlantic, during the Second World War. He was invalided out of the service in 1943 and became Naval Defence Correspondent for the *Evening News*, a post which he held until 1959, when he resigned to become a full-time writer. He is a respected naval historian, and has written a number of books about aspects of naval life and battles, in addition to his novels. He has spent the last twenty years sailing the Caribbean with his wife in their ketch *Ramage*. His books are consistently popular.

He writes both historical and modern sea stories. His best known series is about Nicholas Ramage, serving during the Napoleonic War period. His detail is accurate, and his descriptions colourful. There is a lot of action in the plots, and the battle scenes are particularly convincing. The other series is about the Yorkes: Ned, a buccaneer in the time of Henry Morgan, and Edward, his descendant, serving in the Royal Navy in the Second World War. The Caribbean locations are vivid and full of interest, obviously drawn from the author's own knowledge.

Publications

RAMAGE

Ramage   1966
Ramage and the drum beat   1967
Ramage and the free-booters   1969
Governor Ramage RN   1972
Ramage's prize   1974
Ramage and the guillotine   1975
Ramage's diamond   1976
Ramage's mutiny   1977
Ramage and the rebels   1978
The Ramage touch   1979

Ramage's signal   1980
Ramage and the renegades   1981
Ramage's devil   1982
Ramage's trial   1984
Ramage's challenge   1985
Ramage at Trafalgar   1986
Ramage and the Saracens   1988
Ramage and the Dido   1989

NED YORKE

Buccaneer   1981
Admiral   1982
Galleon   1986
Corsair   1987

EDWARD YORKE

Convoy   1979
Decoy   1983
(All published by Secker & Warburg.)

Now read
Alexander Kent, Philip McCutchan, Patrick O'Brian, C. N. Parkinson.

Reeman, Douglas

British. He also writes under the name of Alexander Kent. Though he came from an Army family, he was fascinated by the Navy in the days of sail, and this prompted him to join the Navy in the Second World War. He served in the Battle of the Atlantic and in the Mediterranean and Normandy campaigns, and his experiences proved valuable as background to his stories of naval action. He actually lived on board his motor yacht for some years.

The novels which he writes under his own name are very different from the Bolitho novels of Alexander Kent. They deal with the naval encounters in the First and Second World Wars, and are stories of high adventure, set at sea. The plots are full of action and excitement, and conditions on board a modern warship are authentically described.

Publications

A prayer for the ship   1958
With blood and iron   1964
Path of the storm   1966
To risks unknown   1969
The greatest enemy   1970
HMS Saracen   1971
The hostile shore   1972
Dive in the sun   1972
Rendezvous South Atlantic   1972
Go in and sink   1973
The deep silence   1973
The pride and the anguish   1973
The destroyers   1974
High water   1975
The last raider   1975
Winged escort   1975
Surface with daring   1976
Strike from the sea   1978
A ship must die   1979
Torpedo run   1981
The volunteers   1985
The iron pirate   1986
In danger's hour   1988
The white guns   1989
Killing ground   1991

BLACKWOOD FAMILY

Badge of glory   1982
The first to land   1984
The horizon   1993
(All published by Heinemann.)

Now read
Brian Callison, Alexander Fullerton, Philip McCutchan.

Styles, Showell

British. Born in 1908, and educated at Sutton Coldfield. He served in the Royal Navy during the Second World War, and retired as a Commander in 1946. Since then he has been a professional author. He is well known as a mountaineer, and led private expeditions to the Arctic and the Himalayas. He has written over a hundred books on mountaineering, travel, biography and naval history, including a series of thrillers about rock climbing, under the name of Glyn Carr. He now lives in Porthmadog, Wales.

He has written a number of novels about naval life in the nineteenth century. Though the plots are full of action, they are not adventure stories in the same sense as the 'Ramage' or 'Halfhyde' novels, but are closer in character to the 'Hornblower' series by C. S. Forester. The details are accurate, and the characterisation is thoughtful. The books are not, perhaps, quite as easy to read as some others in the genre, but worthwhile for the reader who wants to know what life was really like in the Navy of the last century.

Publications

Vincey Joe at Quiberon   1971
Admiral of England   1973
A kiss for Captain Hardy   1979
Centurion comes home   1980
Seven gun broadside   1982
The Malta frigate   1983
Mutiny in the Caribbean   1984
Stella and the fireships   1985
(Published by Faber.)

MR. FITTON SERIES

A sword for Mr. Fitton   1975
Mr. Fitton's commission   1977
The Baltic convoy   1979
The quarterdeck ladder   1982
The lee shore   1986
Gun-brig Captain   1987

HMS Cracker   1988
(Published by Wm. Kimber.)
A ship for Mr. Fitton   Hale   1992
The independent cruise   Hale   1992
Mr. Fitton's prize   Hale   1993

Now read
Patrick O'Brian, C. N. Parkinson.

Trew, Anthony

South African. He served in the South African and Royal Navies during the Second World War, in the Atlantic, the Mediterranean and the Western Approaches, in command of an escort destroyer with the Russian convoys. He then returned to South Africa to resume his post as Director General of the Automobile Association, and wrote his first novel in his spare time. It was published in 1963, an immediate bestseller, and he retired early to become a full-time writer. He now lives in Weybridge, Surrey.

His novels are mainly set in the Second World War, and are full of action and adventure, with fast-moving plots and an element of suspense. They fall equally well into the categories of adventure stories and war stories.

Publications

Two hours to darkness   1963
Smoke Island   1965
The sea break   1967
The white schooner   1969
Towards the tamarind trees   1970
The 'Moonraker' mutiny   1972
Kleber's convoy   1974
The Zhukov briefing   1975
Ultimatum   1975
Death of a supertanker   1978
The Antonov project   1979
Sea fever   1980

> *Running wild*   1982
> *Bannister's chart*   1984
> *Yashimoto's last dive*   1986
> *The road to the river and other stories*   1992
> (All published by Collins.)

Now read
Brian Callison, Philip McCutchan, Douglas Reeman, John Wingate.

Wingate, John

British. He joined the Royal Navy at 13, and served throughout the
Second World War and the Korean War in cruisers, submarines and
destroyers. He became captain of a submarine in 1943, and ended
the war as a First Lieutenant of a destroyer in the Far East. He
believes very firmly that Britain still has a role to play as a sea
power, and that our existence depends on that role. He still maintains
close touch with the Navy and other maritime organisations, and has
become a leading author of books on ships and seafaring.

He writes books full of excitement and adventure, usually about
warships of all types, but sometimes about small craft. The plots
move quickly, the dialogue is crisp, and the details of ships and the
sea totally authentic.

Publications

SUBMARINER SINCLAIR

Sinclair in command   Newnes   1961
Nuclear captain   Macdonald   1962
Sub zero   Macdonald   1963

Never so proud   Heinemann   1966
Full fathom five   Heinemann   1967
Below the horizon   1972
The sea above them   Barker   1975
Oil strike   Weidenfeld   1976
Avalanche   Weidenfeld   1977

Black tide   Weidenfeld   1977
Red mutiny   Weidenfeld   1978
Target risk   Weidenfeld   1979
Seawaymen   Weidenfeld   1979
Frigate   Weidenfeld   1980
Carrier   Weidenfeld   1981
Submarine   Weidenfeld   1982
Go deep   Weidenfeld   1985
The windship race   Weidenfeld   1988

Now read
Brian Callison, Philip McCutchan, Douglas Reeman, Anthony Trew.

Woodman, Richard

British. He served in the Merchant Navy as a midshipman and, after qualifying as a navigator, became an officer in cargo and weather ships. He joined the Trinity House Service in 1967, and has commanded lighthouse tenders and a squadron of Guardships in the English Channel.

He writes about the Navy in the early nineteenth century, in a series featuring Commander Nathaniel Drinkwater. The details are carefully researched, and the battle scenes realistic and credible. The locations vary from the scenes of Nelson's battles to the South Seas and the Arctic.

Publications

NATHANIEL DRINKWATER

An eye of the fleet   1981
A King's cutter   1982
A brig of war   1983
Bomb vessel   1984
The corvette   1985
1805   1985
Baltic mission   1986
In distant waters   1988

Now read on

A private revenge   1989
Under false colours   1991
The flying squadron   1992
Wager   1990
(Published by Murray.)
The darkening sea   Macdonald   1991
Endangered species   Little, Brown   1992

Now read
Alexander Kent, Philip McCutchan, C. N. Parkinson, Dudley Pope,
Showell Styles.

SPY STORIES

This is the sub-genre of the crime novel, which, with some of the classic detective stories, is most closely related to the 'straight' novel. There is enormous depth of plot and character, much psychology, and often quite scholarly research into the workings of the intelligence services. Many of the best known writers of the genre have worked in intelligence, and have first-hand experience of espionage and international politics. Some of the great novelists of the century have written in this genre – Somerset Maugham and Graham Greene, for example – without losing the respect of the literary critics.

The genre has spawned its own sub-divisions: political thrillers, financial thrillers and novels about industrial espionage. It also overlaps with the thriller and war story.

The end of the Cold War and the improvements in East-West relations have necessitated some new directions in this genre. There is no shortage of new angles and fresh ideas.

Allbeury, Ted

British. Born in Stockport, Cheshire in 1917, and educated in Birmingham. He served in the Intelligence Corps, 1940–47, reaching the rank of Lieutenant-Colonel. He went into sales and advertising after the war, and is co-founder of a firm in Tunbridge Wells, Kent. He started writing when he was 54, and says that having a full-time job and writing two novels a year demands a high degree of self-discipline. He says, 'I have tried in my novels to show that people employed in espionage have private lives, and that their work affects their lives.' As a result, his novels explore the dilemmas faced by agents who doubt the morality of what they are doing, and tend to end on a sad note. The early books concentrated on action and adventure, but his later ones portray characters in much greater depth. His experiences in the Intelligence Corps add authenticity and local colour to his stories, particularly to those set in Russia. He also writes as Richard Butler.

Publications

A choice of enemies   1973
Snowball   1974
Palomino blonde   1975
Moscow quadrille   1976
The only good German   1976
The man with the President's mind   1977
The lantern network   1978
(All published by Peter Davies.)
The Alpha list   Hart Davis   1979
Consequence of fear   Hart Davis   1979
The 20th day of January   Granada   1980
The other side of silence   Granada   1981
Secret whispers   Granada   1981
All our tomorrows   Granada   1982
Pay any price   NEL   1983
The reaper   NEL   1983
Shadow of shadows   Granada   1983
The Judas factor   NEL   1984
Codeword Cromwell   Granada   1984

The girl from Addis   Granada   1984
Children of tender years   NEL   1985
The choice   NEL   1986
The seeds of treason   NEL   1986
The crossing   NEL   1987
A wilderness of mirrors   NEL   1988
A time without shadows   NEL   1989
The line-crosser   NEL   1993

as Richard Butler
Where all the girls are sweeter   P. Davies 1975
Italian assets   P. Davies 1976 (Reissued under his
   own name by Firecrest 1989.)
Other kinds of treason   NEL   1990
The dangerous edge   NEL   1991
Show me a hero   NEL   1992

Now read
Clive Egleton, Brian Freemantle, Adam Hall.

Buckley, William F.

American. He was born in New York in 1925, and was educated at the Universities of Mexico and Yale. He is a journalist and political commentator, and has hosted the TV chat show 'Firing Line' since 1966. He also edits *National Review* and has written a syndicated column since 1962. His continuing involvement with politics and contacts with the White House and the Pentagon put him in a very good position from which to write political thrillers. He writes action-filled, ingenious stories, with a good deal of humour, about an agent called Blackford Oakes. The characterisation is not as deep as that of some of the other authors of the genre, but this is compensated for by the fast-moving plots and exotic settings.

Publications

BLACKFORD OAKES

Saving the Queen   1976

Stained glass   1978
Who's on first?   1980
The story of Henri Tod   1984
See you later, alligator   1986
High jinx   1987
Mongoose R.I.P.   1988
(Published by Century Hutchinson.)
Tucker's last stand   Severn House   1991

Now read
John Gardner, Adam Hall.

Deighton, Len

British. Born in London in 1929. He was educated at Marylebone Grammar School and the Royal School of Art and did National Service in the Royal Air Force. He had a variety of jobs – cook, waiter, BOAC steward, teacher, illustrator and photographer, among others – before becoming a full-time writer. He has written cookery books, studies of the Second World War, plays and some straight novels, as well as his two series of spy stories. He now lives in Ireland.

His books are well-crafted, with intricate, imaginative plots and witty dialogue. The main character in the first series is an agent who uses a variety of names; Harry Palmer is the best known, since Michael Caine played him in filmed versions of the books. The locations used are both exotic and atmospheric, with a convincing air of authenticity. The business of espionage, with its double- and triple-crosses, its emphasis on documents as a first resource, and its unique relationship with government, is accurately and minutely described. The later series, about Bernard Samson, has even more intricate plots, and much greater depth of characterisation, while keeping the atmosphere and authenticity, and has put him in the top rank of writers of spy stories.

Publications

The Ipcress file   1962

Horse under water 1963
Funeral in Berlin 1964
Billion dollar brain 1966
An expensive place to die 1969
(All published by Cape.)

BERNARD SAMSON

Berlin game 1983
Mexico set 1984
London match 1985
Spy hook 1988
Spy line 1989
Spy sinker 1990
(*Winter: a Berlin family* 1987 is a pendant to the
    series.)
(All published by Hutchinson.)

OTHERS

Only when I larf Joseph 1968
Bomber Cape 1970
Close- up Cape 1972
SS–GB Cape 1978
Goodbye Mickey Mouse Hutchinson 1982
Mamista Century 1991
City of gold Century 1992

Now read
John Gardner, John Le Carré, Anthony Price.

Egleton, Clive

British, born in Harrow in 1927, and educated at Haberdashers'
Aske's School, London, and the Army Staff College, Camberley. He
served in the British Army, 1945–75, reaching the rank of
Lieutenant-Colonel. His appointments took him all over the world,
and he was involved in Intelligence in Cyprus, the Persian Gulf and
East Africa. He began writing in 1969, and has devoted most of his

time to it since he left the army. He lives on the Isle of Wight.

He regards himself primarily as a writer of suspense fiction, and hopes that his stories will make the reader want to turn over the page to see what happens next. His books are, however, examples of the tough, realistic type of spy story, in which the hero does not emerge triumphant and unbloodied. The plots are exciting and well-constructed, and the locations authentically described. Most concern the conflict between East and West, and the KGB operations are realistically portrayed. He has also written war stories as John Tarrant.

Publications

GARNETT

A piece of resistance   1970
Last Post for a partisan   1971
The Judas mandate   1972

CHARLES WINTER

The Winter touch   1981
The Russian enigma   1983

Seven days to a killing   1973
The October plot   1974
Skirmish   1975
State visit   1976
The Mills bomb   1978
Backfire   1979
A falcon for the hawks   1982
A conflict of interests   1984

Troika   1984
A different drummer   1985
Picture of the year   1987
Gone missing   1988
Death of a Sahib   1989
In the red   1990
Last act   1991
A double deception   1992

Hostile intent   1993
(All published by Hodder.)

as John Tarrant
The Rommel plot   Macdonald   1977
The Clauber trigger   Macdonald   1978

Now read
Ted Allbeury, John Gardner, Anthony Price.

Freemantle, Brian

British. He was born in Southampton in 1936, and educated there. He became a journalist, first on provincial papers, and later as Foreign Editor of the *Daily Sketch* and *Daily Mail*. He worked as a foreign correspondent in thirty countries, including Vietnam, where he organised the only British airlift of orphaned children, before the collapse of South Vietnam. He left journalism in 1975 to concentrate on writing novels.

He says that he tries to make his spy stories good novels, and relies heavily on characterisation to gain that effect, using psychology rather than violent action. The agents are seen, not so much as 'goodies' and 'baddies', but as people caught in the machinations of their superiors. He created, in the character of Charlie Muffin, the hero of a series of novels, what he describes as 'a new kind of spy', courageous but anti-establishment.

Publications

Goodbye to an old friend   1973
Face me when you walk away   1974
The man who wanted tomorrow   1975
The November man   1976
(Published by Cape.)
Deaken's war   1982
Rules of engagement   1984
The Kremlin kiss   1986
The bearpit   1988

The factory Century 1990
Little grey mice Century 1991
(Published by Century Hutchinson.)

CHARLIE MUFFIN

Charlie Muffin 1977
Clap hands, here comes Charlie 1978
The inscrutable Charlie Muffin 1979
Charlie Muffin's Uncle Sam 1980
Madrigal for Charlie Muffin 1981
(Published by Cape.)
Charlie Muffin and Russian Rose 1985
Charlie Muffin San 1987
The run around 1988
Comrade Charlie 1989
Charlie's apprentice 1993
(Published by Century Hutchinson.)

as John Maxwell (Sea stories)
HMS Bounty Cape 1977
The Mary Celeste Cape 1978

Now read
Len Deighton, John Gardner, John Le Carré, Anthony Price.

Gardner, John

British. Born in Northumberland in 1926, and educated at
Newcastle, King Alfred's School, Wantage and St. John's College,
Cambridge, where he gained a BA in Theology. He served in the
Royal Marines in the Second World War, where he spent some time
as a Commando in the Far East. He became a clergyman in 1952,
and spent some time as a Royal Air Force Chaplain. He has also
been a theatre critic for the *Stratford-upon-Avon Herald*. He now
lives in Wiltshire.

He writes in a number of genres – spy stories, suspense stories,
straight novels, thrillers – though he says that he does not like the

classic detective story. He thinks of himself as an observer, through whose eyes the story is told. He brings a new dimension to the spy story: that of humour. He conceived the character of Boysie Oakes as 'an amusing counter-irritant to the excesses of 007'. Oakes is an anti-hero, vulgar, stupid and cowardly, and the books which feature him are black comedies. Ironically, John Gardner has written several sequels to the James Bond books, after the death of Ian Fleming. He has also written two books based on the Conan Doyle character of Moriarty, who he regards as being more interesting than Sherlock Holmes.

His plots are inventive, sometimes bizarre, but full of action. Characters are rounded, if not always credible, and the tension mounts as the plot progresses. The longer novels have an underlying seriousness, as he explores the effects of world events on contemporary characters.

Publications

BOYSIE OAKES

The liquidator   1964
The understrike   1965
Amber nine   1967
Madrigal   1967
Founder member   1969
Traitor's exit   1970
The airline pirates   1970
The champagne communist   1974
A killer for a song   1974
(Published by Muller.)

JAMES BOND

Licence renewed   1981
For special services   1982
Icebreaker   1983
Role of honour   1984
Nobody lives forever   1986
(Published by Cape.)

No deals, Mr. Bond   Cape/ Hodder   1987
Scorpius   Hodder   1988
Win, lose or die   Hodder   1989
Brokenclaw   Hodder   1990
Death is forever   Hodder   1992

MORIARTY

The return of Moriarty   Weidenfeld   1974
The revenge of Moriarty   Weidenfeld   1975

HERBIE KRUGER

The Nostradamus traitor   1978
The garden of weapons   1980
The quiet dogs   1982
(Published by Hodder.)

SECRET GENERATIONS

The secret generations   Bantam   1987
The secret houses   Bantam   1988
The secret families   Bantam   1989

OTHERS

The censor   NEL   1970
Every night's a bullfight   Joseph   1971
To run a little faster   Joseph   1976
The werewolf trace   Hodder   1977
The dancing dodo   Hodder   1978
Flamingo   1983

DEREK TORRY (crime novels)

A complete state of death   Cape   1969
The corner men   Cape   1974

Now read
Len Deighton, Brian Freemantle, Anthony Price.

Hall, Adam

British. A pseudonym for Elleston Trevor. Born in Kent in the 1920s. He was apprenticed as a racing driver on leaving school, but joined the Royal Air Force at the outbreak of the Second World War. He started to write professionally at the end of the war, and writes prolifically, under his own name, and as Warwick Scott, Simon Rattray, Caesar Smith, Roger FitzAlan, Howard North and Lesley Stone. He now lives in Arizona.

As Adam Hall he has written a series of fast-moving, action-filled spy stories about an agent known only as Quiller. The plot and action are stronger than the characterisation, and the tension builds up as the book progresses.

Publications

QUILLER

The Berlin memorandum 1965
The ninth directive 1966
The Striker portfolio 1969
The Warsaw document 1971
The Tango briefing 1973
The Mandarin cipher 1975
The Kobra manifesto 1976
The Sinkiang executive 1978
The Scorpion signal 1980
The Pekin target 1981
Northlight 1985
Quiller's run 1988
Quiller, KGB 1989
Quiller Barracuda 1991
(Published by W. H. Allen.)
Quiller bamboo Headline 1992
Quiller solitaire Headline 1992
Quiller meridian Headline 1993

Now read
Ted Allbeury, William Buckley, Philip McCutchan.

Harcourt, Palma

British. She was born on Jersey, where she still lives. After gaining a degree at St. Anne's College, Oxford, she worked in various branches of British Intelligence. In the course of her job, she travelled widely, and lived in several capital cities. Her books are all set in the diplomatic or intelligence services, and are exciting without being violent. She draws widely on her own background for her plots and locations, and both are totally authentic. The characters are also based on real agents and diplomats with whom she has worked, giving credibility and depth to the stories. Very few women write in this genre; she has done so well and successfully.

Publications

> *Climate for conspiracy*   1973
> *At high risk*   1974
> *A fair exchange*   1975
> *Dance for diplomats*   1976
> *A sleep of spies*   1977
> *Agents of influence*   1978
> *Tomorrow's treason*   1980
> *A turn of traitors*   1981
> *The twisted tree*   1982
> *Shadows of doubt*   1983
> *The distant stranger*   1984
> *A cloud of doves*   1985
> *A matter of conscience*   1986
> *Limited options*   1987
> *Clash of loyalties*   1988
> *Cover for a traitor*   1989
> *Double deceit*   1990
> *The reluctant defector*   1991
> *Cue for conspiracy*   1992
> *Bitter betrayal*   1993
> (Published by Collins.)

Now read
Clive Egleton, Helen MacInnes.

347

Le Carré, John

British. A pseudonym for John Cornwell. Born in Poole, Dorset, in 1931, and educated at Sherborne School and Berne University, before reading modern languages at Lincoln College, Oxford. He joined the Foreign Service in 1959, and served as Second Secretary at Bonn and Consul at Hamburg. His first novel was published in 1961, with immediate success. He left the service in 1964, to become a full-time writer. His work has brought him many literary prizes: British Crime Novel Award, 1963, for *The spy who came in from the cold*; Maugham Award, 1964; Mystery Writers' of America Edgar Allan Poe Award, 1965; Crime Writers' Association Gold Dagger, 1978; Black Memorial Award, 1978.

Le Carré is the most acclaimed writer in the genre, and has been compared with Conrad, Somerset Maugham and Graham Greene. His books are detailed, almost scholarly, and with enormous depth of character. He has an encyclopaedic knowledge of the way in which the diplomatic service works, and of the day-to-day involvement in counter-espionage. The complexities of spying, with its cells, paymasters and safe houses are described with accuracy and insight, and his portrayal of the spy as a pawn in the hands of bureaucracy is chillingly effective. His plots are intricate and involved, and the tension comes from a slow build-up of suspense, rather than action. The characters are complex, and much of the plot revolves around their interaction with colleagues and opponents. The books are not an easy read, requiring considerable concentration, but worth pursuing to the end.

Publications

GEORGE SMILEY

Call for the dead   Gollancz   1961
A murder of quality   Gollancz   1962
The spy who came in from the cold   Gollancz   1963
The looking-glass war   Heinemann   1965
Tinker, tailor, soldier, spy   Hodder   1974
The honourable schoolboy   Hodder   1977
Smiley's people   Hodder   1980
The quest for Carla   Hodder   1982 (omnibus edition)

A small town in Germany   Heinemann   1968
The naive and sentimental lover   Hodder   1971
The little drummer girl   Hodder   1983
A perfect spy   Hodder   1986
The Russia house   Hodder   1989
The secret pilgrim   Hodder   1990
The night manager   Hodder   1993

Now read
Len Deighton, Brian Freemantle, John Gardner, Anthony Price.

MacInnes, Helen

American. Born in Glasgow in 1907, but emigrated to the USA in 1937 and was naturalised in 1951. She was educated in Glasgow, at the High School for Girls and at the University. She became a librarian at the University of Glasgow and with Dumbartonshire Education Service, and gained a Diploma in Librarianship in 1931. She lived in Oxford for a few years before she emigrated, and became involved in the theatre.

Unlike many of the authors in the genre, she does not strive for authenticity in her plots, preferring to tell a good, action-filled story, with pace and excitement. She does, however, research her locations carefully, and her own extensive travels provide background colour. She says that she is interested in international politics, which give her ideas for her plots. The central character in her books is often an amateur agent, drawn into the plot by involvement with others.

Publications

Above suspicion   Harrap   1941
Assignment in Brittany   Harrap   1942
The unconquerable   Harrap   1944
Horizon   Harrap   1945
Neither five nor three   1951
I and my true love   1953
Pray for a brave heart   1955
North from Rome   1958

Decision at Delphi   1961
The Venetian affair   1964
The double image   1966
The Salzburg connection   1969
Message from Malaga   1971
Snare of the hunter   1974
Agent in place   1976
Prelude to terror   1978
The hidden target   1980
Cloak of darkness   1982
Ride a pale horse   1984
(Published by Collins, except where stated.)

Now read
Ted Allbeury, William Buckley, Adam Hall, Philip McCutchan, and see also Adventure stories.

McCutchan, Philip

British. Full biographical details appear under his entry in Sea stories. His spy stories fall into two series: one featuring Detective Chief Superintendent Simon Shard, seconded to the Foreign Office from Scotland Yard, the other about Commander Esmonde Shaw, late of Naval Intelligence, and now working for 6D2. The stories are fast-moving, with plenty of action and excitement, and plots which do not pretend to attain credibility. The pace is kept up throughout the book. The characters are not presented in any great depth, but are real and rounded enough.

Publications

SUPT. SHARD

Call for Simon Shard   Harrap   1973
A very big bang   1985
Blood runs East   1976
The Eros affair   1977
Blackmail north   1979
Shard calls the tune   1980

The hoof   1983
Shard at bay   1985
The executioners   1986
Overnight express   1988
The Logan file   1991
The Abbot of Stockbridge   1992
(Published by Hodder, except where stated.)

COMMANDER SHAW

Gibraltar Road   1961
Redcap   1961
Bluebolt one   1961
The man from Moscow   1962
Warmaster   1963
The Moscow coach   1964
Deadline   1965
Skyprobe   1966
The screaming dead balloons   1968
The bright red businessmen   1969
The all-purpose bodies   1969
Hartinger's mouse   1970
This Drakotny ...   1971
(Published by Harrap.)
Sunstrike   1979
Corpse   1980
Werewolf   1982
Rollerball   1984
Greenfly   1987
The spatchcock plan   1989
Kidnap   1993
(Published by Hodder.)

Now read
William Buckley, Adam Hall, Helen MacInnes.

Price, Anthony

British. Born in Hertfordshire in 1928. Educated at the Kings'

School, Canterbury, and Merton College, Oxford. He did National Service in the British Army, and has spent his whole career in publishing and journalism. His novels have won several awards: Crime Writers' Silver Dagger, 1971, Gold Dagger, 1975; Swedish Academy of Detection Award, 1979. He lives in a village near Oxford.

His novels are complex and ingenious, with a great deal more to them than even the most complicated books by other writers of spy fiction. The linking character in all the books is Dr. David Audley, a highly intelligent academic, drawn into the web of espionage because of his loyalty to his country. Colonel Jack Butler also appears in many of the books, as the controller of the particular intelligence unit for which Audley works. The characters of the agents and their families are explored in depth, and there is a good deal of applied psychology in the relationships with both friends and enemies. In addition to the devious plot concerned with the spying element, there is always an interacting sub-plot, based, the author says, on whatever piece of research he is engaged in at the time. These usually concern some form of military history, ranging from Roman forts, through the Sealed Knot Society to the battles of the American Civil War and the Irish Rebellion. The endings are often tragic, but there is always a clear division between good ('Our side') and bad ('Their side'). The books demand a high level of concentration, but are consistently intriguing.

Publications

DAVID AUDLEY

(in chronological order of reading)
44 vintage   1977
A new kind of war   1987
The labyrinth makers   1970
Alamut ambush   1971
Colonel Butler's wolf   1972
October men   1973
Other paths to glory   1974
Our man in Camelot   1975
War game   1976

Tomorrow's ghost 1979
The Old Vengeful 1982
Gunner Kelly 1983
Sion Crossing 1984
Here be monsters 1985
For the good of the state 1986
A prospect of vengeance 1988
The memory trap 1989
(All published by Gollancz.)

Now read
Len Deighton, John Le Carré.

Sebastian, Tim

British. He was born in London in 1952. He was an investigative reporter for the BBC for ten years, working in Eastern Europe, and was in Poland during the rise of Solidarity. He became the BBC's first television correspondent in Moscow, but was expelled in a tit-for-tat retaliation, and later accused by the Russians of working for British Intelligence. He now lives and works in Washington DC.

He is well qualified to write about the tensions between East and West, and about espionage circles. His books have taut, gripping plots, authentic settings, and good characterisation. His knowledge of the countries about which he writes adds realism to the story.

Publications

The spy in question 1988
Spy shadow 1989
Saviour's gate 1991
(Published by Simon & Shuster.)
Exit Berlin Bantam 1992
Last rights Bantam 1993

Now read
Clive Egleton, Palma Harcourt, John Le Carré, Helen MacInnes.

THRILLERS

A genre which is very closely related to both adventure and detective stories, but differs slightly from both in its content. The plots are more believable than those of adventure stories, where action is more important than credibility, and have less emphasis on police detectives and the process of logical deduction than those of detective stories.

There is a bewildering variety of thrillers, ranging from the ephemeral blood-and-thunder and tough 'private eye' story to the complex psychological drama. We have tried to include examples of most types, choosing authors who write an exciting story, while maintaining a reasonable literary style. Some, like Frederick Forsyth, are very well known; others are comparative newcomers.

Anthony, Evelyn

British. Born in London in 1928. She married in 1955, and has divided her time since then between writing and caring for her husband and six children. She lives in Ireland.

She started her writing career as an historical novelist, and published twelve novels about England and France, between 1953 and 1968. In 1967 her first thriller was published, setting the pattern for her later work. Her novels usually have a political content, and, indeed, a few are actual spy stories. She finds her themes and locations in current events: war crimes, kidnapping, international smuggling. As well as action and excitement, her books have a strong romantic element, and it is often sexual attraction that binds the hero and heroine together. The plots are well-crafted and fast-moving, and the characters are rounded. The locations are described in detail, obviously carefully researched, and the action moves towards a satisfactory solution.

Publications

The rendezvous   1967
The legend   1969
The assassin   1970
The tamarind seed   1971
The Poellenberg inheritance   1972
The occupying power   1973
The Malaspiga exit   1974
The Persian ransom   1975
The silver falcon   1977
The return   1978
The grave of truth   1979

DAVINA GRAHAM

The defector   1980
Avenue of the dead   1981
Albatross   1982
The company of Saints   1983
(spy stories)

> *Voices on the wind*   1985
> *No enemy but time*   1987
> *House of Vandekar*   1988
> *A scarlet thread*   1989
> (All published by Hutchinson.)
> *The doll's house*   Bantam   1992

Now read
Michael Gilbert, Helen MacInnes, Paul Myers.

Clancy, Tom

American. He was born and still lives in Maryland. He is an independent business man, an avid wargamer, and a computer fanatic. He achieved instant success with his first novel *The hunt for Red October*, which set the pattern for his later work.

He writes very long, well constructed thrillers, full of action and adventure. The suspense is maintained to the end, and the plots are intricate and exciting.

Publications

> *The hunt for Red October*   1984
> *Red storm rising*   1987
> *Patriot games*   1987
> *The Cardinal of the Kremlin*   1988
> *Clear and present danger*   1989
> *The sum of all fears*   1991
> (All published by Collins.)
> *Without remorse*   HarperCollins   1993

Now read
Clive Cussler, Peter Driscoll, Gerald Seymour, Craig Thomas.

Cussler, Clive

American. Born in Alhambra, California, and educated at Pasadena

City College, which he left to join the Air Force. He had a successful career in advertising, winning national awards for copy-writing. His first novel won a Mystery Writers of America award, and he is now a full-time writer with an international reputation. In his spare time he is an explorer, specialising in historic shipwrecks, and collects classic cars. He lives in Denver, Colorado.

His stories are adventure thrillers with a marine diving theme, featuring his hero, Dirk Pitt. The plots are inventive and exciting, full of action, and with good descriptive detail about the world of deep-sea diving. Characterisation is secondary to the action.

Publications

> *Raise the Titanic!*   1980
> *Night probe*   1981
> *Pacific vortex*   1983
> *Deep six*   1984
> *Mayday! (The Mediterranean caper*   US and first
>   paperback title) Severn House   1985
> *Cyclops*   1986
> *Iceberg*   1987
> *Treasure*   1988
> *Dragon*   1990
> *Sahara*   HarperCollins   1992
> (Published by Grafton except where stated.)

Now read
Geoffrey Jenkins, Robert MacLeod.

Forsyth, Frederick

British. Born in Ashford, Kent, in 1938, and educated at Tonbridge School. He served in the Royal Air Force, before becoming a journalist, first in Norfolk, and later for Reuters. He joined the BBC in 1967, and worked as a radio reporter and as Assistant Diplomatic Correspondent for BBC Television. He spent a year in Nigeria as a freelance journalist, and then wrote his first novel, *The day of the Jackal*, which won the Mystery Writers of America Edgar Allan Poe

Award in 1971. He lives in Ireland, but spends a good deal of his time travelling, to research locations for his current novel.

His books are essentially stories of suspense, in which an individual is pitted against the forces of bureaucracy. He uses anti-heroes, ruthless and often anti-social, but dedicated to the professional function of the role in which they are cast. The plots are extremely complex, with many changes of emphasis as the action swings from the hero to the organisation, and a wealth of locations as the characters travel around on their different paths, until the final confrontation. Real people and events are described in the background, adding authenticity to the story. The books are long, very well-written, and meticulously researched, justifying his reputation as the leading novelist in his field.

Publications

> *The day of the Jackal*   1971
> *The Odessa file*   1972
> *The dogs of war*   1974
> *The shepherd* (a short novel)   1975
> *The devil's alternative*   1979
> *No comebacks* (short stories)   1982
> *The fourth protocol*   1984
> (Published by Hutchinson.)
> *The negotiator*   Bantam   1989
> *The deceiver*   Bantam   1991

Now read
Robert Ludlum, Gerald Seymour.

Francome, John

British. He is a former National Hunt jockey, who is now a successful trainer. He rode a phenomenal number of winners and was extremely popular with the racing fraternity. He started his writing career with an autobiography in 1985, and turned to novels. His first two books were written in collaboration with James MacGregor.

The books have an authentic racing background, based on his own experience, but with the addition of action-packed plots and sustained tension. The stories are well-crafted, easy to read, and very popular.

Publications

> *Eavesdropper* Macdonald 1986
> *Riding high* Macdonald 1987
> *Blood stock* Headline 1989
> *Stone cold* Headline 1989
> *Rough ride* Headline 1990
> *Stud poker* Headline 1991

Now read
Dick Francis.

Gash, Jonathan

British. He was born in Lancashire, where his family were in the mill trade. He was educated in London and took a degree in medicine. As a practising doctor, he worked in London, Germany, the Middle East and Hong Kong, specialising in tropical medicine, about which he lectured world wide. He has recently retired after working for thirty years in the Faculty of Medicine at London University.

Writing has always been a hobby, ever since his student days, when he saw an advertisement offering cash for short stories. He wrote a series of bodice rippers to eke out his grant, and has written consistently since then. He also developed his love of antiques as a student, when he worked on an antiques stall off Petticoat Lane. He lived in Hong Kong for ten years, and it was there that his first Lovejoy novel was written.

The novels are full of knowledge about antiques, and Gash's own enthusiasm for and love of the subject comes over very clearly. Lovejoy is a loveable rogue, who operates just on the right side of the law, but is not above pulling off the odd scam. He has an uncanny knack for detecting fraud and crime, and becomes involved in solving the cases. The style is witty, with crisp dialogue, and the plots are ingenious and fast-moving. The books have always been widely read, but have greatly increased in popularity since the Lovejoy series appeared on television.

Publications

> *The Judas pair*   1978
> *Gold from Gemini*   1979
> *The Grail tree*   1979
> *The spend game*   1980
> *The Vatican rip*   1981
> *The firefly gadroon*   1982
> *The sleepers of Erin*   1983
> *The gondola scam*   1984
> *Pearlhanger*   1985
> *The Tartan ringers*   1986
> *Moonspender*   1986
> *Jade woman*   1988
> (All published by Collins.)
> *The very last Gambado*   1989
> *The great California game*   1990
> *Paid and loving eyes*   1993
> (Published by Century.)

Now read
Gerald Hammond, John Sherwood, Neville Steed.

Gilbert, Michael

British. Born in Lincolnshire in 1912, and educated at Blundell's School and the University of London, where he read law. He served in the Royal Horse Artillery in the Second World War, and then became a solicitor. He started writing just after the war, and is a founder member of the Crime Writers' Association. He has also been series editor of Hodder's *Classics of Detection and Adventure*, and has written many scripts for television thrillers. He lives in Cobham, Kent.

Some of his stories have a legal background, and feature a firm of solicitors, who become embroiled in detection. The early ones have a police background, with Inspector Hazlerigg as detective, and he later introduces a London police station, with Sergeant Petrella. Most are thrillers with an amateur detective, in differing locations. The plots are ingenious and intriguing, and the characterisation adds humour and spice to the action. He has written consistently since 1947, and still retains his freshness of approach and satisfying conclusions.

Publications

C. I. HAZLERIGG

Close quarters   1947
They never looked inside   1948
The doors open   1949
Smallbone deceased   1950
Death has deep roots   1951
Fear to tread   1953

Sky high   1955
Be shot for sixpence   1956
Blood and judgment   1959
After the fine weather   1963
Game without rules (short stories)   1965
The crack in the teacup   1966
The dust and the heat   1967
The Etruscan net   1969
The body of a girl   1972
Death in captivity   1972
The 92nd tiger   1973
Flash point   1974
The night of the twelfth   1976
Petrella at Q   1977
The empty house   1978
Mr. Calder and Mr. Behrens (short stories)   1982
The long journey home   1985
Young Petrella   1988

Paint, gold and blood 1989
The Queen against Karl Mullen 1991
(All published by Hodder.)

Now read
Tim Heald, John Sherwood, Michael Underwood, Sara Woods.

Haggard, William

British. A pseudonym for Richard H. M. Clayton. Born in Croydon in 1907, where his father was a parson. He was educated at Lancing College and Christ Church, Oxford. He served in the Indian Civil Service, and the Indian Army in the Second World War. He returned to England to work at the Board of Trade, where he became Controller of Enemy Property. He retired in 1969, and is now a full-time writer.

He has a distinctive style of writing, racy, sometimes flippant, sometimes even brusque, but full of pace and humour. His books are political thrillers, almost spy stories, about a fictitious body known as the Security Executive, which exists to protect the higher echelons of the Civil Service. The hero of most of the books is Colonel Russell, a civilised but somewhat irascible man who does not suffer fools gladly. The civil service and political details are very accurate, obviously drawn from his own experience. The plots are fast-moving, and the dialogue is crisp.

Publications

COLONEL RUSSELL

Slow burner 1958
Venetian bird 1959
The arena 1961
The unquiet sleep 1962
The high wire 1963
The antagonists 1964
The powder barrel 1965
The hard sell 1965
The power house 1966

The conspirators 1967
A cool day for killing 1968
The doubtful disciple 1969
The hardliners 1970
The bitter harvest 1971
The old masters 1973
The scorpion's tail 1976
Yesterday's enemy 1976
The poison people 1977
Visa to limbo 1978
The median line 1978
The money men 1981
The mischief maker 1982
The heirloom 1983
The need to know 1984
The meritocrats 1985

OTHERS

The Telemann touch 1958
Closed circuit 1960
The protectors 1972
The kinsmen 1974
The diplomatist 1987
The vendettists 1990
(All published by Cassell.)

Now read
Gerald Hammond, Tim Heald, Gregory McDonald.

Hammond, Gerald

British. Born in 1926 and educated at Wellington College and Aberdeen School of Architecture. He took early retirement to concentrate on writing, and produces books in rapid succession. He also writes detective stories, as Arthur Douglas.

He wrote three books in the mid-1960s about a character called Beau Pepys, which were comedy thrillers. After a long gap, he started a series set in the Scottish Borders, about Keith Calder, a gunsmith and amateur detective. Calder is a likeable rogue, who is often just outside the law, and is closely watched by the local police, who, nevertheless, accept his help in solving cases. The plots all revolve about guns and shooting, a subject about which the author obviously knows a great deal. The plots are fast-moving, and the dialogue is racy and witty. The minor characters, many of whom appear in each book, are vividly portrayed, and are often eccentric. Calder himself is a brusque, tough countryman, with a soft centre as far as his family and friends are concerned, but with a strong sense of justice and fair play, and a horror of guns being misused. In the later novels, Calder's daughter Deborah plays an increasingly large part, as a detective in her own right. The plots are well-constructed, with humour as well as excitement, and the descriptions of the Borders countryside are very authentic. His latest series concerns a dog breeder, John Cunningham, also in the Borders.

Publications

BEAU PEPYS

Fred in situ   1965
The loose screw   1966
Mud in his eye   1967

KEITH CALDER

Dead game   1979
The reward game   1980
The revenge game   1981
Fair game   1982
The game   1982
Sauce for the pigeon   1984
Cousin once removed   1984
Pursuit of arms   1985
Silver City scandal   1986
The executor   1986
The worried widow   1987
Adverse report   1987
Stray shot   1988
A brace of skeet   1989

Let us prey   1990
Home to roost   1990
Snatch crop   1991
Cash and carry   1992
(All published by Macmillan.)

JOHN CUNNINGHAM

Dog in the dark   1989
Doghouse   1989
Whose dog are you?   1990
Give a dog a name   1992
The curse of the cockers   1993

as Arthur Douglas
The decoy murders   1974
Crime without reason   1975
Dead on delivery   1976
Double cross   1977
Luckless lady   1978
The end of the line   1979
The goods   1985
A very wrong number   1986
(All published by Macmillan.)

Now read
William Haggard, Tim Heald, Gregory McDonald, Neville Steed.

Heald, Tim

British. Born in Dorchester in 1944, and educated at Sherborne School and Balliol College, Oxford, where he took a degree in Modern History. He has spent his entire career in journalism, and is a feature writer and critic for many newspapers and magazines. He lives in Richmond, Surrey.

His books are light-hearted mysteries, with an irreverent humour and bizarre settings. His anti-hero, Simon Bognor, is a Special Investigator to the Board of Trade, who is sent to investigate an infringement of the regulations in such areas as dog breeding, restaurants or historic houses, and invariably stumbles upon a murder or some other form of crime. He bungles his way through, with the help of his long-suffering girl-friend, Monica, and eventually solves the crime. The plots are not particularly devious, and the books rely on humour and the ineptitude of Bognor for effect, which works successfully.

Publications

SIMON BOGNOR

Unbecoming habits   1973
Blue blood will out   1974
Deadline   1975
Let sleeping dogs die   1976
Just desserts   1977
Murder at Moose Jaw   1981
Masterstroke   1982
Red herrings   1985
(Published by Hutchinson.)
Brought to book   Macmillan   1988
Business unusual   Macmillan   1989

Now read
Gerald Hammond, Gregory McDonald, Neville Steed.

Kellerman, Jonathan

American. He was born in New York in 1949, but grew up in Los Angeles. He graduated from UCLA, and received a PhD in clinical psychology from the University of Southern California, where he is currently Associate Professor of Paediatrics. As a practising psychologist, he has headed a consulting firm, conducted research into behavioural medicine, and has become a national authority on childhood stress. He lives in Southern California, with his wife, the novelist Faye Kellerman.

The novels are psychological thrillers, mainly concerned with serious issues like serial killing, rape and psychosis. He understands the mind of the criminally insane and the obsessive, and brings a chilling realism to the plots. The main character is Dr. Alex Delaware, a clinical psychologist who is brought in to track down the psychopaths and violent criminals, responsible for crimes against society. The situations are explored in depth, and the procedures are authentically described, drawn from the author's own experience. The plots are well constructed and intricate, and build in tension to a horrifying climax.

Publications

>*Over the edge*   Macdonald   1984
>*When the bough breaks*   Macdonald   1985
>
>ALEX DELAWARE
>
>*Shrunken heads*   1985
>*Blood test*   1986
>*The butcher's theatre*   1988
>*Silent partner*   1989
>*Time bomb*   1990
>*Private eyes*   1991
>(All published by Macdonald.)
>*Devil's waltz*   Little, Brown   1992

Now read
Robert Ludlum, David Morrell, Margaret Yorke.

Ludlum, Robert

American. Born in New York in 1927, and educated to university level in Connecticut. He served in the US Marines, 1945–47, and started his career in the theatre, both as actor and producer. He became a freelance writer in 1969.

He writes political thrillers with a deep awareness of current events and contemporary history. The plots are intricate and inventive, with linked sub-plots and great psychological insight into the characters. The heroes have a strong sense of social justice and patriotism, and engage in power struggles to ensure that right prevails. The books are often violent, even brutal, but are very well-written, and deserve their popularity on both sides of the Atlantic.

Publications

> *The Scarlatti inheritance* 1971
> *The Ostermann weekend* 1972
> *The Matlock paper* 1973
> *The Rhinemann exchange* 1975
> *The road to Gandolfo* 1976
> *The Gemini contenders* 1976
> *The Chancellor manuscript* 1977
> (Published by Hart Davis.)
> *The Matarese circle* 1979
> *The Bourne identity* 1980
> *The Parsifal mosaic* 1982
> *The Aquitaine progression* 1984
> *The Bourne supremacy* 1986
> *The Icarus agenda* 1988
> (Published by Granada.)
> *Trevayne* Grafton 1989
> *The Bourne ultimatum* Grafton 1990
> *The road to Omaha* HarperCollins 1992
> *The Scorpio illusion* HarperCollins 1993

Now read
Frederick Forsyth, David Morrell, Gerald Seymour.

MacLeod, Robert

British. A pseudonym for Bill Knox, whose biographical details appear in the Police work section.

Under this name, he writes fast-moving, action-filled thrillers set mainly in foreign locations. They are pure escapism, well-crafted, but without the intricacy of plot and depth of characterisation found in some writers in the genre. The foreign settings are accurately described, from the author's own experiences as a journalist. There are three series: one featuring Jonathan Gaunt, an agent in the

Scottish Remembrancer's Office, the second about Andrew Laird, a marine insurance claims investigator, and the third about Talos Cord.

Publications

TALOS CORD

Cave of bats 1964
Lake of fury 1966
Isle of dragons 1967
Place of mists 1969
Path of ghosts 1971
Nest of vultures 1973

JONATHAN GAUNT

A property in Cyprus 1970
A killing in Malta 1972
A burial in Portugal 1973
A witch-dance in Bavaria 1975
A pay-off in Switzerland 1977
Incident in Iceland 1979
A problem in Prague 1981
A legacy from Tenerife 1984
The money mountain 1987
Spanish maze game Century 1990

ANDREW LAIRD

All other perils 1974
Dragonship 1976
Salvage job 1978
Cargo risk 1980
Mayday from Malaga 1983
A cut in diamonds 1985
Witchline 1988
(All published by Hutchinson, except where stated.)

Now read
Evelyn Anthony, Clive Cussler, Michael Gilbert.

McDonald, Gregory

American. Born in Shrewsbury, Massachusetts, in 1937. He gained a BA at Harvard University, and became a journalist on the *Boston Globe*, until 1973, when he decided to be a self-employed writer. He won the Mystery Writers of America Edgar Allan Poe Award in 1975 and 1977.

He writes fast-moving, humorous thrillers, with clever plots and likeable characters. He has a real gift for witty wise-cracking dialogue, which carries the book along well. The main character is Irwin 'Fletch' Fletcher, an investigative journalist specialising in crime reporting. He becomes mixed up with eccentric criminals in most of the books, and in one or two becomes involved with the law in the shape of Inspector Francis Xavier Flynn, who also merits a series of his own. Flynn is a quirky detective, with his own peculiar way of approaching a case. The books are thoroughly good reads, if not to be taken seriously.

Publications

FLETCH

(in chronological order of reading)
Fletch won   1985
Fletch, too   1987
Fletch and the Widow Bradley   1981
Fletch   1975
Confess, Fletch   1977
Fletch forever   1978
Fletch's fortune   1979
Fletch's Moxie   1983
Fletch and the man who ...   1984
Carioca Fletch   1984

FLYNN

Flynn   1976
Snatched   1980
The buck passes Flynn   1982
Flynn's Inn   1985
(All published by Gollancz.)

Now read
Gerald Hammond, Tim Heald, Neville Steed.

Morrell, David

American. He is Professor of American Literature at the University of Iowa. He wrote his first book, *First blood* in 1972, with moderate success. It was only when it was filmed as 'Rambo' that he became a bestselling author, and his later books have been highly praised.

He writes tautly-constructed thrillers, full of violent action and mounting tension. The 'Rambo' books are particularly violent, the others less so, though they are uncompromisingly tough. The plots of his later books are intricate and ingenious, with greater depth of characterisation than the early ones.

Publications

First blood   Barrie & Jenkins   1972
Rambo: First blood part II   Arrow   1985

Testament   Chatto   1976
Last reveille
The totem   Pan   1981
Blood oath   Severn House   1989
The hundred-year Christmas

The Brotherhood of the Rose   NEL   1985
The Fraternity of the Stone   NEL   1986
The League of Night and Fog   NEL   1987
The fifth profession   Headline   1990
The covenant of the flame   Headline   1991

Now read
Robert Ludlum, Gerald Seymour.

Myers, Paul

British. He is a record producer, working with classical musicians in major recording studios all over the world. He has also produced recordings of the spoken word, and has been responsible for the soundtracks of films and television programmes. He lived for some years in New York, where he was a frequent broadcaster with his own series.

His novels, not surprisingly, have a musical background. His hero is a concert pianist, Mark Holland, who is also a spy, using his concert tours as a cover. The plots are well-constructed, with plenty of action and intrigue, but have authentic details about the world of music. The characters are rounded, and developed through the books, and the locations are vividly described.

Publications

MARK HOLLAND

Deadly variations   1985
Deadly cadenza   1986
Deadly aria   1987
Deadly sonata   1987
Deadly score   1988
Deadly crescendo   1989
(Published by Constable.)

Concerto   Century   1993

Now read
Evelyn Anthony, Michael Gilbert, Robert MacLeod.

Royce, Kenneth

British. Born in Croydon in 1920. He served in several Rifle Regiments during the Second World War, reaching the rank of Captain, then set up in business as a travel agent in London. He has been a full-time writer since 1973, and lives in Andover.

He wrote a number of adventure stories with foreign settings in the 1960s, with intricate plots and colourful, authentic locations. They were fast-moving and gripping. His later books have been based in England, featuring the XYY department, with Spider Scott and Detective Inspector George Bulman. The first four of the series were adapted for television. This series has greater depth of characterisation, with ingenious plots and a lot of atmosphere. Ken Royce says that he only ever plans a broad outline of a story, and he finds that structure and realism come instinctively.

Publications

> *My turn to die*   Barker   1958
> *The soft-footed Moor*   Barker   1959
> *The long corridor*   1960
> *No paradise*   1961
> *The night seekers*   1962
> *The angry island*   1963
> *The day the wind dropped*   1964
> *Bones in the sand*   1967
> *A peck of salt*   1968
> (Published by Cassell.)
> *A single to Hong Kong*   1969
> *The woodcutter operation*   1975
> *Bustillo*   1976
> *The Satan touch*   1978
> *The third arm*   1980
> *Channel assault*   1982
> *The Stalin account*   1984
> *The President is dead*   1988
> *Fall-out*   1989
> *Exchange of doves*   1990
> *The proving ground*   1991
> *A wild justice*   1992
> (Published by Hodder.)

SPIDER SCOTT AND GEORGE BULMAN

The XYY man   1970
The concrete boot   1971
The miniatures frame   1972
Spider underground   1974
Trap Spider   1974
The crypto man   1984

The Mosley receipt 1985
No way back 1986
(All published by Hodder.)

Now read
William Haggard, Paul Myers.

Russell, Martin

British. Born in Bromley, Kent in 1934, and educated at the Grammar School there. He did National Service in the Royal Air Force, before becoming a journalist working on local newspapers in Kent. He has been a full-time novelist since 1974.

He writes psychological thrillers rather than fast-moving stories full of action. His books are low-key, with the suspense coming from the criminal's actions, and the tension building slowly to an ending which often has an unexpected twist. He explores the criminal mind with depth and precision. He has written one short series, but most of his books are individual studies of criminal motivation.

Publications

No through road 1961
No return ticket 1966
Danger money 1968
Hunt to a kill 1969
Advisory service 1971
Double hit 1973
The client 1975
Double deal 1976
Mr. T. 1977
Dial death 1977
Daylight robbery 1978
A dangerous place to dwell 1978
Touchdown 1979
Catspaw 1980
Backlash 1981
Rainblast 1982

The search for Sara   1983
The censor   1984
Domestic affair   1984
Prime target   1985
Dead heat   1986
The second time is easy   1987
House arrest   1988
Dummy run   1989
(All published by Collins.)

JIM LARKIN

Deadline   1971
Concrete evidence   1972
Crime wave   1974
Phantom holiday   1974
Murder by the mile   1975
(Published by Collins.)

Now read
Margaret Yorke.

Seymour, Gerald

British. He was a travelling reporter for Independent Television News before deciding to become a full-time writer. He lived in the Irish Republic for some years, which provided him with the background for some of his novels, but now lives with his family and dogs in the West Country.

His novels are action-filled political thrillers, often with a theme concerned with terrorism or political unrest. *Harry's game*, which was filmed for television, was about the IRA, and *Red fox* concerned a political kidnapping in Italy. The plots are tough and uncompromising, often violent, but the stories are convincing, and well-constructed.

Publications

Harry's game   1975

> The glory boys   1976
> Kingfisher   1977
> Red fox   1979
> The contract   1980
> Archangel   1982
> In honour bound   1984
> Song in the morning   1986
> Field of blood   1988
> (Published by Collins.)
> Home run   Harvill   1989
> Condition black   Collins Harvill   1991
> Journeyman tailor   HarperCollins   1992

Now read
Frederick Forsyth, Jack Higgins, Robert Ludlum.

Sherwood, John

British. Born in 1913. He worked for the BBC External Service for many years, and wrote his first novel in 1949. He wrote a number of thrillers in the 1950s, and then had a long gap until his retirement. He began to write again with a detective story set in the BBC in the 1930s, and after that began his series featuring Celia Grant, a horticulturalist, who owns a nursery, and whose travels in search of plants and gardens lead her into mystery and adventure. The plots are ingenious and intricate, and full of detail about plants and gardening – John Sherwood is obviously a dedicated and knowledgeable gardener. The books have a good pace, interesting characters, and exotic settings.

Publications

MR. BLESSINGTON

> The disappearance of Dr. Bruderstein   Collins   1949
> Mr. Blessington's plot   Collins   1951
> Ambush for Anatol   Collins   1952
> Vote for poison   Collins   1956

The half hunter   Ian Henry   1977
Honesty will get you nowhere   Gollancz   1977
A shot in the arm   Gollancz   1982

CELIA GRANT

Green trigger fingers   1984
A botanist at bay   1985
The mantrap garden   1986
Flowers of evil   1987
Menacing groves   1988
Bouquet of thorns   1989
(Published by Gollancz.)
Sunflower plot   Macmillan   1990
The hanging garden   Macmillan   1992
Creeping Jenny   Macmillan   1993

Now read
Evelyn Anthony, Douglas Clark, Gwen Moffat.

Steed, Neville

British. He was born in the West Country, and read law at Oxford. He worked in advertising for some years, writing and directing television commercials. He is widely travelled, and his interests – toy collecting, motoring and the cinema – are reflected in his books. He has now returned to the West Country, with his wife and four sons, to write full-time.

His books are fast-moving, witty and intriguing. The hero is Peter Marklin, a dealer in second-hand tin-plate toys, living on the South Coast, who becomes involved in all sorts of crime as he pursues his business. The dialogue is crisp and funny, and Marklin and his eccentric friend Gus are thoroughly likeable characters. There is an element of Chandler and Hammett about the books, though Marklin is by no means as tough as their private eyes. He has recently created a new series, set in the 1930s, about a private eye called Johnny Black.

Publications

PETER MARKLIN

Tinplate 1986
Die-cast 1987
Chipped 1988
Clockwork 1989
Wind up 1990
Boxed-in Century 1991
Dead cold Century 1992

JOHNNY BLACK

Black eye 1989
Black mail 1990

Hallowes hell (a supernatural thriller) Headline 1990
(All published by Weidenfeld & Nicolson except where
stated)

Now read
Gerald Hammond, Tim Heald, Gregory McDonald.

Underwood, Michael

British. His real name is John Michael Evelyn. He was born in
Worthing, Sussex in 1916, and educated at Charterhouse School and
Christ Church, Oxford, where he gained an MA. He was called to
the Bar in 1939, before joining the army. After the war, he joined the
Department of Public Prosecutions, from which he retired in 1976.

His first novel was published in 1954, and he has written
prolifically since then. All his books are connected with the law,
either through police investigation or, more often, through legal
officers and trials. They are well-constructed, with logical plots and
excellent descriptions of the legal process. The characters, whether
police, lawyers or criminals, are credible and the action is sustained
until the end of the story. There are several series, the most recent
featuring Rosa Epton, a young lawyer/detective.

Publications

INSPECTOR SIMON MANTON

Murder on trial   1954
Murder made absolute   1955
Death on remand   1956
False witness   1957
Lawful pursuit   1958
Arm of the law   1959
Cause of death   1960
Death by misadventure   1960
Adam's case   1961
(Published by Hammond & Hammond.)
The case against Philip Quest   1962
Girl found dead   1963
The crime of Colin Wise   1964
The anxious conspirator   1965

RICHARD MONK

The man who died on Friday   1967
The man who died too soon   1968

A crime apart   1966
The shadow game   1969
(Published by Macdonald.)
The silent liars   1970
A trout in the milk   1971
Reward for a defector   1973

NICK ATTWELL

The juror   1975
Menaces, menaces   1976
The fatal trip   1977
Murder with malice   1977
Crooked wood   1978

ROSA EPTON

A pinch of snuff   1974
Anything but the truth   1979
Smooth justice   1979
Victim of circumstances   1980
Crime upon crime   1980
Double jeopardy   1981
Goddess of death   1982
A party to murder   1984
Death in camera   1984
The hidden man   1985
Death at Deepwood Grange   1986
The uninvited corpse   1987
The injudicious judge   1987
Dual enigma   1988
Rosa's dilemma   1990
Dangerous business   1990
The seeds of murder   1991
Guilty conscience   1992
(All published by Macmillan.)

Now read
Michael Gilbert, Sara Woods.

Woods, Sara

British. Born in Bradford in 1922, and educated privately. She worked in a bank and in a solicitor's office in London during the Second World War, and then became a pig breeder. She went back to office work as a company secretary, 1954–58, and then emigrated to Nova Scotia, where she was Registrar at Saint Mary's University, Halifax. She died in 1987.

Her books are all concerned with the legal process, and feature trial scenes. They feature a London barrister, Antony Maitland, and his irascible uncle, Nicholas Harding, Head of Chambers. Maitland is a crusader, always on the side of the underdog, which leads him to take on seemingly impossible cases, and to act as unofficial detective to find new evidence in his clients' favour. The books are urbane and civilised, with touches of humour, and a wealth of detail about the work of barristers. The plots are often slightly implausible, but the action carries them along and sustains the reader's interest. There are good contrasting characters in Maitland and Harding, and domestic interest in Maitland's wife Jenny and their friends outside the legal profession. Most of the books are set in London, but a few are set in the Yorkshire Dales, where the Maitlands have farmer friends.

Publications

Bloody instructions   1962
Malice domestic   1962
The taste of fears   1963
Error of the moon   1963
Trusted like the fox   1964
This little measure   1964
The windy side of the law   1965
Though I know she lies   1965
Enter certain murderers   1966
Let's choose executioners   1966
The case is altered   1967
And shame the devil   1967
Knives have edges   1968
Past praying for   1968
Tarry to be hanged   1969
An improbable fiction   1970
Serpent's tooth   1971
The knavish crown   1971
They love not poison   1972
(All published by Collins.)
Yet she must die   1973
Enter the corpse   1973
Done to death   1974
A show of violence   1975
My life is done   1976
The law's delay   1977
A thief or two   1977
Exit murderer   1978

This fatal writ   1979
Proceed to judgment   1979
They stay for death   1980
Weep for her   1980
Cry guilty   1981
Dearest enemy   1981
Enter a gentlewoman   1982
Villains by necessity   1982
Most grievous murder   1982
Call back yesterday   1983
The lie direct   1983
Where should he die   1983
The bloody book of law   1984
Murder's out of tune   1984
Defy the devil   1984
An obscure grave   1985
Away with them to prison   1985
Put out the light   1985
Nor live so long   1986
Naked villainy   1987
(All published by Macmillan.)

Now read
Michael Gilbert, Michael Underwood.

Yorke, Margaret

British. Born in Surrey in 1924, and educated at Godalming. She served in the WRNS in the Second World War. She worked as a school secretary, and in bookselling, for a time, and she was an Assistant Librarian at St. Hilda's College, Oxford, 1959–60, and Library Assistant at Christ Church, Oxford, 1963–65. Researching her books has given her an interest in penology and law reform.

She was Chairman of the Crime Writers' Association in 1979. She lives in Aylesbury, Buckinghamshire.

Her first books were family stories about the problems of ordinary people, but she says that she was tempted to stir up the plots with some violent action. This feeling led naturally on to crime fiction, and she modelled her style on other successful women authors. Her later books have not been so much 'whodunnits' but what she calls 'whydunnits', and have been concerned with the motivation for crime. She is a master of the psychological thriller, concentrating on character rather than action.

Publications

PATRICK GRANT

Dead in the morning   Bles   1970
Silent witness   Bles   1971
Grave matters   Bles   1973
Mortal remains   Bles   1974
Cast for death   1976

No medals for the Major   Bles   1974
The cost of silence   1977
The point of murder   1978
Death on account   1979
The scent of fear   1980
The hand of death   1981
Devil's work   1982
Find me a villain   1983
The smooth face of evil   1984
Intimate kill   1985
Safely to the grave   1986
Evidence to destroy   1987
Speak for the dead   1988
Crime in question   Mysterious Press   1989
Admit to murder   Mysterious Press   1990
A small deceit   1991
Criminal damage   1992
(All published by Hutchinson, except where stated.)

Now read
Martin Russell.

385

WAR STORIES

Surprisingly, in view of the enormous interest which is still shown in both the First and Second World Wars, there are very few novelists who write about them. There are a number of rather violent and ephemeral paperbacks, without any discernible literary merit, but not many well-constructed novels. Fortunately, the authors who do write war stories tend to write consistently and fairly frequently.

Some of the books listed would fall equally well into other categories; Sea stories and Adventure stories in particular. They appear here, though, because they are about specific areas of war, and follow the fortunes of one particular character or group of characters.

Bickers, Richard Townshend

British. He was born in India, and educated in England at St. Paul's School. He volunteered for the RAF at the beginning of the Second World War, and served as a regular officer until 1957. Since then he has travelled widely, and lived in many countries. He is a linguist, with a fluent knowledge of nine European and four Oriental languages.

He writes straightforward, action-filled novels about the pilots of the RAF in the Second World War. His own experiences add realism and accuracy to his descriptions of service life in conditions of war, and its effect on pilots. The flying sequences and battles are vividly and graphically portrayed, with an atmosphere of tension. He writes similar stories about the First World War, as Richard Leslie.

Publications

Summer of no surrender   1976
Desert falcons   1977
My enemy came nigh   1978
Beaufighters   1979
Air strike   1980
Operation Fireball   1980
Sea strike   1980
Battle climb   1981
Bombs gone   1981
Operation Thunderflash   1981
Burning blue   1982
Panther Squadron   1982
Target ahead   1982
Eagles, crying flames   1983
The killing zone   1983
Bomb burst   1985
While fates permit   1985
The bombing run   1986
Cauldron   1987
Torpedo attack   1987

DAEDALUS QUARTET

The gifts of Jove   1983

A time for haste   1984
Too late the morrow   1984
The sure recompense   1985

as Richard Leslie
Dusk patrol   1980
Bloodied hawks   1981
The sky aflame   1981
Fire's breath   1982
Night raiders   1982
Sunset flight   1982
Fire of spring   1983
No wrath of men   1983

THE HERACLES TRILOGY

Trouble in the wind   1984
The fateful dawn   1984
Under a shrieking sky   1984

The thundering line   1984
Dawn readiness   1985
The raging skies   1985
Hunters   1986
(All published by Hale.)

Now read
Robert Jackson, Leo Kessler.

Cornwell, Bernard

British. He was born in London and grew up in South Essex. He graduated from London University, and worked for the BBC for seven years, mostly as a producer on 'Nationwide', before going to Northern Ireland to take charge of the Current Affairs Department. In 1978, he became Editor of 'Thames at Six' for Thames Television. His wife is an American, and they lived in the USA for several years before returning to England to settle in the West Country.

He writes war stories set in the period of the Peninsular War. The hero is Richard Sharpe, a member of a regiment of foot, who sees action throughout the campaign in Northern Spain and Portugal. The novels are deeply researched and historically accurate. The battle scenes are vividly and authentically described, and the details about army life in the nineteenth century realistic and honest. The feelings of men at war in a foreign country are convincingly portrayed, and there is an atmosphere of tension which pervades the books.

Publications

SHARPE

Sharpe's rifles   1988
Sharpe's eagle   1980
Sharpe's gold   1981
Sharpe's company   1982
Sharpe's sword   1983
Sharpe's enemy   1984
Sharpe's honour   1985
Sharpe's regiment   1986
Sharpe's siege   1987
Sharpe's Waterloo   1990
(All published by Collins.)
Rebel   HarperCollins   1993

Wildtrack   Michael Joseph   1988
Sea lord   Michael Joseph   1989
Crackdown   Joseph   1990
Scoundrel   Joseph   1992 – all four are sea stories

Now read
Sea stories for books about the war at sea in the period.

Harris, John

British. He was born in Rotherham in 1916, and started work as a reporter on a local weekly newspaper in 1932, progressing to writing features on a provincial daily. He gave up his job, and set out to cycle to Cornwall, where he found a job as deckhand on a tanker. He returned to England to join the RAF at the start of the Second World War, and flew until he was shot down. After six months in hospital, he went back to the Navy, and served in Africa and the Channel in high-speed launches. After the War he returned to journalism as a cartoonist on the *Sheffield Telegraph*, but became a full-time novelist in 1954. He lives near Chichester.

His adventurous career has given him a wealth of experience, which he uses as background to his novels. He writes books about the Second World War, in all spheres of action, but mainly in Italy and North Africa. Though the books are full of action and adventure, they are based on actual campaigns in the war, and the details are authentic. The plots are well-constructed, and the characters and dialogue convincing. He has also written books about military history, and some fiction for children. As Max Hennessey, he wrote sea stories, books about the RFC in the First World War, and a trilogy about the army in Victorian times. John Harris died in 1992.

Publications

> *The lonely voyage*   1951
> *Hallelujah corner*   1952
> *The sea shall not have them*   1953
> *The claws of mercy*   1955
> *The sleeping mountain*   1958
> *The road to the coast*   1959
> *Sunset at Sheba*   1960
> *Covenant with death*   1961
> *Getaway*   1961
> *The spring of malice*   1962
> *The unforgiving wind*   1963
> *Vardy*   1964
> *The Cross of Lazzaro*   1965
> *The old trade of killing*   1966
> *Light Cavalry action*   1967
> *Right of reply*   1968
> *A kind of courage*   1972
> *Ride out the storm*   1975

Take or destroy 1976
Army of shadows 1977
Fox from his lair 1978
Corporal Cotton's little war 1979
Swordpoint 1980
North strike 1981
Live free or die 1982
Harkaway's Sixth Column 1983
Funny place to hold a war 1984
Up for grabs 1985
Thirty days war 1986
China Seas 1987
Picture of defeat 1988
So far from God 1989
Flawed banner 1991
The quick boat men 1992

IRA PENALUNA

The mustering of the hawks 1971
The mercenaries 1968
The Courtney entry 1970 (about the early days of
  aviation)

as Max Hennessey

KELLY MAGUIRE

The lion at sea 1977
The dangerous years 1978
Back to battle 1979

CAVALRY TRILOGY

Soldier of the Queen 1980
Regimental lance 1981
The iron stallions 1982

The bright blue sky 1982

The challenging heights　1983
Once more the hawks　1984
(All published by the Hutchinson Group.)

Now read
Robert Jackson, Douglas Scott.

Jackson, Robert

British. Born in 1941, and educated at Richmond School, Yorkshire. He has been a full-time author since 1969, specialising in aviation and military history. He has travelled extensively, can speak five languages, and has flown every type of aircraft from gliders to jets. He was Public Relations Officer for the Royal Air Force Volunteer Reserve for many years, and is a consultant to a helicopter company in the north-east of England. He lectures on pilot navigation in his spare time.

He writes about the RAF in the Second World War, and after, in action-packed novels about Hurricane Squadron. The plots are fast-moving, and the books are easy to read. Plot is more important than character, but he captures the atmosphere of war, and the tension experienced by pilots, in an authentic way.

Publications

HURRICANE SQUADRON

Yeoman goes to war　1978
Squadron scramble　1978
Target Tobruk　1979
Malta victory　1980
Mosquito Squadron　1981
Operation Diver　1981
Tempest Squadron　1981
The last battle　1982
Operation Firedog　1982
Korean combat　1983
Venom Squadron　1983
Hunter Squadron　1984

Desert commando   1986
Partisan!   1987
Attack at night   1988
Wind of death   1990
Battle of Britain: a novel of 1940   1990
The Romanov mission   1991
The last secret   1991
(Published by Weidenfeld & Nicolson.)

Now read
R. T. Bickers/R. Leslie, Leo Kessler.

Kessler, Leo

German. Born in 1926. He came to England before the Second World War, and joined the 52nd Armoured Reconnaissance Regiment as a volunteer in 1943. He studied in England and Germany after the war, and became a University teacher in England and America, and later in Germany, where he also acted as German Correspondent for the *Times Educational Supplement*. He became a full-time writer in 1973, and writes under several pseudonyms.

He writes prolifically about the German Forces in the Second World War. The books are little more than thrillers with a wartime setting, but are extremely popular, and have the advantage of presenting the war from the opposing side. Most of the books are in series, about all aspects of the armed forces. Most of them appeared in paperback originally.

Publications

COSSACKS

Black Cossacks   Severn House   1977
Sabres of the Reich   Futura   1976
The mountain of skulls   Severn House   1978
Breakthrough   Futura   1979

OTTO STAHL

Otto's phoney war   1981

Otto's blitzkrieg   1982
Otto and the Reds   1982
Otto and the Yanks   1983
Otto and the SS   1984
Otto and the Himmler love-letters   1984

ROMMEL

Ghost division   1981
Massacre   1979

SEA WOLVES

Sink the Scharnhorst   1982
Death to the Deutschland   1982

STORM TROOP

Storm troop   1983
Blood mountain   1983
Valley of the assassins   1984
Red assault
Himmler's gold   1986
Fire over Kabul   1982
Wave of terror   1983
Fire over Africa   1984

STUKA SQUADRON

The black knights   1983
The hawks of death   1983
The tank busters   1984
Blood mission   1984

WOTAN/PANZER DIVISION

SS Panzer Division   1975
Death's head   1978
Claws of steel   1978
Guns at Cassino   1978
The Hess assault   1987
The march on Warsaw   1988

Devil's shield   1979
Blood and ice   1987
The sand panthers   1987
Hammer of the Gods   1979
Forced march   1986
Counter attack   1979
Hell fire   1978
Panzer hunt   1979
Slaughter ground   1980
Flash point   1980
Cauldron of blood   1981
Schirmer's head hunters   1981
Whores of war   1986
Schirmer's death legions   1983
Death ride   1986
Slaughter at Salerno   1985
March or die   1986
The outcasts   1986

REBEL

Cannon fodder   1986
The die-hards   1987
Death match   1988
Breakout   1988

SUBMARINE

The wolf pack   1985
Operation deathwatch   1985
Convoy to catastrophe   1986
Fire in the west   1986
Flight to the Reich   1987
(Dates given are for hardback editions.)

(Published by Macdonald and Century in hardback
   and Futura in paperback.)

SS WOTAN

Assault on Baghdad   Severn House   1992

Flight from Moscow   Severn House   1992
Fire over Serbia   Severn House   1993

Operation long jump   Severn House   1993

 as Charles Whiting
Sabres in the sun   Century   1991
The Baltic run   Severn House   1993

Now read
R. T. Bickers, Sven Hassel.

MacAlan, Peter

British. Born in Coventry in 1943. He is an investigative journalist. His novels are all set in the Second World War, but with a background of suspense and intrigue, in the Intelligence Service, rather than actual battle scenes. They have taut plots, and good characterisation, with the tension sustained to the end.

Publications

The Judas battalion   1983
Airship   1984
The confusion   1985
Kitchener's gold   1986
The Valkyrie directive   1987
The doomsday decree   1988
(All published by W. H. Allen.)

Now read
Douglas Scott; see also Adventure stories.

Scott, Douglas

British. Born in Dundee in 1926. He was educated at the Dundee School of Navigation, and joined the Merchant Navy, serving in the

Second World War. He became a journalist after the war, but turned to writing fiction in 1977.

He writes long, exciting stories of the Second World War, with either an intelligence or a naval setting. The plots are intricate and well-constructed, and the scenes of action are gripping and authentic. There is a greater depth of characterisation in his work than in some of the other writers in the genre.

Publications

> *The spoils of war* 1977
> *The gifts of Artemis* 1979
> *The burning of the ships* 1980
> *Die for the Queen* 1981
> *In the face of the enemy* 1982
> *The hanged man* 1983
> *Chains* 1984
> *Eagle's blood* 1985
> *The albatross run* 1986
> *Shadows* 1987
> *Whirlpool* 1988
> (All published by Century Hutchinson.)

Now read
Peter MacAlan; see also Sea stories and Adventure stories.

WOMEN DETECTIVES

A whole new field is developing in the genre of detective stores. There have always been women detectives, from the 'golden age' of the 1930s, when Miss Marple and Miss Silver were created, to their modern equivalents like Melinda Pink and Celia Grant. Some of them have been listed in the first edition of *Now read on*. All these ladies, were, however, gifted amateurs, who were allowed to assist the police in their enquries.

The contemporary woman detective is a professional; either a member of the police force or a licensed private detective. They solve cases, not through intuition, but by using orthodox police methods. All of them have to compete in what has been essentially a man's world.

It is no surprise to find that the authors in this new field are, without exception, women.

Cross, Amanda

American. Real name Carolyn Heilbrun. Born in New Jersey in
1926. Educated at Wellesley College, Mass. and Columbia
University, New York, where she is now Professor of English. She
writes literary biography and criticism under her own name, but has
written several detective stories under her pen name. These feature a
university lecturer, Professor Kate Fansler, as detective, and are
usually set on a university campus or in academic circles.

The books are of a very high literary standard, without undue
violence, though they usually include a murder. The characterisation
has real depth and the situations have been carefully researched to
provide authenticity. The author says that she began to write
detective stories because she could find none that she wanted to read,
and because she wanted to create a female character in the genre
who did not provide a mere decoration or sex object. She
acknowledges that accusations of snobbery are probably justified. 'I
am myself, that apparently rare anomaly, an individual who likes
courtesy and intelligence, but would like to see the end of
stereotyped sex roles, and convention that arises from the fear of
change. I loathe violence, and do not consider sex a spectator sport.
One day Kate Fansler sprang from my brain to counter these things I
loathe, to talk with wit, and to offer to those who like it the company
of people I consider civilised.'

Publications

KATE FANSLER

In the last analysis   1964
The James Joyce murder   1967 (rep. Virago   1989)
Poetic justice   1970
The Theban mysteries   1972
The question of Max   1976
A death in the faculty   1981
Sweet death, kind death   1984 (rep. Virago   1988)
(All published by Gollancz.)
No word from Winifred   Virago   1987
A trap for fools   Virago   1989

Now read
P. D. James, D. L. Sayers.

Fraser, Antonia

British. Born in London in 1932, the daughter of Lord and Lady Longford, both prolific writers. She was awarded a BA in History from Lady Margaret Hall, Oxford in 1953. She married Hugh Fraser in 1956, and had six children. She began writing children's books in 1954, and moved on to historical biography, winning the Black Memorial Prize in 1970. She is now married to Harold Pinter, the playwright.

Her detective stories are uncomplicated, but well-researched, and have as their heroine an investigative TV journalist, Jemima Shore. The backgrounds are authentic, and the characterisation is rounded. Some of the plots are wildly improbable, but are totally in keeping with the author's style, which has zest and humour, with fast-moving action.

Publications

JEMIMA SHORE MYSTERIES

Quiet as a nun 1977
The wild island 1978
A splash of red 1981
Cool repentance 1982
Oxford blood 1985
Jemima Shore's first case (short stories) 1986
Your royal hostage 1987
(All published by Weidenfeld & Nicolson.)
The Cavalier case Bloomsbury 1990
Jemima Shore at the sunny grave and other stories
  Bloomsbury 1991

Now read
Amanda Cross, Lesley Grant-Adamson, Martha Grimes, John Sherwood.

Fyfield, Frances

British. She was born in South Derbyshire, and started her career as a criminal lawyer in Nottingham. She now lives and works in London, where most of her novels are set.

The main character, Helen West, is a Crown Prosecutor, who combines her work for the Home Office with some detection, in conjunction with her partner, Detective Chief Inspector Geoffrey Bailey. The novels are very atmospheric, written with sensitivity and perception. The feeling of psychological suspense is sustained throughout the book, enhanced by the ingenuity of the plots, Her villains, are, for the most part, misfits, and there is a great deal of empathy with their character flaws, though a sense of evil is also apparent. *Deep sleep* won the Crime Writers' Association Silver Dagger Award in 1991. She also writes psychological thrillers/horror stories under the name of Frances Hegarty.

Publications

> *A question of guilt*   1988
> *Shadows on the mirror*   1989
> *Trial by fire*   1990
> *Deep sleep*   1991
> (Published by Heinemann.)
> *Shadow plan*   Bantam   1993
>
> as Frances Hegarty
> *The playroom*   1991
> *Half light*   1992
> (Both published by Hamish Hamilton.)

Now read
Amanda Cross, Lesley Grant-Adamson, Jenny Melville.

Grafton, Sue

American. She was born in 1940, and is the daughter of C. W. Grafton, who is also a well-known writer of crime novels. Her writing career began with scriptwriting for the cinema and television, and she published straight novels before turning to crime. She now lives in Santa Barbara, California, which is the inspiration for her books. The novels feature Kinsey Milhone, a tough wisecracking private investigator. They are set in the fictional town of Santa Teresa, so named as a mark of her admiration for the thriller writer Ross Macdonald, whose novels are also set there. The plots are crisp and ingenious, and the dialogue is full of humour.

Publications

KINSEY MILHONE

A is for alibi   1985
B is for burglar   1986
C is for corpse   1987
D is for deadbeat   1987
E is for evidence   1988
F is for fugitive   1989
G is for gumshoe   1990
H is for homicide   1991
I is for innocent   1992
J is for judgment   1993
(All published by Macmillan.)

Now read
Susan Moody, Marcia Muller, Sara Paretsky.

McDermid, Val

British. She was born in Scotland, and has worked as a journalist since 1975, spending some time as a reporter for *The People* in Manchester. She is active in the National Union of Journalists, and is a former member of the NUJ Equality Council. All her novels are set in the world of investigative journalism, and reflect her own experience in their authenticity of detail, and knowledge of procedure. Her women characters are all feminists, and the detective featured in the first three novels, Lindsay Gordon, is a lesbian.

The plots are intricate and well-crafted, and the settings unusual: a girls' public school, the Greenham Common Peace Camp, and large-scale company fraud. Lindsay is assertive, shrewd and prepared to face personal danger to solve a case. The books show a sympathetic insight into the domestic life of lesbian couples, and the prejudices which they encounter.

Publications

LINDSAY GORDON

Report for murder   1987
Common murder   1989
Final edition   1991

KATE BRANNIGAN

Dead beat   1992
Kick back   1993
(All published by Women's Press.)

Now read
Sue Grafton, Marcia Muller.

McGown, Jill

British. She was born in Argyll in 1947, but moved to Corby at the age of ten. She started work in a solicitor's office, then joined the British Steel Corporation. She had the occasional short story published, and, on being made redundant, she turned to full-time writing. Her first novel, *A perfect match*, was published in 1983.

Her novels are police procedurals, set in a provincial town. Her detective, Judy Hill, was originally a Detective Sergeant, working with Detective Inspector Lloyd, her immediate superior and lover. In the last two novels, she has been promoted to Detective Inspector, and moved to a neighbouring town, in charge of her own team. Judy is a conscientious detective, proud of her achievements, and determined to be accepted on the same level as her male colleagues.

The novels are complex, with several sub-plots interwoven into the main thread. Characterisation is explored in depth, both in the police, and in the people they encounter in the course of their investigations. A good deal of research obviously goes into the setting of the book, whether it is in a school, a factory, or the life of a local VIP. Jill McGown also knows a good deal about the police force and the way in which it carries out its duties. The somewhat turbulent domestic life of Lloyd and Hill forms a secondary plot in all the books, and dovetails neatly with their police routine.

Publications

LLOYD AND HILL

A perfect match   1983
Redemption   1988
Death of a dancer   1989
The murder of Mrs. Austin and Mrs. Beale   1991
The other woman   1992
Murder… now and then   1993
(All published by Macmillan.)

Now read
Gwendoline Butler, Erica Quest.

Moffat, Gwen

British. She served in the ATS during the Second World War, and wanted to continue in an outdoor life afterwards. She took up climbing, and became the first woman guide to be appointed by the British Mountaineering Council. She has also been involved with Outward Bound schemes and Mountain Rescue. She lived for many years in the rock-climbing areas of Wales and the Lake District.

She wrote her first mystery story in 1973, and has also written travel books and a volume of autobiography. Her novels are very much concerned with climbing, and her detective, Melinda Pink, is a retired civil servant, still involved in mountaineering. The plots are intricate and well-constructed, with totally authentic detail of location and climbing techniques. Her last few books have been set in Canada and the United States, and arose from journeys that she made to Arizona and Colorado in particular. Again, the descriptions of the country and its people are accurate and perceptive. Her style is spare and crisp, with good dialogue, and her characterisation is penetrating and rounded.

Publications

MELINDA PINK

Lady with a cool eye   1973
Deviant death   1974
The corpse road   1975
Miss Pink at the edge of the world   1975
Hard option   1976
Over the sea to death   1976
A short time to live   1977
Persons unknown   1978
Die like a dog   1982
Last chance country   1983
Grizzly trail   1984
(Published by Gollancz.)
Snare   1988
The Stone Hawk   1989
Rage   1990
Raptor zone   1990
Veronica's sisters   1992

Pit bull   1991
The outside edge   1993
(Published by Macmillan.)

Now read
Frances Fyfield, John Sherwood.

Moody, Susan

British. She lives in Bedford, and is active in the field of creative writing, teaching and encouraging young authors. She is a former Chairman of the Crime Writer's Association and represents Britain in the International Association of Crime Writers. Her detective is a six-foot, beautiful, black woman called Penny Wanawake. Penny is probably the female equivalent of James Bond, with his taste for the good things in life. She handles tough situations with charm and humour, but can easily hold her own when the fighting starts. The novels are fast-moving with action filled plots, and wise-cracking dialogue, and are stylishly written.

Publications

> *Penny black*   1983   Macmillan
> *Penny dreadful*   1984   Macmillan
> *Penny post*   1985   Macmillan
> *Penny royal*   1986   Macmillan
> *Penny wise*   1988   Michael Joseph
> *Penny pinching*   1989   Michael Joseph
> *Penny saving*   1991   Michael Joseph

Now read
Sue Grafton, Val McDermid, Marcia Muller, Sara Paretsky.

Morice, Anne

British, real name Felicity Shaw. Born in Kent in 1918, and educated in London and Europe. She lived in Henley-on-Thames, until her death in 1991. Most of her family are connected with the theatre, and her husband is a film director.

All her books have a theatrical setting, and her main character is an actress, Tessa Crichton, married to a Scotland Yard Chief Inspector, Robin Price. Light-hearted and humorous, her books are in the tradition of the domestic murder story, without a great deal of violence. Her knowledge of the theatre gives authenticity to both plot and characters, and her dialogue is convincing.

Publications

TESSA CRICHTON SERIES

Death in the grand manor   1970
Murder in married life   1971

Death of a gay dog 1972
Murder on French leave 1973
Death and the dutiful daughter 1973
Death of a heavenly twin 1974
Killing with kindness 1974
Nursery tea and poison 1975
Death of a wedding guest 1976
Murder in mimicry 1977
Scared to death 1978
Murder in outline 1978
Death in the round 1980
The men in her death 1981
Hollow vengeance 1982
Sleep of death 1982
Murder post-dated 1983
Getting away with murder 1984
Dead on cue 1985
Publish and be killed 1986
Treble exposure 1987
Design for dying 1988
Fatal charm 1988
Planning for murder 1990
(All published by Macmillan.)

Now read
Simon Brett, Agatha Christie, Antonia Fraser, Ngaio Marsh, Patricia Moyes.

Muller, Marcia

American. She lives in northern California. In addition to her work as a novelist, Marcia Muller is an anthologist and critic. She has edited several collections of mystery stories, and produced in 1986 *The aficionado's guide to mystery and detective fiction*.

She pioneered the contemporary female private investigator novel, when she wrote *Edwin of the iron shoes* in 1977. Her main character is Sharon McCone, a tough Los Angeles private eye, who brings intelligence and perception to the seedy world in which she operates.

The plots are taut and well-characterised, and the dialogue moves at a cracking pace.

Publications

SHARON McCONE

Edwin of the iron shoes   Mysterious Press NY   1977
   Women's Press   1993
Ask the cards a question   Hale   1983
The Cheshire cat's eye   Hale   1984
Games to keep the dark away   Mysterious Press   1985
Trophies and dead things   Mysterious Press   1990
   Women's Press   1992
Where echoes live   Mysterious Press   1991
   Women's Press   1992
There's something in a Sunday   Women's Press   1992
The shape of dread   Women's Press   1992
Pennies on a dead woman's eyes   Women's Press 1993

Now read
Val McDermid, Susan Moody, Sara Paretsky.

Paretsky, Sara

American. She was born and brought up in Kansas, but now lives in Chicago with her husband and their golden retriever. She has a degree in finance and a PhD in history. She has had a variety of jobs, but now writes full-time. The novels are set in Chicago, and her knowledge of the city adds authenticity to the plots and their locations. Her detective is a tough, intelligent, uncompromising insurance investigator, V. I. Warshawski, known simply as V. I. Her books have received much critical acclaim, and she won the Crime Writers' Silver Dagger award in 1988 with *Toxic shock*. Some of the stories have recently been adapted for radio and the movies, with Kathleen Turner as V. I. The novels are very well written, with excellent detail in both plot and characterisation. The dialogue is witty and the style literary, though the action does not flag.

Publications

V. I. WARSHAWSKI

Indemnity only   Gollancz   1982
Deadlock   Gollancz   1984
Killing orders   Gollancz   1986
Bitter medicine   Gollancz   1987
Toxic shock   Gollancz   1988
Burn marks   Hamish Hamilton   1990
Guardian angel   Hamish Hamilton   1992

Now read
Frances Fyfield, Susan Moody, Marcia Muller.

Quest, Erica

British. The pseudonym of a husband and wife, whose real names have not been disclosed, though they are both successful authors.

These novels are police procedurals, set in the Cotswolds, and featuring Detective Chief Inspector Kate Maddox, recently promoted, and in charge of a murder squad, composed mainly of men. She has to battle with the resentment of her male colleagues, some of whom think that a woman is not capable of leading a team, while still coming to terms with the deaths of her husband and child in a car crash. The plots are credible and well-written, and the police procedures realistic and carefully researched. The characters are explored in depth, and grow in stature as the series proceeds.

Publications

KATE MADDOX

Death walk   Piatkus   1989
Cold coffin   Piatkus   1990
Model murder   Piatkus   1991
Deadly deceit   Piatkus   1992

Now read
Jennie Melville, Jill McGown.

Rowlands, Betty

British. Her career was in teaching, specialising in busines French and English, and in writing English language courses for foreign executives. She lives in Gloucestershire, and has three children and four grandchildren.

She won the *Sunday Express*/Veuve Clicquot Crime Short Story of the Year competition in 1988, and turned her hand to writing full length novels. Her detective is a crime writer, Melissa Craig, who has bought a cottage in the Cotswolds in which to write in peace. She stumbles on mysteries quite by accident, but her fertile imagination leads her into solving them.

The plots are well crafted, in the tradition of the straight-forward detective story. The dialogue is crisp, and there is a good deal of humour in the books, She draws on her own experience in teaching for some of the details and locations.

Publications

MELISSA CRAIG

A little gentle sleuthing   1990
Finishing touch   1991
Over the edge   1992
Exhaustive enquires   1993
(All published by Hodder.)

Now read
Gwen Moffat, John Sherwood.

LITERARY PRIZES AND AWARDS

Novels which have featured as prizewinners or runners-up in British and American genre fiction competitions are listed below; prizes awarded for literary-type fiction are not included. In cases where competitions make awards for non-fiction as well as fiction, only the fiction winners are cited here. The compilers acknowledge the assistance of the administrators of the prizes and awards in assembling this Appendix.

Angel Literary Prize
(East Anglian writers)

1984	Norman Lewis	*Voices from the old sea* (Penguin)
1987	Jan Marks	*Zeno was here*
1988	Ruth Rendell	*A house of stairs* (NAL Dutton)
1989	Rose Tremain	*Restoration* (Hamilton)
1990	Mike Ripley	*Angel hunt* (Collins)
1992	Elspeth Barker	*O Caledonia* (Hamilton/Penguin)

Boot's Romantic Novel of the Year
See Romantic Novelists Association Boot's Romantic Novel of the Year Award

British Science Fiction Association Award – novel

1990	Terry Pratchett	*Pyramids* (Gollancz)
1992	Dan Simmons	*The Fall of Hyperion* (Headline)

Arthur C. Clarke Award – for a science fiction novel

1989	Rachel Pollack	*Unquenchable fire* (Century Hutchinson)
1991	Colin Greenland	*Take back plenty* (Grafton)
1992	Pat Cadigan	*The synners* (Grafton)

Now read on

Catherine Cookson Award
(Work written in the Cookson tradition)

1992	Valerie Wood	*The sea is my companion* (Bantam)

Crime Writers' Association Awards

(Cartier Diamond Dagger – special achievement; Golden Handcuffs – substantial contribution to the genre; Last Laugh Award – humorous crime novel; '92 Award – for a novel set mostly in Europe; Rumpole Award – for a crime novel with a legal background; Gold Dagger – best crime novel; Silver Dagger – runner–up; John Creasey Memorial Award – best crime novel by a previously unpublished writer)

1955	Winston Graham	*The little walls* (Bodley Head)
	Runners-up	
	Leigh Howard	*Blind date*
	Ngaio Marsh	*Scales of justice* (Collins)
	Margot Bennett	*The man who didn't fly*
1956	Edward Grierson	*The second man*
	Runners-up	
	Sarah Gainham	*Time right deadly*
	Arthur Upfield	*Man of two tribes*
	J. J. Marric	
	(John Creasey)	*Gideon's week* (Ulverscroft)
1957	Julian Symons	*The colour of murder* (Papermac)
	Runners-up	
	Ngaio Marsh	*Off with his head* (Collins)
	George Milner	*Your money and your life* (Linford Mystery)
	Douglas Rutherford	*The long echo*
1958	Margot Bennett	*Someone from the past*
	Runners-up	
	Margery Allingham	*Hide my eyes* (Hogarth Press)
	James Byrom	*Or be he dead*
	John Sherwood	*Undiplomatic exit*
1959	Eric Ambler	*Passage of arms* (Fontana)
	Runners-up	
	James Mitchell	*A way back*
	Menna Gallie	*Strike for a kingdom*

1960	Gold Dagger	Lionel Davidson	*The night of Wenceslas* (Chivers)
		Runners-up	
		Mary Stewart	*My brother Michael* (Hodder)
		Julian Symons	*Progress of a crime*
1961	Gold Dagger	Mary Kelly	*The spoilt kill*
		Runners-up	
		John le Carré	*Call for the dead* (Penguin)
		Allan Prior	*One away*
1962	Gold Dagger	Joan Fleming	*When I grow rich* (Collins)
		Runners-up	
		Eric Ambler	*The light of day* (Oxford)
		Colin Watson	*Hopjoy was here* (Methuen)
1963	Gold Dagger	John le Carré	*The spy who came in from the cold* (Pan)
		Runners-up	
		Nicholas Freeling	*Guns before butter* (Penguin)
		William Haggard	*The high wire*
1964	Gold Dagger	H. R. F. Keating	*The perfect murder* (Mysterious Press)
	Best Foreign	Patricia Highsmith	*The two faces of January* (Heinemann)
		Runners-up	
		Gavin Lyall	*The most dangerous game* (Pan)
		Ross Macdonald	*The chill* (Allison & Busby)
1965	Gold Dagger	Ross Macdonald	*The far side of the dollar* (Allison & Busby)
	Best British	Gavin Lyall	*Midnight plus one* (Pan)
		Runners-up	
		Dick Francis	*For kicks* (Pan)
		Emma Lathen	*Accounting for murder* (Penguin)
1966	Gold Dagger	Lionel Davidson	*A long way to Shiloh*
	Best Foreign	John Ball	*In the heat of the night*
		Runner-up	
		John Bingham	*The double agent*

Now read on

Year	Award	Author	Title
1967	Gold Dagger	Emma Lathen	*Murder against the grain*
	Best British	Eric Ambler	*Dirty story* (Fontana)
		Runner-up	
		Colin Watson	*Lonely heart 4122* (Methuen)
1968	Gold Dagger	Peter Dickinson	*Skin deep*
	Best Foreign	Sebastian Japrisot	*The lady in the car* (No exit Press)
		Runner-up	
		Nicholas Blake	*The private wound* (Dent)
1969	Gold Dagger	Peter Dickinson	*A pride of heroes* (Mysterious Press)
	Silver Dagger	Francis Clifford	*Another way of dying*
	Best Foreign	Rex Stout	*The father hunt*
1970	Gold Dagger	Joan Fleming	*Young man I think you're dying* (Ulverscroft)
	Silver Dagger	Anthony Price	*The labyrinth makers* (Gollancz)
1971	Gold Dagger	James McClure	*The steam pig* (Coronet)
	Silver Dagger	P. D. James	*Shroud for a nightingale*
1972	Gold Dagger	Eric Ambler	*The Levanter* (Fontana)
	Silver Dagger	Victor Canning	*The rainbird pattern*
1973	Gold Dagger	Robert Littell	*The defection of A. J. Lewinter*
	Silver Dagger	Gwendoline Butler	*A coffin for Pandora*
	Creasey Award	Kyril Bonfiglioli	*Don't point that thing at me*
1974	Gold Dagger	Anthony Price	*Other paths to glory*
	Silver Dagger	Francis Clifford	*The Grosvenor Square goodbye*
	Creasey Award	Roger L. Simon	*The big fix*
1975	Gold Dagger	Nicholas Meyer	*The seven per cent solution* (Ulverscroft)
	Silver Dagger	P. D. James	*The black tower*
	Creasey Award	Sara George	*Acid drop*
1976	Gold Dagger	Ruth Rendell	*A demon in my view* (Hutchinson)
	Silver Dagger	James McClure	*Rogue eagle*
	Creasey Award	Patrick Alexander	*Death of a thin-skinned animal*
1977	Gold Dagger	John le Carré	*The honourable schoolboy* (Hodder)

	Silver Dagger	William McIlvanney	*Laidlaw* (Coronet)
	Creasey Award	Jonathan Gash	*The Judas pair* (Arrow)
1978	Gold Dagger	Lionel Davidson	*The Chelsea murders* (Cape)
	Silver Dagger	Peter Lovesey	*Waxwork* (Mysterious Press)
	Creasey Award	Paula Gosling	*A running duck* (Macmillan)
1979	Gold Dagger	Dick Francis	*Whip hand* (Pan)
	Silver Dagger	Colin Dexter	*Service of all the dead* (Macmillan)
	Creasey Award	David Serafin	*Saturday of glory* (Ulverscroft)
1980	Gold Dagger	H. R. F. Keating	*The murder of the Maharajah* (Mysterious Pr.)
	Silver Dagger	Ellis Peters	*Monk's hood* (Macmillan)
	Creasey Award	Liza Cody	*Dupe*
1981	Gold Dagger	Martin Cruz Smith	*Gorky Park* (Collins)
	Silver Dagger	Colin Dexter	*The dead of Jericho* (Macmillan)
	Creasey Award	James Leigh	*The ludi victor*
1982	Gold Dagger	Peter Lovesey	*The false Inspector Dew* (Macmillan)
	Silver Dagger	S. T. Haymon	*Ritual murder*
	Creasey Award	Andrew Taylor	*Caroline Minuscule* (Gollancz)
1983	Gold Dagger	John Hutton	*Accidental Crimes* (Portway)
	Silver Dagger	William McIlvanney	*The papers of Tony Veitch* (Hodder)
	Creasey Award	Carol Clemeau	*The Adriadne clue*
	(TIE)	Eric Wright	*The night the gods smiled* (Collins)
1984	Gold Dagger	B. M. Gill	*The twelfth juror* (Hodder)
	Silver Dagger	Ruth Rendell	*The tree of hands* (Hutchinson)
	Creasey Award	Elizabeth Ironside	*A very private enterprise* (Fontana)
1985	Gold Dagger	Paula Gosling	*Monkey puzzle* (Macmillan)
	Silver Dagger	Dorothy Simpson	*Last seen alive* (Sphere)
	Creasey Award	Robert Richardson	*The Latimer mercy*

Now read on

1986	Gold Dagger	Ruth Rendell	*Live flesh* (Hutchinson)
	Silver Dagger	P. D. James	*A taste for death* (Faber)
	Creasey Award	Neville Steed	*Tinplate* (Weidenfeld)
1987	Gold Dagger	Barbara Vine (Ruth Rendell)	*A fatal inversion* (Viking)
	Silver Dagger	Scott Turow	*Presumed innocent* (Bloomsbury)
	Creasey Award	Denis Kilcommons	*Dark apostle* (Bantam)
1988	Gold Dagger	Michael Dibdin	*Ratking* (Faber)
	Silver Dagger	Sara Paretsky	*Toxic shock* (Gollancz)
	Creasey Award	Janet Neel	*Death's bright angel* (Constable)
1989	Gold Dagger	Colin Dexter	*The wench is dead* (Macmillan)
	Silver Dagger	Desmond Lowden	*Shadow run* (Deutsch)
	Creasey Award	Annette Roome	*A real shot in the arm* (Hodder)
	Last Laugh	Mike Ripley	*Angel hunt* (Collins)
1990	Cartier Diamond Dagger	Julian Symons	(crime writer of the year)
	Gold Dagger	Reginald Hill	*Bones and silence* (Collins)
	Silver Dagger	Mike Phillips	*The late candidate* (Joseph)
	Creasey Award	Patricia Daniels Cornwell	*Postmortem* (Macdonald)
	Last Laugh	Simon Shaw	*Killer Cinderella* (Gollancz)
	'92 Award	Michael Dibdin	*Vendetta* (Faber)
	Rumpole Award	Frances Fyfield	*Trial by fire* (Heinemann)
1991	Cartier Diamond Dagger	Ruth Rendell	(crime writer of the year)
	Gold Dagger	Ruth Rendell	*King Solomon's carpet* (Viking)
	Silver Dagger	Frances Fyfield	*Deep sleep* (Heinemann)
	Creasey Award	Walter Mosley	*Devil in a blue dress* (Serpent's Tail)
	Last Laugh	Mike Ripley	*Angels in arms* (HarperCollins)
	'92 Award	Barbara Wilson	*Gaudi afternoon* (Virago)
1992	Cartier Diamond Dagger	Leslie Charteris	(lifetime achievement)
	Golden Handcuffs	Catherine Aird	*Catherine Aird collection* (Pan)

	Gold Dagger	Colin Dexter	*The way through the woods* (Macmillan)
	Silver Dagger	Liza Cody	*Bucket nut* (Chatto)
	Creasey Award	Minette Walters	*Ice house* (Macmillan)
	'92 Award	Timothy Williams	*Black August* (Gollancz)
	Rumpole Award	Peter Rawlinson	*Hatred and contempt* (Chapmans)
1993	Cartier Diamond Dagger	Ellis Peters	(lifetime achievement)

Fawcett Society Book Prize
(Substantial contribution to the understanding of women's position in society)

1983	Pat Barker	*Union Street* (Virago)
1985	Zoe Fairbairns	*Here today* (Methuen)
1987	Sheena McKay	*Redhill rococo* (Heinemann)
1989	Stevie Davies	*Boy blue* (Women's Press)
1991	Jennifer Dawson	*Judasland* (Virago)

David Higham Prize
(For a first work of fiction)

1989	Timothy O'Grady	*Motherland* (Chatto)
1990	Russell Celyn Jones	*Soldiers and innocents* (Cape)
1991	Elspeth Barker	*O Caledonia* (Hamilton/Penguin)
1992	John Loveday	*Halo* (Fourth Estate)

Historical Novel Prize in Memory of Georgette Heyer
(Outstanding previously unpublished historical novel)

1978	Rhona Martin	*Gallows wedding*
1979	Norah Lofts	*Day of the butterfly* (Ulverscroft)
1980	Lynn Guest	*Children of Hachiman*
1981	Valerie Fitzgerald	*Zemindar* (Bodley Head)
1982	No prize awarded	
1983	Kathleen Herbert	*Queen of the lightning* (Bodley Head)
1984	Alan Fisher	*The Terioki crossing* (Charnwood)
1985	Susan Kay	*Legacy* (Bodley Head)
1986	Michael Werron	*The cage* (Charnwood)

Now read on

1987	Patricia Wright	*I am England* (Bodley Head)
1988	No prize awarded	
1989	Margaret Birkhead	*The trust and treason* (Bodley Head)
1990	Janet Broomfield	*A fallen land* (Bodley Head)
1991	No prize awarded	

Winifred Holtby Prize
(For a regional novel)

1989	Shusha Guppy	*The blindfold horse* (Heinemann)
1990	Hilary Mantel	*Fludd* (Viking)
1991	Nino Ricci	*Lives of the saints* (Allison & Busby/ Minerva)
1992	Elspeth Barker	*O Caledonia* (Hamilton/Penguin)

Hugo Awards
(For science fiction in various categories, awarded by the World Science Fiction Convention; novels only are listed here)

1958	Fritz Leiber	*The big time* (Severn House)
1959	James Blish	*A case of conscience*
1960	Robert A. Heinlein	*Starship troopers*
1961	Walter M. Miller	*A canticle for Leibowitz*
1962	Robert A. Heinlein	*Stranger in a strange land* (New English Library)
1963	Philip K. Dick	*The man in the high castle* (Penguin)
1964	Clifford Simak	*Way station* (Eyre Methuen)
1965	Fritz Leiber	*The wanderer* (Dobson)
1966	Roger Zelazny	*And call me Conrad*
(TIE)	Frank Herbert	*Dune* (Gollancz)
1967	Robert A. Heinlein	*The moon is a harsh mistress* (New English Library)
1968	Roger Zelazny	*Lord of light* (Methuen)
1969	John Brunner	*Stand on Zanzibar* (Arrow)
1970	Ursula K. LeGuin	*The left hand of darkness* (Futura)
1971	Larry Niven	*Ringworld* (Gollancz)
1972	Philip José Farmer	*To your scattered bodies go* (Panther)
1973	Isaac Asimov	*The gods themselves* (Gollancz)
1974	Arthur C. Clarke	*Rendezvous with Rama* (Gollancz)
1975	Ursula K. LeGuin	*The dispossessed* (Panther)
1976	Joe Haldeman	*The forever war* (Futura)

1977	Kate Wilhelm	*Where late the sweet birds sang*
1978	Frederik Pohl	*Gateway* (Futura)
1979	Vonda N. McIntyre	*Dreamsnake* (Gollancz)
1980	Arthur C. Clarke	*The fountains of paradise* (Gollancz)
1981	Joan Vinge	*The snow queen* (Futura)
1982	C. J. Cherryh	*Downbelow Station* (Severn House)
1983	Isaac Asimov	*Foundation's edge* (Granada)
1984	David Brin	*Startide rising* (Bantam)
1985	William Gibson	*Neuromancer* (Gollancz)
1986	Orson Scott Card	*Ender's game* (Century)
1987	Orson Scott Card	*Speaker for the dead* (Century)
1988	David Brin	*The uplift war* (Bantam)
1989	C. J. Cherryh	*Cyteen* (3 volumes) (Warner)
1990	Dan Simmons	*The fall of Hyperion* (Headline)
1991	Lois McMaster Bujold	*The vor game* (Baen Books)
1992	Lois McMaster Bujold	*Barrayar* (Baen Books)

Macmillan Silver Pen Award
(For fiction)

1989	Molly Keane	*Loving and giving* (Deutsch/Sphere)
(TIE)	Marina Walker	*The lost father* (Chatto)
1990	V. S. Pritchett	*A careless widow* (short stories) (Chatto)
1991	Pauline Melville	*Shape-shifter* (Women's Press)
1992	John Arden	*Cogs tyrannic* (short stories) (Methuen)

Nebula Awards
(Science Fiction Writers of America; novels category only given here)

1965	Frank Herbert	*Dune* (Gollancz)
1966	Daniel Keyes	*Flowers for Algemon* (Gollancz)
(TIE)	Samuel R. Delany	*Babel-17* (Gollancz)
1967	Samuel R. Delany	*The Einstein intersection*
1968	Alexei Panshin	*Rite of passage* (Methuen)
1969	Ursula K. LeGuin	*The left hand of darkness* (Futura)
1970	Larry Niven	*Ringworld* (Gollancz)
1971	Robert Silverberg	*A time of changes* (Gollancz)
1972	Isaac Asimov	*The gods themselves* (Gollancz)
1973	Arthur C. Clarke	*Rendezvous with Rama* (Gollancz)

1974	Ursula K. LeGuin	*The dispossessed* (Panther)
1975	Joe Haldeman	*The forever war* (Futura)
1976	Frederik Pohl	*Man plus* (Gollancz)
1977	Frederik Pohl	*Gateway* (Futura)
1978	Vonda N. McIntyre	*Dreamsnake* (Gollancz)
1979	Arthur C. Clarke	*The fountains of paradise* (Gollancz)
1980	Gregory Benford	*Timescape* (Sphere)
1981	Gene Wolfe	*The claw of the conciliator* (Arrow)
1982	Michael Bishop	*No enemy but time* (Bantam)
1983	David Brin	*Startide rising* (Bantam)
1984	William Gibson	*Neuromancer* (Gollancz)
1985	Orson Scott Card	*Ender's game* (Century)
1986	Orson Scott Card	*Speaker for the dead* (Century)
1987	Pat Murphy	*The falling woman* (Headline Books)
1988	Lois McMaster Bujold	*Falling free* (Baen Books)
1989	Elizabeth Scarborough	*The healers war* (Bantam)
1991	Ursula K. LeGuin	*Tehanu: the last book of Earthsea* (Bantam)
1992	Michael Swanwick	*Stations of the tide* (Avon)

Romantic Novelists Association Boot's Romantic Novel of the Year Award

1980	Joanna Trollope	*Parson Harding's daughter* (Hutchinson)
1980	Mary Howard	*Mr. Rodriquez* (Collins)
1981	Gwendoline Butler	*Red staircase* (Collins)
1982	Valerie Fitzgerald	*Zemindar* (Bodley Head)
1983	Eva Ibbotson	*Magic flutes* (Century)
1984	Sheila Walsh	*High respectable marriage* (Hutchinson)
1985	Rosie Thomas	*Sunrise* (Piatkus/Fontana)
1986	Brenda Jagger	*Song twice over* (Collins)
1987	Marie Joseph	*A better world than this* (Century Hutchinson)
1988	Audrey Howard	*The Juniper bush* (Century Hutchinson)
1989	Sarah Woodhouse	*The peacock's feather* (Century)
1990	Reah Tannahill	*Passing glory* (Century)
1991	Susan Kay	*Phantom* (Doubleday/Transworld)
1992	June Knox-Mawer	*Sandstorm* (Weidenfeld)
1993	Cynthia Harrod-Eagles	*Emily* (Sidgwick)

Sagittarius Prize
(For a first novel by a writer over the age of 60)

1991	Juddith Hubback	*The sea has many voices* (Aiden Ellis)
1992	Hugh Leonard	*Parnell and the Englishwoman* (Deutsch)

W. H. Smith Thumping Good Read Award

1992	Robert Goddard	*Into the blue* (Bantam)

Sunday Times Book of the World Award – fiction

1988	David Lodge	*Nice work* (Secker & Warburg/Penguin)
1989	Rose Tremain	*Restoration* (Hamilton)
1990	J. M. Coetzee	*Age of iron* (Secker & Warburg)
1991	Michael Frayn	*A landing on the sun* (Viking)
1992	Hilary Mantel	*A place of greater safety* (Viking)

Betty Trask Prize and Awards
(For a first novel of a traditional or romantic nature by an author under 35)

1984	Ronald Frame	*Winter Journey* (Bodley Head)
(TIE)	Clare Nonhebel	*Cold showers* (Century)
	Runners-up	
	James Buchan	*A parish of rich women* (Hamilton)
	Helen Harris	*Playing fields in winter* (Century Hutchinson)
	Gareth Jones	*The disinherited* (Gollancz)
	Simon Rees	*The Devil's looking glass* (Methuen)
1985	Susan Kay	*Legacy* (Bodley Head)
	Runners-up	
	Gary Armitage	*A season of peace* (Secker & Warburg)
	Elizabeth Ironside	*A very private enterprise* (Hodder)
	Alice Mitchell	*Instead of Eden* (W. H. Allen)
	Caroline Stickland	*The standing hills* (Gollancz)
	George Schweiz	*The earth abides for ever*
1986	Tim Parks	*Tongues of flame* (Heinemann)
	Runners-up	
	Patricia Ferguson	*Family myths and legends* (Deutsch)
	Philippa Blake	*Mzungu's wife* (Bodley Head)
	Matthew Kneale	*Whore banquets* (Gollancz)
	J. F. McLaughlin	*The road to Dilmun*

Now read on

	Kate Saunders	*The prodigal father* (Cape)
1987	James Maw	*Hard Luck* (Quartet Books)
	Runners-up	
	Peter Benson	*The levels* (Constable)
	Helen Flint	*Return Journey* (Heinemann)
	Catharine Arnold	*Lost time* (Hodder & Stoughton)
	H. S. Bhabra	*Gestures* (Michael Joseph)
	Lucy Pinney	*The pink stallion* (Hodder & Stoughton)
1988	Alex Martin	*The general interruptor* (Viking/Penguin)
	Runners-up	
	Candia McWilliams	*A case of knives* (Bloomsbury)
	George Andrewes	*Behind the waterfall* (Pandora Press)
	James Friel	*Left of North* (Macmillan)
	Glenn Patterson	*Burning your own* (Chatto & Windus)
	Susan Webster	*Small tales of a town* (Simon/Schuster)
1989	Nigel Watts	*The life game* (Hodder)
	Runners–up	
	William Riviere	*The watercolour sky* (Hodder)
	Alasdair McKee	*Uncle Henry's last stand* (Chatto)
	Paul Houghton	*Harry's last wedding* [Unpublished]
1990	Robert McLiam Wilson	*Ripley Bogle* (Deutsch)
	Runners–up	
	Elizabeth Chadwick	*The wild hunt* (Joseph)
	Rosemary Cohen	*No strange land* [Unpublished]
	Nicholas Shakespeare	*The vision of Elena Silves* (Collins/Penguin)
1991	Amit Chaudhuri	*A strange and sublime address* (Heinemann)
	Runners-up	
	Suzannah Dunn	*Quite contrary* (Sinclair-Stevenson)
	Lesley Glaister	*Honour thy father* (Secker & Warburg)
	Simon Mason	*The great English nude* (Constable)
	Nino Ricci	*Lives of the saints* (Allison & Busby)
	Mark Swallow	*Teaching Little Fang* (Macmillan)
1992	Liane Jones	*The dream stone* (Heinemann)
	Runners-up	
	Tibor Fischer	*Under the frog* (Polygon)
	Eugene Mullan	*The last of his line* [Unpublished]
	Peter Michael Rosenberg	*Kissing through a pane of glass* [Unpublished]
	Edward St. Aubyn	*Never mind* (Heinemann)

INDEX OF AUTHORS

Now read on

Now read on

INDEX OF SERIES AND RECURRING CHARACTERS

Now read on

Now read on

Now read on